To Bess & Fred
In pleasant
memories of your
parents John & Jessie &
with Best Regards
Bill & Lucille

XMAS-1981

The Sword and the Gavel

by

The Last of the Nuremberg Judges
William J. Wilkins

an Autobiography

with
Eleanor Elford Cameron

The Writing Works
A Division of Morse Press
Seattle, Washington

Library of Congress Cataloging in Publication Data
Wilkins, William J. (William John), 1897-
The sword and the gavel.

Included index.
1. Wilkins, William J. (William John), 1897- . 2. Judges—United States—Biography. 3. Krupp Trail, Nuremberg, 1947-1948. I. Title.
KF373.W465A37 347.73'14 81-16409
ISBN 0-916076-46-4 347.30714 (B) AACR2

Printed in the United States of America

Published by The Writing Works
Division of Morse Press, Inc.
417 E. Pine Street
Seattle, WA 98122

Library of Congress Catalog Number: 81-52988
ISBN: 0-916076-46-6

Contents

To Lucille, the world's best pal for over fifty years, who prodded me into writing my memories of things past, deciphered my scribbling, typed long hours and wrote a few chapters herself, which you will doubtless recognize.

Acknowledgments

The author extends a special acknowledgment to the late Eleanor Elford Cameron, long-time friend and author of several books, whose editing, writing skill and encouragement made this book a *fait accompli.* She has my eternal gratitude.

Also my special thanks to the following:

J. Ronald Wilby, Professor Emeritus, Seattle University and former British consul general to the Pacific Northwest; Edward T. Stone, retired former managing editor, *Seattle Post-Intelligencer;* Dr. George E. Taylor, Professor Emeritus, University of Washington; Ross L. Cunningham, retired editorial director, the *Seattle Times;* Ralph Bushnell Potts, lawyer and author; the late Joseph M. Donnelly, my platoon commander in World War I; Robert G. Forman, executive director, University of Michigan Alumni Association; Professor William E. Porter, department of communications, University of Michigan; Robert M. Leach, assistant vice-president, Ferris State College; Professor William Manchester, distinguished author of several books and fellow of Wesleyan University; the *Seattle Argus,* the *Ontonagon Herald, Seattle Post-Intelligencer, Seattle Times* and the Society of the Fifth U.S. Division.

Foreword

It seems but yesterday to those of us who were adults during the dark days of World War II when our way of life was hostage to a gang of obscene bandits led by a maniacal little Austrian housepainter named Adolf Hitler.

Thus it is hard to realize that whole generations have grown up around us for whom those terrible events have as little present day reality as the American Civil War, something embalmed in history books in school libraries.

And even we, whose memories should serve us better, tend to forget. It came as a shocker a few days ago when Bill Wilkins, a friend of long standing, remarked off-handedly that he was the last survivor of the panel of distinguished jurists who sat with him in judgment in Nuremberg, Germany on the monstrous crimes against humanity by Hitler's Nazis.

How could I forget that Bill, whom I had long admired during our contemporary professional lives in Seattle, for his fairness and integrity as a King County superior court judge, had indeed participated actively in one of the great landmark events of human history? For the Nuremberg trials established the principle in international law that evil men who seize power for their own selfish ends and make brutal war against their own people and neighboring nations, may be brought to book as common criminals.

As a newspaper editor *(Seattle Post-Intelligencer),* I had known Bill casually during those years when he was working his way upward in a Seattle political structure devoted to clean government leading eventually to his appointment to the superior court bench, thus fulfilling a lifelong dream.

But it was only when we both neared what Bill himself describes as the green pastures of retirement that I became more intimately acquainted with him through mutual friends and realized the Horatio Alger story in the man, a story which began with childhood in a poor immigrant family from Cornwall, England, laboring in the copper mines of Northern Michigan.

Bill tells the story himself in fascinating detail in the chapters that follow. Of his mother he writes:

"She lives in memory—her strength of character, her absolute faith in God, her kindness and generosity.... A conversation with her when (I was) about 10 comes to mind. 'Mom' I said 'when I grown up I want to be a judge.'" She patted me on the back and said: 'Wonderful, Willie. Work hard and keep your mind on that course and you'll be a judge and a good one.'"

On January 2, 1940 the black robe of a superior court judge was draped over Bill's shoulder. "I recalled with emotion that conversation with my mother 32 years before and wished she could be there to see my childhood dream come true."

In those 32 years Bill Wilkins never lost sight of his shining goal. But the way upward was steep and often hard. Blacksmith's apprentice at 16 in the little mining town of Mass City, Mich.; working in the copper mines at $2.50 a day; grocery clerk at the general store for $65 a month—these were some of Bill's jobs while he was trying to get through high school.

On April 6, 1917, the United States declared war on Germany. A month later Private William J. Wilkins, still short of graduation from high school was on his way to war. Nine months later, homesick and seasick, he was on a troop ship bound for "Over There." By June, 1918, now a sergeant in the famous Red Arrow Division, he was in the thick of the trench warfare in Lower Alsace. On September 25 he was commissioned a second lieutenant and assigned to the 5th Division. Six weeks later he led his platoon in a vital crossing of the Meuse River in the face of withering fire of enemy machine guns entrenched on the east bank. On November 7, four days before the Armistice, he led another mission that broke up a German machine gun nest and was awarded the Silver Star for gallantry in action. Quite a record for a lad not yet out of high school!

Discharged from the army in 1919, he enrolled in Ferris Institute in Big Rapids, Mich., to finish high school. Washing dishes at a boarding house netted him three meals a day. His grade average at Ferris was high enough to allow him to enter the University of Michigan as a sophomore in 1922. A job as a bellhop at a nearby resort earned him the magnificent sum of $350 in savings to help finance his years in Michigan's noted law school. Other odd jobs along the way kept him going.

In his senior year, at the suggestion of two friendly lawyers for whom he had worked during summer vacation, he transferred to George Washington Law School in Washington D.C., where he received his degree of Doctor of Law.

Some years before, Bill had heard vaguely of an Indian town named Seattle somewhere in the western wilds. A former classmate who was practicing law in Seattle persuaded him to visit the place and Bill liked it so much he decided to stay, a full-fledged lawyer without a job. This was in 1928.

Then one enchanted evening he met Lucille. Lucille Schreiner, a lovely vivacious young woman was the daughter of a Yakima rancher. Lucille and Bill joined hands and forces in a happy marriage that has lasted more than 50 years. She is a talented artist and devoted scrounger for unique furniture and decorative oddments that have made their various homes in Seattle charming gathering places for their many friends.

Which brings us to the greatest venture of their married life and in my view the most thrilling chapter in Bill's autobiography. After 24 years of childless marriage they adopted in one fell swoop an orphaned family of three brothers and two sisters ranging in age from 5 to 15 and with loving devotion reared them to happy and successful manhood and womanhood. To me this is bigger than Nuremberg.

Bill calls his story "The Sword and the Gavel." An apt title, but if it had been left to me, a quondam avid reader of Horatio Alger, I would have called it "Luck and Pluck or the American Dream."

Ed Stone

CHAPTER I

In the Beginning

(1897-1917)

My father, William Wilkin—the "s" was added later—was one of the Cousin Jacks, those daring young Cornishmen who emigrated from Cornwall in the latter part of the nineteenth century to the mining areas of America—the Black Hills of South Dakota, Butte in Montana, the iron and copper mines of Michigan and Minnesota, and the Grass Valley of California.

In 1895 at Negaunee, Michigan, my father met and married my mother, Selina Ann Folland, a widow with three children—George, Ada and Christopher. The story is that the comely young widow supported herself and children by taking boarders, among them William Wilkin and Johnnie Northey who vied for her affections. They were serious rivals, but after Selina gave Father the nod, they became good friends. In fact, "Uncle Johnnie," as we kids called him, often visited us and it was for him I was given the middle name of John.

Shortly after their marriage my parents moved to Ironwood where, in 1896, Alice was born. I came along the next year, and Howard, who was to be my pal and partner in mischief, two years later. In time, Elsie, Mabel and Mildred were born, making us a family of nine children. It seemed to me there was always a baby in our house. Our family had such a warm and happy relationship it wasn't until I was 10 I learned that George and Ada and Chris were half brothers and sister.

In 1899 we moved to Greenland, Michigan, where Father was to work in the hard-rock copper mine owned by the Adventure Mining Company. Young as I was, one of the most vivid images of things remembered is the day we arrived by train—the old Copper Range Railroad. For a two-year-old boy his first train ride isn't just a ride; it's an adventure.

To me the engine was a monstrous dragon belching clouds of smoke accompanied by loud hissing noises. Inside the coach were green plush seats and swaying gas lanterns and a big pot-bellied stove. Mother had packed a picnic lunch which we ate as we bounced up and down, pointing to the countryside as it whizzed by. At last, the train chugged and chuffed into the station and wheezed to a stop, leaving a tattered ribbon of smoke trailing across the hot blue sky. The Wilkin family, spit and polished to a Sunday shine, peered out the windows with curious eyes and were surprised to see a crowd on the platform. It soon became evident they were other Cornish families, already established in Greenland, come to meet their former countrymen.

The Cornish people were warm and outgoing, and though transplanted to a new land, they retained a strong sense of clan characteristic of all Celts. Here in Greenland they rushed to welcome us, and their enthusiastic acceptance soon put the Wilkin family inside rather than out. Mercifully, the ceremonies were brief. The long confinement on the train had made us restless, and it was hard to obey our parents' hasty admonishment to be on our best behavior. Lined up before our parents, we stood at attention through a spirited rendition of several hymns by the Ladies Methodist Choir and a short prayer by the Reverend Hoard, who later became our spiritual advisor and close personal friend.

Typical of most Cornishmen, Father was of medium height and slender build; a handsome man with dark brown hair brushed forward and combed to the side across his brow, blue-green eyes and a handlebar mustache of which Mother was very proud. Once, in payment of a lost bet, he shaved off, not only every hair on his head, but the mustache as well. Samson shorn! Mother broke into tears when he appeared, but fortunately time took care of it.

He had a bit of the dandy about him, taking pride in his apparel for church services and occasions such as this. Across his vest he sported a gold hunting case watch and chain. Later a glass charm, with Mother's picture on one side and Mabel's when a baby on the other, was attached to the chain.

Beside him on the platform stood my mother wearing a black bombazine dress with leg-of-mutton sleeves. She was plump and jolly with brown eyes and wore her long dark hair swept up in a chignon. In her arms she held two-month-old Samuel Howard dressed in a long white starched gown. At some time during the ceremony, failing to stop the baby's crying with a pacifier, Mother opened the front of her dress and offered him one of her ample breasts. That solved the problem.

From the station we were escorted down the board sidewalk to our new home in one of the duplexes which lined the long dirt-paved street. These houses were built by the mining company and rented to the miners for $4 a month. They were substantial two-story buildings painted a drab gray, able to withstand the severe winters to be expected in northern Michigan but unsoftened by greenery. We lived in this duplex until 1909 when we moved two miles to Mass City, where Father was in charge of the surface compressors for the Mass Consolidated Mine.

Like most small towns Greenland had one main street; its name was, of course, Main Street. There were some fairly prosperous businesses too—Powers Drug Store, Driscoll's Livery Stable, the First National Bank, a Chinese laundry, the telephone office, a barber shop and a butcher shop whose owner slaughtered cattle and hogs in a vacant lot nearby; the village blacksmith and the Town Hall which also served as the Fire Hall because it had such a loud bell. When I was about seven, at mention of the Marshal's name, I'd run home and hide under Mother's bed for fear he'd arrest me. We kids'd been throwing our caps at the train as it passed.

Mass City was separated from Greenland by The Ridge. Here, in the stately Victorian homes of that period, lived the elite of the two towns. Incongruously, the two most popular saloons were also situated on The Ridge. One, operated by a Mrs. Brunsky, was an unscrupulous operation. On pay days men often left her place drunk, little or nothing left of their paychecks. The other, run by Henry Barbera, showed more concern for the men, sending them home before they lost both their sobriety and their pay. In the two towns there were 18 saloons, not unusual in a mining community; Hurley, Wisconsin boasted 75 saloons in four blocks and was the most wide-open, hell-raising town in the Midwest.

Perhaps this extreme consumption of alcohol was due in part to the hazards faced by the miners every time they went underground. Conditions were poor, hours long—from 7 a.m. to 5 p.m.—six days a week. Pay was low and was not "portal to portal." Shifts started from arrival at the shaft and ended there. There were no child labor laws, no minimum wage, no compensation for injuries or illness, or aid to dependents when death occurred as the result of an accident in the mine. Many men contracted miners' consumption and were laid off for long periods without pay. Father fell a victim to this disease in 1905 and wasn't able to work for several years. Until then we'd had no serious financial problems, but during his illness we all had to find ways to contribute to the family's welfare.

To appreciate how hazardous hard-rock mining was, you have to realize that in those days mining in all aspects was primitive. Mining gear consisted of heavy leather hobnailed boots extending to the knee, flannel underwear covered by denim jackets and overalls. Because there was no place to change clothes at the mine, the men wore their work clothes back and forth to their homes. Later washrooms and lockers, referred to as "the dry," were installed.

A cap held a single candle which furnished the only light underground. In time, candles were supplanted by wick lamps filled with petroleum wax. The lighting was better but the resulting smoke and smell left much to be desired. An improved carbide lamp was used when I started working underground at sixteen; later, the battery-operated head lamp was invented and is in common use today.

There were no drilling machines; the work was done by hand. Miners worked in teams of three, two swinging their sledges on the drill which was held and turned by the third man. The holes were then filled with dynamite connected by fuses to dynamite caps which were lighted in proper succession for the blast. In this way miners sank their shafts through the hard rock, drove their drifts at one hundred foot levels and cross-cuts from one drift to another to stope out the precious metals between levels.

Later the chippy, a heavy drilling machine weighing about two hundred and fifty pounds, was introduced. Operated by two miners, it was fastened to a steel post jacked from the footing to the hanging of the drift. This was a piston type machine operated throughout the mine by air pumped from an air compressor on the surface. As the chippy drove into the breast of the drift, a helper turned the drill, squirting water into the hole to keep down the hard-rock dust. Many improvements in hard-rock mining were made after 1910.

Workmen known as muckers and rock pickers worked behind the miners, sorting poor rock from copper rock. Poor rock was broken up with sledge hammers and deposited between chutes as a fill. Copper rock was dumped in the chutes by rock pickers and carted to the shaft in tram cars; trammers pushed the cars over iron rails to the skip which transported the rock to the surface. After being processed by rock crushers at the shaft house, the copper ore was taken by railroad to the stamp mills at Keewenah Bay on Lake Superior for refining.

At the end of each shift sticks of dynamite and long fuses with caps attached were tamped into holes. Before the fuses were lighted, the cry, "Fire!" echoed through the long damp corridors, warning the men to leave the stopes and drifts. After these blasts gas permeated the underground area, and though compressed air pumps were started to drive out the gas, some hung in the air causing havoc with the men coming on shift. Often the presence of gas could not be detected until men experienced severe headaches or unconsciousness. Working under such conditions over long periods of time affected the lungs and was the cause of miners' consumption.

I suppose some people would say we were poor; if so, we didn't *feel* poor. We always had a nice house, good clothes and plenty to eat. Winter and summer we enjoyed the best of sports and always, wherever we went, there was music and song.

A cow supplied us with plenty of fresh milk and chickens with eggs and an occasional chicken in the pot. From the garden came the potatoes, cabbages and rutabagas kept in the cellar through the winter along with a barrel of Baldwin apples. In the fall we gathered hazel nuts, stowing them in the attic to dry for the holidays. Through the summer months everyone big enough to pick berries went to The Astick where they grew wild. We rode free on the Copper Range passenger run, courtesy of Mr. James, the engineer of Engine 52, who bought the berries for 50 cents a pail and sold them in Houghton. This was a three-way deal—we earned money, had a free outing and ate all the berries we could hold.

Twice a week Mother made the famous Cornish pasties, a meat pie, which she made by rolling out rich dough into sheets, piling each with meat, potatoes, onions, carrots and parsley, folding over and crimping the edges and baking. They were graduated in size according to the ages of the family, and were equally delectable cold—a favorite with the men in their dinner buckets for their underground meal. Saturdays she baked bread, a dozen loaves at a time. Saffron cake and buns, Devonshire dumplings in chicken stew and the thick rich Devonshire cream we spread on our toast with jelly or jam were delicacies of the house.

We all had our chores for the home, the girls helping with the housework. The boys kept wood supplied for the stove and earned what money we could on the side. During Father's illness, in addition to her heavy duties at home with a big family, Mother earned money by helping the company doctor on maternity cases and doing laundry. With our little red wagon Howard and I collected baskets of laundry which she washed and ironed for one dollar a basket.

There was no electricity, no piped-in running water, so my mother stood bent over a large tin tub set up on chairs in the kitchen, vigorously washing clothes on a washboard. That same tin tub became the Saturday night bathtub, used in rotation from the youngest to the eldest.

Water was heated in large pans to add to that of the reservoir on the side of the stove. A neighborhood well between our houses supplied the water which was carried in buckets.

A happy day came when a washing machine was bought through the Sears Roebuck Catalog. It was primitive—a wooden tub built on a stand with four sturdy legs and a handle on top which permitted the tub to be manually rotated in a semi-circular motion back and forth, thus agitating the tub full of clothes. What an improvement over the old tub and washboard! Everyone was delighted to have a turn operating the mechanical miracle.

Our duplex was shared by another Cornish family, and all our neighbors were English except for the Millards and the Coffeys who were Irish. Old Man Coffey was a real character in our town. Over a hundred, he lived a few blocks up the street in the log house he built when he came from Ireland at the end of the Civil War. Sturdy and irascible, Old Man Coffey spoke with a heavy brogue and always carried a shillelagh. In his orchard, conveniently close to the street, was an apple tree. On the way home from school we kids used to sneak in and pick his prize apples. The day he caught us he ran through the orchard, brandishing the shillelagh, and roared to his dog, "Sic 'em!" We scattered in a hurry, anxious not to connect with the end of that shillelagh or have the seat of our pants removed by his dog.

Another time, Gertrude Amos, fourteen, pretty and buxom, who cleaned his house on Saturdays, was making the bed when he started to chase her around the room.

"I'm 'orney!" he shouted.

Poor Gertrude ran out of the house and all the way home, never to return. Pretty good for a lad in his second century.

When I was a second grader and Howard in kindergarten, we shared a schoolroom, and Nellie Coffey, a no-nonsense old maid schoolmarm, was our teacher. One day Howard got into trouble; taking him by the ear, Nellie led him to the little red stool facing the corner reserved for such occasions. She didn't know that she had a bear by the tail! He screamed and cried, fought, kicked and tried to bite her. During this disturbance I raised my hand, showing two fingers. When Nellie nodded permission, I ran all the way home to tell Mother Miss Coffey was killing Howard.

"Well, Willie," she said, "you look after the baby and I'll go see what this is all about." When she returned, she had an amused expression on her face. "Everything's all right, Willie," she assured me. "You can go back now."

"She'll beat me," I remonstrated.

"No, she won't."

With some apprehension I returned to school. I wasn't punished, but I had to stay late and make up the time I'd been away.

Howard had a temper and was a fighter; unfortunately, he usually drew an antagonist larger than he. One day he got into a fight with John Millard, who was older and bigger than I, but when Howard was getting the worst of it, I felt duty bound to pitch in and help. Then John's older brother Jordan came in after me, which brought Chris in after him. Then Mrs. Millard, a fighting Irish woman without peer, came running toward us, on the way grabbing a 10-foot maple pole used to prop up her heavy sagging clothesline. Chris was then a grocery delivery boy, and fortunately his horse Leo was hitched to the delivery wagon nearby. The three of us made a dash for it, urged old Leo to get going, and escaped the blows from Mrs. Millard's clothes pole.

Like all Celts, the Cornish people were a bit fey and enjoyed a good ghost story. Often after supper on winter evenings, while Dad had his beer or porter (a dark brown ale favored by Britishers) and Mother a glass of her homemade wine, we would sit around the kitchen stove and listen to tales that sent chills crawling up our spines. On Saturday nights, when we delivered the weekly paper, the *Ontonagon Herald,* Howard and I, remembering those stories, ran like rabbits when we passed the cemetery. For a while there was a rumor that a strange light appeared at various times over a certain tombstone. Many folks swore they had seen this strange light; in the telling the story got even more chilling. The rumor continued for several weeks until someone observed that the light disappeared when the windowshade was down in Dr. Larned's office which faced the cemetery. Even so, Howard and I gave it a wide berth.

Dr. Larned was the Adventure Mine company doctor and came to Greenland immediately on graduation from medical school at the University of Michigan. No years of internship or residency or training in a specialty in those days. Aside from maternity cases, for which he received $25, his sole income was $1 for each married man and 50 cents for bachelors a month which was withheld at the mine office. He was dedicated to the care of the miners and their families; in turn, they had great respect and affection for him.

A practical expression of their affection, and their wit, came when he was married. On their return from their honeymoon, he and his bride were met at the train by the miners, who had replaced the doctor's horse with a cow between the shafts of the buggy and personally escorted the bride and groom to their new home.

The horse, called Dr. George, was kept in Driscoll's Livery Stable about a mile from the office. Each morning he was hitched to the buggy, the lines thrown around the whipstock, and sent, driverless, to the office, where he waited patiently until hours there were over and house calls began. When they got home, Dr. Larned turned him toward the livery stable and sent him on his way. We kids used to steal rides in the buggy, but if Dr. George saw us first, he broke into a trot. We soon learned how to circumvent that problem. He wore blinders, so we waited until he passed us, then sneaked up behind the buggy, climbed aboard and got a free ride downtown.

Ours was a strict Methodist family. Every Sunday we were scrubbed and laundered and went to church *en famille*. Sunday School at nine; after that, the regular service—a long session for active children. We had pennies for the collection box, but often on our way to church we detoured into old Mrs. Cosgrove's candy shop and squandered a penny, sometimes two.

No playing cards were allowed in the house, though we had games like Authors, Old Maid, checkers and dominoes. On Sundays, baseball games were played between Greenland, Mass City and other small towns, but we weren't allowed to watch. The Sabbath was a Holy Day, and we were taught that to watch sports on Sunday was a sin. If that belief were prevalent today, television would have rough going and Heaven would be a ghost town. Nonetheless, when we passed the ball field on our way home, we boys dawdled, watching the game out of the corner of our eyes. If our sisters tattled, we suffered the consequences, usually a trip to the woodshed for a tanning.

As I've said, miners were noted for their alcoholic consumption; Cornish miners drank beer or porter, seldom whiskey, which was more costly. They couldn't handle it either and, generally, had the sense to leave it alone. On a few occasions when Father got hold of some, he became pugnacious, spoiling for a good fight.

Every Saturday Tom Robson, agent for Marquette and Miller Life beer, delivered a case of Marquette to our home and one Miller Life to John Millard our neighbor. Father didn't like to drink in a saloon, so when the beer ran out, Howard and I were given the tea container of his dinner bucket and sent to McDonald's saloon for a schooner. On one occasion, while returning home, we stopped at the town pump and tried out the beer; one drink led to another until we'd consumed half the container. That presented us with a problem, which we solved by filling it with water, a fact Father discovered on his first swallow. Back to the woodshed for Howard and me, and we never did that again. Tom Robson also operated a coal yard, so with his beer agencies on one hand and the coal yard on the other, he kept the miners warm inside and out.

Our favorite comic, "The Katzenjammer Kids," got Howard and me into more trouble. Intrigued with one of their escapades, we decided to pretend we were "The Kids" and try it ourselves. Blond, I was Hans; Howard, brunette, was Fritz. That particular day Father played right into our hands. He sat on the porch, his chair propped against the house, smoking his pipe. Waiting until he dozed off, we tied a rope to our dog's neck, the other end to the leg of Father's chair. Just as we were about to call Rover and pull Father's chair out from under him, he woke up.

"Damme!" he swore. "You could 'ave broken my blawdy neck!"

That tanning put an end to "The Wilkins Kids."

Father had a great sense of humor though, and sometimes he would regale us with stories of his adventures in Montana and the Black Hills. Our favorites were the ones about Buffalo Bill and Wild Bill Hickok. Father had been in the saloon where Wild Bill was killed some years before. Come to think of it, quite a few "wild" characters had the name of Bill.

He was also a tease. One way he could always get a rise out of us was to brag about the British Empire, reminding us the sun never set on it, which it didn't then. He knew we'd all stand up for the USA. No country in the world was as great as this wonderful land of ours. Of course, he didn't really mean it. In 1904, with three other miners, he went to Ontonagon and received his certificate of citizenship from the circuit judge of the county. The men were very proud, as we all were, when they got off the train wearing American flags in their lapels. They were also very exuberant as the result of celebrating in an Ontonagon saloon.

The Cornish were sentimental people and loved to sing the old songs learned in their homeland. Like the Welsh, the miners often sang at work and on their way home, their voices blending in perfect harmony. While quite young, Ada had taken music lessons, and somehow our parents managed to buy a Storey & Clark organ, which arrived from Chicago on Christmas Eve in a blizzard. Many a long winter evening we all gathered round the organ for a songfest. Father and George sang bass, Chris baritone, Howard tenor, and I carried the lead. The girls joined in but they were all sopranos—not an alto or contralto among them.

This love of music and song has remained one of our greatest pleasures. Some years ago my wife, Lucille, and I bought our first organ, and though we've had pianos, the organ remains our real joy. Music comes as naturally to Lucille; both her parents had good voices, and there was always music in their home. Hardly a day goes by we don't enjoy some impromptu music. Our friends tell us the highlight of our parties is when Lucille sits at the organ and everybody sings.

In addition to music we had drama of a sort. Lewie James, a hard-rock miner from Cornwall, had had some acting experience in England and recited or sang with great pathos and drama at family gatherings or in the saloons. I remember one song very well.

The lawyer for the prosecution
At the widow commenced to frown,
And politely asked 'is 'onor
If 'e'd order 'er to sit down.
'e said it was disgraceful
And a gross insult indeed
For 'is 'onor to sit on that bench
And allow that woman to plead.
The widow's eyes flashed fire
And 'er cheeks turned deathly pale,
While turning to the jurymen
These words they 'eard 'er say:
Remember I'm a widow
And the prisoner there's my son,
And gentlemen, remember
It's the first crime that 'e's done.
Don't send my boy to prison
For that will drive me mad,
Remember I'm a widow
And I'm pleading for my lad.

His rendition of "The Face on the Bar Room Floor" was a favorite with the habituées of the saloons.

Even more dramatic was the murder trial that shook our own community. At 13, it made a lasting impression on me. Charlie Stannard, one of the brothers who owned the general store on The Ridge, had a strong taste for alcohol and was one of Mrs. Brunsky's regular customers. He had a devoted and loyal wife, two sons and two daughters. When he died suddenly, an autopsy revealed his death was due to poison. His wife admitted putting a powder in his coffee supposed to destroy his taste for alcohol. Unfortunately, the powder contained strychnine. She was charged with murder and confined in the county jail in Ontonagon where she awaited trial throughout the summer while relatives looked after her children.

Sympathy for Mrs. Stannard ran high in the community and the main topic of conversation was the forthcoming trial. The adults thought it outrageous she be held in jail as a murderess, away from her young children. As the trail progressed, the townspeople discussed the evidence and the concerted opinion was she ought to be acquitted, which she was.

The Harry K. Thaw-Stanford White murder case of world-wide fame stirred up a lot of feeling in our area too. The men felt Thaw was right in killing White to uphold the honor of his wife, Evelyn. If it had been left to them, Thaw wouldn't have had to plead insanity—merely "not guilty."

Looking back, I realize even then I was affected strongly by such incidents which may have pointed the way to a long hard climb to a seat on the bench.

One of the most important celebrations was the Fourth of July; every porch was decked with red, white and blue bunting with the American flag hung high above them. Housewives spent days preparing food for picnic feasts at the park on Cole's Bluff. Kids spelled each other off at the ice cream freezer, making dibs to lick the spoon or paddle.

The day started early when miners coming off the graveyard shift set off dynamite in isolated places. In addition to the usual speeches and impromptu ball games and picnic meals everyone shared with everyone else, there were sulky races on Main Street in Greenland. On The Ridge, teams of miners competed in a hammer and drill contest; the prize, a keg of beer, went to the team which drilled the deepest hole in a specified time.

Christmas and Thanksgiving were celebrated much as now, except instead of a turkey we had a big plump chicken which Father had been feeding up for those occasions. The Christmas tree was festooned with whatever ornaments we'd acquired through the years supplemented with cookies and gingerbread men which disappeared soon after the festivities were over. Miraculously, how I've often wondered, there were always presents for everyone, gaily wrapped and set around the tree. We believed Santa Claus *did* deliver the presents on Christmas Eve, and he *did* come down the chimney, and we could not go in the parlor until all was ready on Christmas morning.

Up there in northern Michigan heavy snowfalls began as early as October some years and provided wonderful opportunities for winter sports—skiing, tobogganing and ice skating—but we had to make our own facilities. A large level snow area was trampled and watered down, and overnight we had a first-rate skating rink. Stout tree limbs with curved ends made fine hockey sticks. Our first skis were fashioned from barrel staves; later we received professional ones for Christmas. Even the snow on the boardwalks froze, and it wasn't unusual to look out the window and see gaily scarfed and capped skaters skimming along, waving to friends as they went by. One of the ski runs we made started high up on the bluff behind our house, went through our back yard, ending at the 5-foot fence which we had to jump—or else. Once I ran into the clothesline and ended up with a real shiner. Today one of the finest ski runs in northern Michigan is at the site of the old Adventure mine.

There were hayrides on a large hayrack set on a long sleigh drawn by a team or teams of horses, depending on the load, and we had buffalo robes to keep us warm. Nights were cold and clear, the stars like candles in the sky. Sometimes a full moon, a great silver globe, lighted our way. As the long runners slid over the trails, voices were raised in song accompanied by the jingle of sleigh bells on the horses ahead.

When the weather was too severe to venture out, we amused ourselves by putting on amateur plays. On one occasion I was the minister and performed the wedding ceremony. Ada played the organ; Alice, the bride, wore one of our old lace curtains for a veil. Howard, in Dad's long pants and black hat, was the groom; Elsie and Mabel, the bridesmaids, and little Mildred, the flower girl. After that Dad called me "Parson Tate."

There were no tennis courts or public pools, but in summer we swam in the swimming holes along the creeks, rode our bicycles through the countryside and in nearby streams fished for speckled trout. There were also competitive sports such as baseball and basketball.

I loved and respected both my parents, but it was my mother who had the greatest influence on my life. She was kind, compassionate, not one to lose her head in an emergency, and though her life was a hard one, she was essentially a happy person. Her faith was indomitable. While Father was ill and unable to work, we had rough going financially. Ada was at Marquette Normal School, and Mother was determined she continue. I remember the time she didn't have a two-cent stamp for her weekly letter to Ada; that same day Howard and I were walking on the boardwalk and found a 50-cent piece under the steps to the saloon. We ran all the way home to give it to Mother. Her response was, "The Lord always provides."

It is said that every family has at least one skeleton to rattle, and we were not without ours. Mother, the eldest of eight children, was born Selina Ann Sloman in Devon, England. When she was sixteen, her mother ran away to Wales with a man named Oliver. Following her father's death, my mother received a letter from her wayward mother, asking forgiveness and saying someday she, Selina Ann, would understand. Mother never answered the letter. Though I am sure she loved her mother, she never could understand, nor could she forgive her mother for leaving her family with Selina Ann charged with the burden of running the household and the care of the younger children.

Mother was devoted to her family in Devon and spoke of them

often, especially her father who, at 92, fell off a hayrack and died of a broken neck.

Frequently the women visited together evenings after the younger children went to bed, and one of my greatest treats was when Mother would say, "Come, Willie, let's go over to Mrs. Hodge's house." Like Mother, Mrs. Hodge came from Devon and was her closest friend and confidante. While the ladies talked in the parlor, I got to stay up late and play with the Hodge kids in the kitchen where they had a Victor Gramophone with the cylinder-type records. It was on one of those occasions while eavesdropping I learned George, Chris and Ada were half brothers and sister.

What I heard was that when she was 18, my mother had married her first husband, George Folland, in Whitchurch, a small fishing village in Devon, where George and Ada were born. Shortly after, their father came to America, settled in Negaunee, Michigan, went to work in the iron mines and was soon able to send for his family. Chris was born just before his father was killed in a mine accident within a year of the family's reunion. The half brother and sister relationship made no difference in our feelings toward each other. We were a united family and loved each other.

All mining communities have tragedy, poverty and disease in common, and ours was no exception. In spite of the exhilaration of sports and hayrides, winters brought with them the constant threat of sickness. Temperatures were below zero for days at a time, and without the benefit of modern medicine the dread scourge of communicable diseases ran rampant. Often we saw the familiar red sign posted on houses to indicate contagion within—entrance forbidden. We all had antitoxin shots, even the babies, but despite this Howard had diphtheria and I pneumonia at the same time. Alice had the measles which settled in one of her eyes. Father took her to an eye specialist in Houghton who had to remove her eye.

Mother nursed us through these serious illnesses, often sitting up nights while carrying on her other duties during the day. She grieved over Alice and the loss of her eye, and for George who suffered a mental breakdown while working in the mine and had to be sent to a mental institution at Newberry. After several months he returned but was always a hypersensitive young man.

Psychiatry and the private sanatoriums of today did not exist then. I have always thought George, being the eldest of Mother and George Folland's children, had suffered more than Ada from the imagined rejection of his father when he left them in Devon. His death soon after their arrival in America, Mother's remarriage and the rivalry of eight siblings, all contributed to George's problems.

The most tragic time for our family began the winter of 1908. In

November George, Elsie and Alice came down with typhoid fever. Mother had been caring for a family where there were two cases. One evening George went with her, and evidently while she was busy nursing the family, he used one of their drinking glasses. In a few days he was down with the fever, and the others took it from him. Mother was up night and day with the three of them. Elsie and Alice finally recovered but in spite of Mother's valiant efforts we lost George.

Being her first-born and having required more protection through the years since they left England, he was always her first concern. I heard her say she was relieved he died before she did as she had worried about his future.

Within one month of George's death, early in 1909 Mother died of typhoid. Weakened by long hours nursing the family in addition to three days and nights on a difficult maternity case, she was unable to fight the fever. Early that morning Father called us. He came to our bedrooms, little Mildred in one arm, a lamp in the other hand. "If you want to see your mother alive for the last time," he said, his voice strange in that early morning quiet, "come to our bedroom." Rushing to her room, we saw her there, barely breathing. We hovered over her, crying for her not to leave us, but she did not hear. Quietly, without our realizing it, she slipped away.

Reverend Hoard, who had been such a wonderful minister to us while in Greenland, made a special trip back from southern Michigan to conduct the services. Later, on that cold winter day in the midst of a blizzard, we stood beside Mother's grave, tears streaming down our cheeks, and watched the snow cover the mound of raw earth. Today caskets are stored throughout the winter and not buried until the ground has thawed in the spring.

She lives in memory—her strength of character, her absolute faith in God, her kindness and generosity in all ways, and her wise guidance of us in our formative years. A conversation I had with her when about 10 comes to mind. "Mom", I said, "when I grow up I want to be a judge." She patted me on the back and said: "Wonderful, Willie! Work hard, keep your mind on that course and you'll be a judge—and a good one!" She also had plans for Chris to attend Albion college, a Methodist school, to study for the ministry.

After Mother's death the duties of the household fell on Alice; before going to school, she got breakfast, did the dishes and put up lunches. The school janitor, Denny Coffey, knew she ran all the way to avoid being marked tardy and kept pulling the school bell rope until she got there.

After Mother died, Father went into a bad depression. He lost his jovial disposition and began to frequent the saloons which he'd never done before. Sometimes, when Howard and I went looking for him, we had a hard time persuading him to come home, but after we moved to Mass City he straightened out. Until 1919, when the mine closed down, he was in charge of the surface compressors. After that he moved to Lansing where he lived with my youngest sister, Mildred, until his death in 1925.

While we still lived in Greenland, Ada got her first teaching job in Mass City. Since there was no regular transportation between the two towns, she boarded with a family during the week. Her roommate at Normal School, Jennie Frances, taught in Greenland, however, and her family arranged for Grandpa Dubuque to hitch their horse to the buggy or sleigh, depending on the weather, so I could drive her back and forth on the weekends.

One Monday morning during the winter, as I left Ada at school and was turning the horse, I cut the turn too short and the sleigh tipped over, spilling me, swathed in a buffalo robe, out in the snow. My shame and embarrassment weren't helped by the picture I must have made as I ran up the road, trailing the buffalo robe behind me, to catch the runaway horse. The kids roared with laughter as I went by. Fortunately a man coming in the opposite direction grabbed the horse's bridle and stopped him; otherwise I'd have had to walk home. Grandpa Dubuque, who lived to be 108, was always waiting to take over the horse so I could get to school on time—another instance of the many kindnesses from our wonderful neighbors and friends.

Our house in Mass City was larger than the one in Greenland and seemed like a palace. We even had a butler's pantry, and though we didn't have a butler, it got plenty of use. The kitchen had a pump and a Monarch range with a water reservoir and warming oven. In the combination sewing and living room there was a box stove, and a coal stove in the parlor that burned all night through the winter. The greatest luxury was the enclosed walkway to the outhouse—a three-holer graduated to accommodate all sizes—couldn't have the little ones falling through. For all this we paid the company ten dollars a month.

Ada spent a lot of time, hard work and money furnishing the house. On Mother's death we received $1,000 insurance from her lodge, The Fraternal Order of Maccabees, which to us was a fortune. Ada employed a Finnish housekeeper named Julia, who was paid $20 a month. She deserved a lot more, for we gave that dear woman many a bad time.

Neither Father nor Mother had gone beyond the fourth grade, and it was one of their greatest hopes that we would all get a good education. To this end Mother saw that we always had plenty of reading material, taking time to go to the school library with us and help select the books. It wasn't easy, though, to comply with our parents' desires.

Ada's teaching salary was $50 a month, most of which went into the family treasury during that time when Father was ill. To help support our large family, George had dropped out of school at 14 to become a miner's helper at the Adventure. Chris left school at 14 for a job as a grocery clerk and delivery boy at Stannard Brothers Grocery on the Ridge. He did complete an International Correspondence School course, graduated in accounting from Ferris Institute, served in the Navy during World War I, then went with Ford Motor Company where he later became head of the accounting division. I made it through the end of my first year of high school when the company doctor gave me my first job driving his spirited team, Kit and Nell, hitched to his fancy rubber-tired buggy.

Dr. Hanna was a typical family doctor—gray-haired, gentle, kind and out-going. He always reminded me of that old painting of the doctor seated at the bedside of a sick child. He and his wife, Olive, were a handsome charming couple, and to them I attribute much of my early training in good character, second only to that of my mother. He exemplified the greatest values in life—compassion, understanding, tolerance, sacrifice and kindness to his fellow man. We got to be good companions when he took me on fishing trips to their log cabin at Six Mile Lake where we also hunted deer and partridge.

Our house was a block from the Hanna's, the barn and pasture midway between. When the doctor had a night call, he stopped at our house to tell me to harness the horses so we could be on our way. Sometimes it meant a drive as far as 20 miles for a maternity case. I'd put the horses in the patient's barn and sit in the kitchen to keep warm while I visited with the family. Sometimes I had to assist the doctor. I seriously considered making medicine my profession, and Dr. Hanna encouraged me in this, giving me access to his medical magazines and books. As time went on, however, I knew it was not for me.

I have said mining was a hazardous business, and during the time I worked for Dr. Hanna, I saw firsthand what could happen to a miner as the result of an accident. Two cases stand out in my memory.

One hot summer night a call came at 2 a.m. Toivo Jarvenen, working the night shift as one of the dumper crew, had leaned over the steel rail on which the skip, loaded with copper rock, was pulled to the surface. Toivo's arm was severed between the elbow and shoulder. A tourniquet was applied at the mine, and two husky miners rushed him to the small surgery next the doctor's office. No nurses were available. The patient was placed on the operating table, his clothes removed, and under the doctor's orders we prepared him for amputation.

I was assigned to administer the anesthetic, holding a piece of gauze over Toivo's nose with one hand and letting chloroform drop from the bottle I held in the other onto the gauze, drop by drop. The two miners removed their boots and stood on either side of the patient to hold him steady and pass the instruments to Dr. Hanna. As the doctor cut the flesh back from the bone so he could saw the jagged ends, one of the miners fainted. His pal said, "Doctor, I think I should take Oscar outside and revive him." Seeing the pal was about to pass out too, Dr. Hanna agreed. So, at two in the morning of that hot summer night, while two strong men were stretched out on the lawn, under the light of a gas lamp Dr. Hanna, with only my inept help, managed to saw the bone, retaining enough skin to sew a flap over the stump.

The other case involved Tony Sankovich. As the result of a mine accident his right leg had to be amputated 6 inches below the knee. Tony had to stay in the hospital for three weeks, as a bad strep infection developed. During that time I was assigned to change the dressings when the doctor or day nurse weren't available. The stench from the pus oozing from the wound nauseated me. A courageous soul, Tony saw my problem and said "Never mind, Will. I'll help." I have often wondered how Tony and Toivo got along in life, handicapped as they were.

In 1914 Dr. Hanna bought a Ford runabout, one of the first automobiles in our town. I'd seen my first horseless carriage in 1909, a Ford parked in front of Swanson's saloon where it attracted a lot of attention. The driver was filling his carbide lamp container, and from the smell I got the idea the car operated on carbide. Later, a large red Winton Six touring convertible drove through our town; it cut quite a swath in the community. The rear seat was elevated, so passengers had two levels. In time other townspeople owned automobiles.

When Dr. Hanna got his runabout, so did Joe Bice, the master mechanic at the mine, and Harry Mullen, the mine surveyor. In 1913 John Matson, the operator of a saloon at Mass City, bought a Buick which he used to transport people around "the Loop" to Greenland and back; it was Mass City's first taxi.

I'd worked for Dr. Hanna one year, receiving $25 a month—fair compensation—but when I turned 16, I felt I should be earning more money. My next job was as a blacksmith's apprentice, swinging the 6-, 8- and 10-pound sledges which developed my muscles to an impressive degree. I also played basketball for Mass City against the Greenland, Rockland and Ontonagon teams. Community enthusiasm ran so high that the town council found it necessary to erect a wire partition to separate the players from the crowd of spectators. Our greatest fan was Mrs. Kidd, whe rang her cow bell or banged the poker against the tall wood-burning stove in our support. Winter evenings when we didn't play basketball Julius Lukkarilla, our star player, and I walked to The Ridge twice a week to take courses from two Greenland high school teachers. Following World War I, at Ferris Institute I received credits in English Literature and Geometry for these courses. Those good teachers would never accept any compensation for their time other than our warm thanks.

One of the main jobs at the blacksmith's shop was to heat and sharpen the drills used underground by the operators of the Murphy and Water-liner machines. When the drills were white hot, my boss placed them on the anvil; my job was to strike the pinion, or head, with the heavy sledges. For this I was paid $1.50 a day for a nine-hour shift. One day, as I swung the 8-pound sledge to strike the pinion which was held on the drill by the boss, I missed it and knocked it out of his hand. It flew 10 feet from the anvil. Fortunately he wasn't hurt, but I realized it could have resulted in serious injuries for him and told him so, apologizing for my error. He came back at me with a line of profanity so loud everybody in the shop heard it. John Westlake, the blacksmith foreman, was outraged at his outburst and told him to "Break it off!"

When things calmed down, I went to Mr. Westlake and told him I was quitting. He was very understanding and gave me a good recommendation. Thus, at 16, I became a rock picker in B shaft, equipped with shovel, pick, sledgehammer and wheelbarrow. I sorted copper rock from poor rock, filled the wheelbarrow with copper rock and dumped it down the chute. From there it was loaded by the trammers, my next job. I was 5′7″ and weighed 140 pounds; pushing those tram cars on the steel rails to the shaft several hundred feet away was hard work, so I was lucky to draw a husky Finnish partner, Matt Ahola. We were a good team, and more than once made a record, dumping more cars than the other trammers on the night shift, thus creating jealousy among our opposite numbers!

The job of operating a jack-hammer came next, one that put me in the classification of a miner, and my pay was increased to $2.50 a day. By 1915 many improvements had been made in underground operations, but one of the most interesting changes over the years was in the men themselves. Cornish miners had been largely supplanted by Finns who were able to out-produce the slightly built men of Cornwall under whom some Finns had trained. The majority of the population in Mass City was now Finnish or of Finnish extraction. I pay tribute to those Finns and their descendants. They were good law-abiding citizens and made a great contribution to our civic and community life.

Typical of the Finnish miners was one known to everyone as Nancy, his last name. Six feet two, powerfully built, he could wrestle a

Murphy machine up the tall stopes and erect his staging on the heavy poles and planks with ludicrous ease. He worked hard and fast and produced six to eight holes in the breast of the rock each shift. One day, as often happens in the mines, tragedy struck Nancy down; he was buried under a bad rock fall and killed, leaving a widow and three children.

We always kept a careful eye on the hangings and cracks which appeared periodically and attempted, by the use of long bars, to pry loose dangerous rocks above us to make our area as safe as possible, but one never knew. More than once on a beautiful summer night, as we went underground, I wondered if I would ever see daylight again. Finally I decided to give up hard-rock mining and went to work for Nara Brothers store as grocery clerk and delivery man at a salary of $65 a month.

Nara's was the general store—meat, groceries, dry goods and general merchandise. There were three horse and wagon delivery routes; mine was the one covering Old Mass, The Ridge and Greenland. I liked my job, especially visiting with the housewives as I took their orders for the next day. Most of my customers were English, but there were some Finns. I got pretty good at speaking Finnish, but what I remember best are the expressive swear words which, if translated literally, would have to be blanked out and marked: "Expletive deleted."

By then our family was doing well. Father had his job at the mine; Howard and I were working at Nara's; Ada and Alice had been happily married for some time and Chris was working his way through school at Ferris Institute at Big Rapids. That year I got myself on wheels—a secondhand Oakland touring car that cost $600; $150 down, and with Howard's help, $50 a month.

How we all enjoyed that car during that summer. The heavy snowfall in November, however, necessitated putting it in the barn on jacks for the winter, and we weren't able to take it out on the road again until April, 1917.

Ours was a small isolated community; the *Ontonagon Herald,* a weekly paper, was practically our only contact with world news. In 1914 we heard rumbles of the war in Europe, but the only way in which it touched our lives was the reaction of the foreign-born miners in our midst—Italians, Germans, Austrians, Russians, and those from the various Balkan countries.

A few immediately returned to their homelands. Two German miners, members of the naval reserve in the Fatherland, were called back for duty in the submarine service; several of their countrymen followed. Others remained, severing their ties to become ardent supporters of the Allied cause as time passed and we were drawn into the conflict.

The assassination of Archduke Francis Ferdinand, heir to the Austrian throne, at Sarajevo in Bosnia was the match that lighted the wildfire which was to sweep across the world. One month later Austria declared war on Serbia. August 1, Germany declared war on Russia; August 3, on France, and marched its troops into Belgium. August 4, Great Britain declared war on Germany, and August 25, on Austria.

In one month an isolated act of violence by a small group of terrorists had ignited a blaze that was to run, like the wildfire, around the globe.

Woodrow Wilson tried desperately to keep the United States neutral. Even after the sinking of the *Lusitania,* though 128 American lives were lost, he fought stubbornly against a declaration of war. By April 1917, however, Britain, by tightening the blockage of Germany, and the latter by stepping up its submarine attacks, had made traffic of any kind on the high seas impossible. America had lost much—ships and cargoes, crews and passengers. On April 6, 1917, the United States of America declared war on Germany. So, within one month of the time the Oakland was on the road again, so was I.

We left Houghton by special troop train, our destination Fort Wayne, Detroit to join our more seasoned comrades of G Company, 33rd Mighigan National Guard Regiment. The second generation of American immigrants—the Cornish, the Finns, the Irish, Germans, French, Poles, Austrians, Italians, Scandinavians, along with sons of native American families were on their way with a warning to the Kaiser to "Beware!" We Americans were coming "over there" to "stop 'is 'orses."

Saturday afternoon underground shift in front of the Mass Consolidated "dry." (1915)

My mother with George Henry, Jr. and Ada—just before leaving Liverpool by ship to join her husband at Negaunee, Michigan, 1892.

Wilkins family picture, 1903. Standing, back row: Christopher, Ada, George. Second row: Father, Elsie, Mother with Mabel on her knee; standing, Alice. Seated in front: Willie. (Mildred came later)

CHAPTER II

Nobody Wins A War!

(1917-1919)

I do not pretend to be a student of history; I am only one of millions who helped shape it. The first World War, however, is far enough behind us to give historians a proper perspective, to make a fairly accurate evaluation of things gained and things lost. Certainly World War I did not fulfill the cherished dreams of those idealists who believed we were fighting "to make the world safe for Democracy." History itself has destroyed the myth and the dream.

On April 6, 1917, however, when President Wilson declared war against Germany, the American people believed in the myth and the dream. For this they sent their fathers, their brothers, their husbands and their sons into battle.

They sent guns and ammunition; they sent their technical knowledge and their skill. They gave of their time, their money and their love for mankind to show the world how strong was their belief that every man was entitled to life, liberty and the pursuit of happiness.

Even at war's end, President Wilson still believed in the myth and the dream. He saw the world united by a common sorrow, and envisioned, not a world of nations, but one world dedicated to the premise that thenceforth man would put down his gun and take his place at the conference table where human rights would prevail. Early in the war Wilson had made it clear that this was a war against the German military leaders, not the German people. But the bitterness and hatred felt toward the German nation by the Allies was so great that secret treaties, already entered into by then, defeated Wilson's purpose. Thus, at Versailles, though some of Wilson's "Fourteen

Points'' were included, such as the insistence on democratic forms of government for new nations, much was lost. The German people were left with a crushing reparations bill. The teeth of a League of Nations, which was eventually formed, depended on the United States being a member. In the end the United States Senate rejected both the League of Nations and the Versailles Treaty, which we have never signed.

The dreadful fact is, that in spite of the sacrifice so nobly given, the world failed to learn the lesson spelled out in sweat and blood and tears.

The price is too great! It can never be marked: ''PAID IN FULL.'' Nobody wins a war.

Families, lines of descent were broken. Children, who should have been, were never born. So many men who, by their very numbers, might have taught us the lesson, never lived to try.

But my story here does not presume to be a judgment, nor does it concern the moral question involved in the war itself or the aftermath. Rather, it is the story of one raw recruit from a small town in America and *his* war. It is an almost day-to-day account of his experiences in that war, of his journey from the training camps of America to those in France, of his progress to the front line trenches where he was the day the Armistice was signed, of his service in the Army of Occupation, and finally, of his coming home.

In 1916, after putting in a year's duty on the Mexican border, the 33rd Michigan Regiment, National Guard had been mustered out except for G Company of Houghton, its complement reduced to half, and stationed at Fort Wayne, Detroit. Immediately war was declared Lieutenant Merrit Lamb of G Company was dispatched to Houghton and Ontonagon Counties to recruit men and bring the company up to required strength.

On May 7, 1917, following a brief session with Lieutenant Lamb, with two close friends, Bud Robson and George Bennetts, I was in the doctor's office undergoing a physical exam preparatory to induction into G Company. First Lieutenant Lamb was a dedicated soldier and true patriot, a man of great courage concerned for and patient with his men who regarded him with both respect and affection. Later, he was promoted to captain, served as intelligence officer at Regimental Headquarters in the Meuse-Argonne offensive, was killed there and buried in France.

Members of the Red Cross, that organization which did so much for the boys during the war, met our train at Marquette with coffee and boxes of food. The next stop was Fort Wayne. After training there, we went to Selfridge Air Base at Mt. Clemens for guard duty. From the ore docks at Ashland, Wisconsin, we left for Camp MacArthur, Waco, Texas, to undergo more intensive training. Our official title became G

Company, 125th Infantry of the famous Red Arrow 32nd Division, which the French called "Les Terribles." From Waco, Texas, we left for France.

Fort Wayne, named for "Mad Anthony" Wayne, Revolutionary War General, had long been used as an army post. The parade grounds where we underwent basic training were surrounded by two-story red brick Georgian buildings which served as our quarters. On the first floors were kitchens, mess halls and drill rooms where we stacked our rifles and other military gear. The second floors were dormitories where we slept on double-decked army cots at the foot of which we kept our army footlockers containing all our worldly goods.

The day after our arrival we were issued complete olive drab uniforms—underwear, socks, shoes, canvas leggings, overcoats, ponchos and broadbrimmed campaign hats like those worn by the men under General "Black Jack" Pershing in their skirmish with Pancho Villa on the Mexican border. When completely outfitted, we were required to send our civilian clothes home; thereafter it was a courts-martial offense to be caught in them.

The rifles issued to us were bolt-action Springfields, superior to the Lee Enfield rifles with which the British and a few of our divisions were equipped. We had a healthy respect for our guns, side arms and bayonets; in combat our lives would depend on them. The old campaigners taught us the manual of arms and the proper cadence while marching of 120 steps per minute, 30 inches to each step.

We had to memorize the "Duty of a Soldier," the nomenclature of the Springfield and the .45 Colt automatic pistols issued to the officers and noncommissioned officers. We learned to take the rifles and pistols apart and put them together again without assistance. Within a few days Company G was adept enough to be invited to participate in a Memorial Day parade in Detroit. We were standing "at ease" in one of the side streets, waiting to join the parade when I heard a young girl say to her mother as they passed, "Mother, they all look so young!"

During our first week at Fort Wayne we copper country boys were required to have the necessary shots and vaccinations. It was a beautiful sunny spring day, so the army surgeon and his staff moved their equipment to tables outside the infirmary. Shedding our long sleeved shirts, we stood in undershirts and watched what was going on at the end of that long white line. Everything went by the alphabet, so I was always near the end, even for payroll. One soldier fell to the ground, then another. Rumors came back the shots were extremely painful and would make us ill. Anxiety built up. To add to the tension, we saw four recruits seated by the doctor *before* receiving their shots. Psychological trauma! But there were no fatalities. Everybody got the necessary three shots plus the vaccinations and wound up with sore and swollen arms for several days.

My third day at camp I drew K.P. (kitchen police.) My job was to peel a 100-pound sack of onions for our dinner. There I sat, all by myself, in our basement kitchen storeroom surrounded by onions and peelings, tears streaming down my cheeks. It wasn't only the onions. I was homesick!

The most important guard duty was Post No. 1 at the guardhouse. The O.D. (officer of the day) and commanding officer passed there frequently, and you had to be alert or you'd find yourself inside with the prisioners instead of out.

First sergeants have a reputation for being tough, hard-hearted men, but our top sergeant, Joe Caspary of Houghton, was quite the opposite. An excellent drillmaster, he was kind and considerate, always concerned for the welfare of his men.

July 5, G Company was ordered to Selfridge Airfield, then being constructed near Mt. Clemens, Michigan, for further training and guard duty until the men of the aero squadrons could take over at the new airfield. We were now up to our full strength of 150 men and three officers. Captain Tommie Smith, in command of the company since the Mexican border patrol in 1916, was ably assisted by two officers, Lieutenants Lamb and Elmer Theriault.

At Selfridge, I was promoted to the rank of corporal with a pay increase to $36 a month, but those two stripes meant far more to me than the money. My assignment was the provost guard, stationed in the evenings at the busiest corners in Mt. Clemens where we policed the conduct of men in uniform while off duty. At the end of the evening Dick Delbridge, Bert Colenso and I, sometimes joined by Sergeant Caspary, rode up the St. Clair River to the air base on the patrol boat. All Cornish descendants, we harmonized as we rode up the river in the moonlight, singing popular war songs, "Over There," "Long, Long Trail A-Winding" and others.

One night, having taken into custody a drunken member of G Company, we were concerned if he'd sober up by drill time the next morning. Someone suggested we get him a can of tomatoes from the storeroom next to the kitchen for that purpose. Finding it locked, Dick Delbridge crawled in through the window and was in the act of taking a can when the mess sergeant caught us. We gave him our reason, using our drunken comrade as Exhibit A. The mess sergeant said it was a serious offense, called it burglary, and took our names, stating he would report us to the captain in the morning. Unknown to us, others had broken into the storeroom and the sergeant was endeavoring to catch the real culprit.

As I crawled into my bunk that night I had visions of being court-martialed, spending time in the guard house, worst of all, losing my two cherished stripes. For days we waited anxiously but nothing happened. Evidently the sergeant didn't report the incident. The anguish we experienced during that wait, though, was punishment enough.

August 30 our guard duties were assumed by the men of the aero squadrons. The Curtis biplanes had arrived and were flown day and night by the newly trained crews. That same day we left by train for Ashland, Wisconsin, for temporary duty guarding the two large ore docks there. October 10 we departed for Camp MacArthur at Waco, Texas, named for General Douglas MacArthur's father. There, the 32nd (Red Arrow) Division was being formed from the national guard regiments of Michigan and Wisconsin, then being federalized.

Large squad tents were already in place on our arrival. The 6-foot walls and floors were of board planks; on top were the canvas tents which allowed greater head space for the eight men quartered in each tent. G Company of the 33rd Michigan was now G Company of the 125th U.S. Infantry with six officers and 250 men. Each company had 32 squad tents in straight rows stretching from the mess hall at the top of the company street to the latrines and showers at the foot. Eight sergeants, of which I was one, having received a second promotion earlier in October, were quartered in a tent at the head of the line next to the mess hall. In addition to our army cots we had a small wood-burning stove in the center. Nights in that part of Texas were cold, and we appreciated the warmth of those stoves. Days were hot and windy, the air filled with a fine sandy grit. At reveille, we raced down the company street in our longies to the cold water showers and latrines, and back. Several mornings there were icicles hanging from the shower heads.

Many replacements joined us to bring our numbers up to new wartime strength, among them First Lieutenant Joseph M. Donnelly, a lawyer from Ontonogan, who was put in charge of the 4th Platoon to which I was assigned. He was a fine officer, admired and respected by us all. "Dad" Blair, the oldest man in the company, a veteran of the Spanish-American War, was our hard-driving drill sergeant. We spent long hours at bayonet drill, charging into straw dummies; at gas drills, becoming familiar with all types of gas used by the Germans. Hours were spent on the rifle range where many of us qualified as sharpshooters and were awarded medals for our expertise. Instructors from overseas demonstrated the use of hand grenades and rifle grenades which were fitted over the barrels of our rifles. We were taught to read topographical maps and the ability to orient ourselves with varying terrains. There were more drills by French instructors on assaulting an objective in platoon and company fronts spaced at specific intervals, and in trench warfare. Our hours were so filled with drills of all kinds we seldom went to the nearby town of Waco.

I went only once to purchase an electric device for our Victrola. Boarding the city bus at the camp gate, not knowing the seating regulations in the South, I took a seat in the rear. I noticed the driver looked me over rather carefully and wondered why. As we proceeded toward the city center, the rear of the bus filled with blacks but I thought nothing of it. In 1970, while attending a show by Don Ho, the Hawaiian entertainer, I heard him tell this story which recalled that incident in Texas.

"I was in the Air Force during World War II, stationed in Texas. I boarded a bus. The driver looked at me. I looked at him. Then he said, 'I guess you better sit in the middle.'" When the laughter died down, Don Ho said, "I guess my color is beige."

At Christmas Sergeant "Chub" Dickens, whose bunk was in our tent, received a quart of peaches which he shared with us. Actually, it was whiskey with the peaches for camouflage. That was my first taste of hard liquor. It made for a most convivial Christmas Eve. The phonograph, sent to us by the Masonic Lodge of Houghton and installed in the mess hall, played all during the holidays.

Our division was well trained, equipped and ready for overseas, and we knew our movement to the port of embarkation was imminent. Some fathers came all the way from northern Michigan to visit their sons. One was Jud Ingram's father, who saw him for the last time, as Jud was one of our first casualties in the Battle of the Marne at Chateau-Thierry.

One day Lieutenant Lamb took six of us noncommissioned officers for a hike in the country. We brought vegetables from the company kitchen and after a few hours hike built a fire to cook our lunch. From a nearby farmhouse one of the men had purloined a stray chicken which Lieutenant Lamb cooked over an open fire without utensils, encasing it, feathers and all, in a ball of clay which hardened as it cooked and turned. When done, the feathers and skin came off with the clay and the chicken was juicy, tender and delicious. It was typical of Lieutenant Lamb that before we left he went to the farmhouse and paid for the chicken.

The end of January found us entrained for Camp Merritt, New Jersey. For security reasons our route was not disclosed to us. Coaches were blacked out and locked as we sped on our way; we didn't know we passed through Detroit during the dead of night. How we would have cherished an opportunity to see friends and loved ones for even a short visit on the station platform. Our troop trains went from Detroit into Canada and reentered the United States at the Canadian Niagara Falls, where we were allowed to detrain and view the falls. A real treat for us country lads.

At Camp Merritt we were given a rigid inspection and issued equipment for overseas. While there, our entire division was assembled in an immense auditorium to listen to a stirring address by former President Teddy Roosevelt. He was popular with the men of Michigan and Wisconsin, both progressive states which supported him during the "Bull Moose" campaign. As he entered the hall, the Wisconsin band struck up "On Wisconsin," and our band played "Michigan, My Michigan," much to Teddy's delight. What an enthusiastic ovation those ten thousand men gave him! In turn, he flashed his toothy smile, kept clapping his hands and saying, "Bully! Bully!" His address was emotional and inspiring and buoyed our spirits for the "great adventure." That high-pitched voice seemed odd coming from such a robust barrel-chested man dressed in formal morning attire.

Rumor had it Teddy was hoping to command a division overseas. From our reception it was apparent he would have been welcomed as our commanding general. He'd led his famous "Rough Riders" up San Juan Hill; we felt he could lead us successfully on the battlefields of France. Of course, it was not to be. President Woodrow Wilson had won a squeaker over Charles Evans Hughes on his record that he had kept us out of war. A Democratic administration would not countenance Teddy, a progressive Republican, becoming a war hero.

By one of those strange quirks of Fate, our outfit captured the town of Fismes and the Bois des Jomblettes during the Chateau-Thierry counteroffensive. There we found the grave of Teddy's aviator son, Quentin, who was shot down by enemy aircraft. The grave was surrounded by a neat white birch-pole fence and someone had cared enough to keep it trimmed.

At 5 a.m. on February 7, 1918, we entrained for Hoboken, our port of embarkation, where the Red Cross served us coffee and rolls. As we marched through the city to board our troop ship, newsboys were calling "Read all about it." The *Tuscania* had been sunk while in a convoy off the coast of France with heavy loss of life. Aboard that ship were some of the advance men of our division headquarters. Thus, in spite of all the Army's precautions for secrecy, the whole world then knew that the 32nd Division was on its way to France. We were the sixth full division to arrive there, followed by 30 other full divisions by Armistice Day.

Our ship, the old North German Lloyd freighter, *Bremen,* renamed the U.S. *Antigone,* had four decks. Our 4th Platoon was assigned to C deck, grateful it wasn't D, as the air was bad enough where we were. Quarters were almost filled by four-decker bunks; in this case it was better to be at the bottom. Some men were seasick before we even pulled away from the dock. As we got under way, we were blacked out, no lights except faint blue lights used by the ship as running lights. All port holes were closed, adding to the foul air on the lower decks. It was a rough crossing. The number of seasick passengers increased daily; I was one of them. Often during that 14-day trip Bud Robson and I met at the latrine where we commiserated over our *mal de mer.* Added to our physical discomfort was our sorrow at the loss of our men on the *Tuscania,* many of whom were known personally to us. The occasional concerts by the 125th Infantry band were real morale boosters on that voyage.

Lookouts and guards were posted under the supervision of the navy—on each side of the forward deck, on the afterdeck, and in the crow's nest. The convoy consisted of five transports—*Von Steuben, Finland, Martha Washington, President Lincoln,* and *Antigone*—escorted by the heavy cruiser *Pueblo.* Tension began to build as we neared the coast of France. Two days out of Brest we were joined by eight destroyers, at which time the *Pueblo* turned and headed back to the States.

Enemy submarines were reported in the area, and no wonder. A full moon laid a wide path across the water, creating ideal submarine weather. Other destroyers joined us a day out of France when some of our transports took off under escort for St. Nazaire. The *Antigone* entered the harbor of Brest on February 24, and we debarked the following day, marching over cobblestone streets to Pontonazin Barracks. We were a sad-looking bunch of seasick soldiers. It was raining, and after 14 days on a transport with little opportunity to exercise, we bent under the load of bedding rolls, steel helmets and overcoats.

French kids, shouting, "Soldats Americains," ran beside us as we trudged the six miles up the hill to the assigned barracks. Bud Robson and I had studied French together from dictionaries given us by the YMCA so I decided to try it out. To a little boy running at our side I said, slowly and carefully, "Kome—ah—voo—sa—pell—e—voo?" He stared at me, then said, "Eh?" So much for my first attempt to fraternize.

The Pontonazin Barracks were built during the reign of Louis II; later they were occupied by Napoleon's cavalry troops. We were told it was a rest camp where we would have a few days to relax and stretch our muscles. There was no straw for our bed ticks, so we slept on the stone floors where Napoleon's horses had been stabled. Our only rations were those we carried with us in our packs—hardtack and bully beef. Some rest camp!

At 4:30 the next morning we were awakened with orders to hike back to Brest to entrain for our new destination. At Brest we had our first experience with French trains and their small compartments, the only entrance outside doors, and running boards along the sides. Each compartment was supposed to hold eight men, but now we also carried ammunition belts, a full canteen, as well as a small army pick and shovel for digging foxholes, and eight soldiers with all their equipment made it a very tight fit.

The whole day was spent loading the train, and we did not leave Brest until late evening. About 2 a.m. we stopped at a station where the French Red Cross served us hot coffee and rolls. As the morning dragged on, with sleep impossible because of crowded conditions, we made several such stops, always greeted by the Red Cross with hot coffee and croissants. A welcome treat! Occasionally the train stopped for what seemed no reason at all. On investigation we learned it was a "nature" stop for the engineer and fireman.

As we chugged along, some men chose to ride the running boards outside, clinging to the door handles. Some of us more adventuresome fellows rode on top of the coaches where we stood, waving and shouting at the farmers in the fields. An adventure that almost cut us down before we'd had a go at the Jerries. As the coach ahead entered a tunnel, I saw there was less than 3 feet clearance and yelled, "Duck!" We flattened out just in time. If we hadn't, we'd have been knocked over and mangled under the wheels of the following coaches. When we were through the tunnel, we lost no time climbing down to our seats inside.

At last, we arrived at our first camp in France, Gievres, where the storage depot for American Expeditionary Forces was located. Nearby was Romarantin, headquarters for the American Air Forces. We were issued iron cots, straw to fill our bed ticks and assigned to commodious barracks. After the first hot meal in three days, we were ready to sack out for a much needed sleep.

We had no idea how long we were to be in Gievres, or what we were to do, but we didn't have long to wait. Work details were called for by the engineer officers in charge of the base and Second Battalion; 125th Infantry became a labor battalion with work ranging from loading and unloading the French box cars and gondolas to grading road beds and laying track. The men of the battalion were of every trade, and there wasn't a job they couldn't handle. Bert Colenso had been a locomotive engineer in Hancock and had a great time running the little antiquated Belgian engine and tooting its high-pitched squeaky whistle.

Some men were assigned to guard duty; I was sergeant of the guard at the prison compound—three barracks enclosed by a high wire fence. First lieutenant Paul R. Des Jardin, an all-American football player from the University of Chicago, in charge of the stockade, was my immediate officer and one of the finest officers I knew. Bud Robson, a corporal of the guard, the lieutenant and I worked together.

Some 50 men in the compound awaited courts-martial, most for being AWOL (absent without leave). They came from several American units then in France including three from our own Company G who had taken off for Gay Paree. One day I found one of them sitting on the edge of his cot, holding his genitals and crying like a baby. He'd contracted a serious and painful venereal disease on his wild spree. I was sorry for him and did all I could to help him. He must have been cured, as he went on to serve with distinction in the Meuse-Argonne offensive where he was killed.

Once, during a crap game, an altercation between one of our men from Detroit and a black man from a stevedore outfit came to blows. The black, who was getting the worst of it, broke off and ran toward his barracks. Someone yelled, "He's going to get his razor!" We guards placed both men in solitary, broke up the dice game, and put all the other prisoners to work.

The depot at Gievres covered an area 6 by 13 miles and was in the process of a tremendous building program when we arrived, but stores and supplies were coming in faster than they could be taken care of. Rolling stock was in such demand in France that material was unloaded at once to be stored later. Great cone-shaped stacks of wheelbarrows and shovels were left uncovered. Buildings were erected *around* piles of material rather than the conventional procedure of putting same inside buildings. The situation was chaotic and getting worse for lack of manpower, but our battalion got the wheels turning. Things soon changed and order took the place of disorder. Buildings went up all over the place and were promptly filled with war materiel. The wheelbarrows, shovels, boxes and crates vanished; in their places were neat rows of storage buildings. The work of our battalion was highly commended by the colonel of Engineers in charge of the depot.

April 4 we were relieved of our duties and ordered to our training area at Nouvelles les Champlite where our 2nd Battalion, under command of Major Guy M. Wilson, was to be billeted. Traveling by train, we reached our new station the next evening. This was the heart of the 10th Training Area allotted for training purposes for the entire 32nd (Red Arrow) Division, now together again as a fighting unit. Billets had been secured for the battalion in French homes. Those who had ideas each man would have a private room in some cozy farmhouse or townhouse and be catered to by the householders were soon disillusioned. We were led in groups from five to 20, depending on the size of the billet, into stables, barns, haylofts, any available space. With two squads of our platoon I was assigned to a bare room on the second floor of a dilapidated building. Seventeen straw ticks were spread out on the floor, 2 feet apart. Morale was good, however, as we now entered our final phase of training before moving on to the big show.

When the 32nd Division arrived in France, General Pershing's headquarters at Chaumont had decided ours was to become a replacement division and not kept together as a combat unit. Thus, while we were at Gievres, several men of our 128th Infantry Regiment had been sent as replacements to the 1st and 42nd Divisions which were then on the front lines. Upon arrival in France, our commanding General, Brigadier General Haan, hastened to Chaumont to confer with General Pershing, his mission to convince Pershing and his staff that we were a well-trained division ready for the front. He must have had clout, as he succeeded in having the orders changed and the 32nd Division retained as a combat division. The 41st Division, consisting of the Oregon and Washington National Guard troops then arriving in France, took over as a replacement division. Later, as I said, the 32nd Division fought so fiercely we were called "Les Terribles," proud to justify the confidence Pershing and Haan had in us.

The middle of April, while we were listed as a replacement division, prior to General Haan's conference with General Pershing, an order was received from Regimental Headquarters requiring the transfer of about 30 men from G Company to the 128th Regiment, which outfit had been whittled down to a skeleton force as a result of replacements sent to the 1st Division. Rather than make an entirely new regiment from replacements it was decided to take men from each remaining company in the division. Company commanders were left no choice in the matter of transfers. An arbitrary ruling was made, as a result of which several of our buddies of G Company who had been with us since Detroit were drawn by lot and transferred to the 128th Regiment.

Training at Nouvelle les Champlits was the most intensive we had had. We drilled eight hours a day, rain or shine. The detailed training schedules came from Regimental Headquarters for a progressive system with close order drill, trench warfare and open warfare formations. Battle-trained French and American officers gave us the benefit of their combat knowledge. Work on the rifle range was intensified, special attention given to gas drills and the use of grenades, personally supervised by Major Wilson, who was an expert.

After long hours of drilling, relaxation came with nightly Victrola concerts in our mess hall. Within a week all the kids in town came to listen followed by the older townspeople, none of whom had ever heard a phonograph. Major Wilson was most anxious the men of his command be on friendly terms with the French people. When he paid a courtesy call on the town mayor, the mayor's only request was that the citizens be permitted to listen to the wonderful music box. Interest was so great many had to stay outside and listen through the open windows. Our donors back home were pleased their gift was so widely appreciated.

Of course, we were active boisterous young soldiers, not all angels. Our first payday men flocked to the town's cafes and restaurants and generally raised a "little hell." Vin rouge and vin blanc flowed freely. Despite Major Wilson's admonitions, some men got out of hand.

One midnight the "call to arms" was sounded. This was an alert ordering us to form a company line in the street, *on the double,* and stand at attention. On our way we grabbed our guns and clothing. Speculation ran rife. Had the Germans broken through? Were they, even then, on their way to our town? Standing at attention in company front, we saw a strong light move down the line. When a soldier was asked to step forward three paces, Major Wilson, his staff holding gas lanterns, scanned his face closely, then passed on.

After the order to dismiss came, we learned that one of our drunken soldiers had raped a French woman. She'd reported it immediately to our headquarters, stating the culprit had a mustache. That was why the call to arms; the men with mustaches told to step forward. When they were brought before the victim, the man she identified confessed at once. The next day our battalion was ordered to form a square on our drill field, all men facing inward. Major Wilson and his staff stood in the center. Two guards brought out the rapist, and Major Wilson addressed the men.

"Men of the 2nd Battalion: we have come over here to fight for these brave French people against a common enemy. The men of Nouvelle, old and young, have had to leave their families behind and are even now fighting to save their homes, their loved ones and their country. One of our number, a member of H Company, has committed rape of a woman of Nouvelle whose husband and son are fighting at the front. How would you men feel if someone were to commit such a dastardly crime against one of your loved ones while you were away?

"I could have this man tried by courts-martial, but that would mean a prison term, here or at home, and that means a loss of manpower which we sorely need in this war. So, this is what I am going to do. I am turning this soldier over to the men of his company to mete out such punishment as they deem adequate. I suggest each member of the company go in those woods nearby and cut a branch, that you form two lines, commonly referred to as a 'hot ass line,' that you make him run the length of the line and use your clubs to the extent you feel it sufficient punishment to deter him from *ever* committing such a crime again."

After that address there wasn't a man in the battalion that wouldn't have joined with H Company. Later, we learned, as the rapist ran the line, he fell down several times from blows but each time was picked up and made to go on. He had no broken bones, but his bruises were such he was confined to the infirmary for two weeks. When he returned to duty, he was transferred to another outfit.

I have often thought of the astute way in which Major Wilson handled this affair. Not only was the culprit punished with the full approval of his fellow soldiers, but the army hadn't lost a man.

Another demonstration of on-the-spot justice came while in Nouvelle. Soldiers were billeted in every nook and cranny of that small town. Two inquisitive soldiers learned the owner of the main cafe had several big barrels of wine in his cellar. One night they entered the cellar, removed the bung of a barrel near the partly opened window and inserted a suction hose which led outside. As evening approached and few people were on the streets, the men sat by the window and took long hearty draughts of the wine, enjoying their ingenious little trick for some time until their exuberance led them to share it with other buddies.

Noticing the mob of soldiers near the window, the cafe owner soon discovered his barrel of vin rouge was almost empty. He came at the soldiers, gesticulating and shouting, "Mon Dieu! Sacre Bleu!" Then he called our military police. The result: our sipping cronies were made to pay the cafe owner the total value of the barrel of wine which sum was deducted from their pay.

On May 13 we got the order we had been waiting for—a transfer of the division to the front at lower Alsace. Transportation was by freight cars, the famous "Quarantes Hommes ou Huites Chevaux"—40 men or eight horses to a car—detraining at Mortzwiller, a town in mountainous terrain deep in the woods of Alsace.

I will never forget those first sounds of the guns of war. Around 3 a.m., as we hiked down the mountain road toward our assignment in the little town of Oberbruck, guns in the nearby hills opened up. The explosions reverberated through the Alsatian mountains, scaring hell out of us. Thinking we were under fire, we proceeded with the utmost quiet. The guns, however, were those of our allies, the French 75's being fired by Italian mountain troops at the enemy. Because of its accuracy and speed of firing, the famous 75 millimeter gun (soixante-quinze) was the most efficient piece of artillery in the war.

In Oberbruck I was billeted with two squads of our 4th platoon in the hayloft of a great old Alsatian farmhouse. Typical of local architecture, it was built of sandstone and timbers with an extension housing the farm equipment, animals and fowl, our loft above. A vast manure pile out front was evidence of the affluence of our farm family.

As we sacked out in our new quarters we could hear the bucolic sounds of cows, sheep, horses and pigs below us as they munched their food and communicated with each other. So peaceful, I thought. So normal. It was hard to believe that within a few miles men waited with guns to destroy us all—animals and men alike.

The farm family spoke German, as Alsace had been part of Germany since the Franco-Prussian War. Now it was part of France again, the French troops having captured this portion of Alsace north of the Swiss border at the start of the war in 1914. The woman of the house was very kind to us. In turn, we gave her and her little daughter, then seven years old, chocolate, soap and other items hard to come by.

Alsace is a beautiful country, almost heartbreakingly so that spring. The fruit trees were in bloom, the fields tender green, the well-cultivated gardens in lush growth. How could you explain all that life, and death waiting just down the road? But you couldn't often stop to question or philosophize. War took precedence over everything else.

Our 1st battalion, under command of Major Gus Gansser, occupied the trenches in the Doller Sector along the banks of the Doller River. The 3rd battalion was in support at the town of Kirchberg. Our 2nd battalion was in reserve at Oberbruck and Dollern. First Lieutenant Elmer Theriault was now in command of G Company.

French officers were assigned us as instructors, teaching us more about offensive and defensive trench fighting and liaison work in those two weeks than we'd learned during all previous training.

June 9, Company G moved to the city of Sentheim and occupied a new section of trenches in the Michelbach sector. This battered village, on a knoll overlooking the action, was strategically located. It had been shelled so often not a building was intact. We were billeted in dugouts in and about the town, which had long since been deserted except for an elderly couple who refused to leave.

On the night of June 11 we quietly entered our sector of the trenches for the first time and by midnight had completed our relief of the French. Obviously, the enemy was not aware that the French had been relieved by Americans for there was no shelling, only scattered machine gun fire.

These were front line trenches. Then there were communication trenches which led in a zigzag pattern to the rear. It was by these trenches our dog-robbers, as we called the K.P.'s, brought us buckets of hot soup and coffee which two men carried slung over a pole across their shoulders.

Observation balloons, looking like large sausages, were posted along our lines and hurriedly pulled down when enemy planes were sighted. At times the observers in the small baskets underneath had to parachute to the ground.

I was placed in command of a contingent of 30 men, and we occupied a deep dugout. The former French occupants had constructed bunks of boards and wire, so we felt quite comfortable. The trenches ran in front of the dugout with large protective parapets in front of which stretched several strands of barbed wire. The French had placed duck boards the full length of the bottom of the trenches which enabled us to keep our feet above the water. Contrary to the general impression and the first British method of trench warfare, trenches were not held by placing men shoulder to shoulder along the parapet, but by isolated groups, a squad or more, in the intervals between the supporting troops.

All officers were now equipped with Very pistols for shooting up flares to communicate with artillery to the rear and to light up no-man's-land when suspicious of Boche raiders approaching.

While relieving our French counterparts, I set my heavy pack down by my assigned bunk and went to post my men. Later, I discovered the pack had been ransacked and the straight-edged razor my father gave me when I started to shave had been stolen. My attempts to inquire of the French were parried by, "Pas comprends!" Worse than losing my razor was the feeling of "bad cricket" to be treated thus by someone I had come to help.

We'd been told this was a rest area for both French and German troops and, at different times during the day, they gathered on their own side of the Doller River to wash their clothing, exchange greetings and, later in the day, fire a few rounds at each other's positions. All that was changed now. We opened fire on any movement we observed, and the Germans returned it so we had plenty of action.

One night I had charge of a raiding party. Eight of us, including Bud Robson, cut through our wire, using extreme care, as both sides of no-man's-land were constantly lighted with flares which descended slowly on small parachutes. Any movement could easily be detected, so we lay perfectly still until the flares went out. Crawling on elbows and knees, we reached the enemy's barbed wire. Absolute quiet was vital for we could hear voices at an outpost inside their wire; any noise would draw instant fire. Two of our huskiest men crawled under the wire, jumped into the outpost, took the two men there by surprise and muffled them so fast no outcry was made.

We had no trouble getting our prisoners back to our lines. They'd been in the war since 1914 and were glad to be out of it. The minute we got to our trenches they asked, "Haben sie cigaretten?"

The night of June 14 the Germans made a raid on our front where our battalion joined that of the Senegalese, French territorial troops who held the sector to our left. The raid lasted an hour in which we were subjected to intense artillery barrage. The Senegalese suffered several casualties before they drove the Germans back. The next morning I saw my first victims of war. The bodies of four Senegalese were laid out on the ground, ferocious even in death with their many facial scars. They were fierce fighters and feared by the Germans. Carrying scimitars, a curved single-edged sword, they often made quiet raids into no-man's-land, sneaking their way through the wire and rapping on the parapet with their swords. When the guards raised their heads to ascertain the noise, the Senegalese whacked them off. Though we sent many patrols into no-man's-land and conducted raids on the enemy trenches, no casualties were suffered.

The company returned to Sentheim to a reserve position for a so-called rest period. It was a change but not exactly what we mean when we say rest. The entire outfit was put to work from 5 a.m. to 5 p.m. covering the whole reserve position in reconnaissance and occupation.

On Memorial Day the battalion hiked to Massevaux to parade and take part in the celebration, a welcome diversion. Our division commander, Major General Haan, was an honored guest. With several French officers and civilians he reviewed our battalion.

On the night of July 11 the battalion returned to the Doller sector to the right of our old position. G and H Companies were once again on the front with E Company in support and F Company in reserve. From now on our patrols were out every night, our star shells were fired constantly, and no-man's-land was ours. We used to sing this song in the trenches:

Keep your head down, Allemand,
Keep your head down, Allemand,
Last night by the pale moonlight
We saw you—we saw you—
You were mending your broken wire
As we opened rapid fire—
If you want to see your father in your Fatherland,
Keep your head down, Allemand!

When an enemy patrol member, entangled in our wire, was captured, he claimed he came to give himself up. He was taken to Battalion Headquarters where he gave valuable information about the location of ammunition dumps and artillery positions. As a result, our artillery was able to open fire and wreak havoc on the enemy.

While occupying trenches and bunks the French had used for years, we were bothered with lice—huge voracious "cooties"—as big as large ants, which covered our bodies with red welts. During a lull we sat in the sunshine, "reading our undershirts" as we expressed it, picking the lice off and cracking them between our thumbnails. The only delousing method we had, for DDT was unheard-of.

Our withdrawal from the Alsace Sector began on July 19 when orders came to move north at once to join the counteroffensive on the Marne. At last, we were to be in a major operation. We hiked back to Mertzwiller and La Collogne where we reorganized. On July 22, at Autremont, we entrained in freight cars, passing through Paris and detraining at Veriberie, west of Soissons where General Foch's great counteroffensive was taking place. From there we hiked to Nery where we remained for two days as part of the general reserve of the army corps fighting around Soissons.

July 26 we moved 75 miles by motor truck to Chateau-Thierry and spent the night in the Verdilly woods close to Chateau-Thierry, which had just been liberated. The city was a wreck. The bridge across the Marne was down. The railroad depot was pockmarked with shell holes, and few buildings were left undamaged. Evidence of a hasty German retreat was everywhere. German bodies, dead horses and war materiel were strewn over the fields. That first night we had to select our sleeping positions with care so as not to wake up in the morning with a dead German beside us. The night of the 27th we moved our position to the rear of the 42nd and 28th Divisions which were on the line near the village of Fresnes. July 28 was spent in the woods under constant shell fire. We'd not had a hot meal in four days and were hoping to see the rolling kitchens, which did ultimately arrive.

On July 29 we received orders to relieve the 28th Division then at Courmont fighting for the woods on the heights beyond the city. That day was spent in preparation for the move into the combat zone. As it turned out, I did not go.

While we were still in the trenches in Alsace, a communication came from army headquarters stating truck drivers were needed and for interested personnel to make application. I had discussed it with Lieutenant Donnelly and his reply was: "Hells Bells (his strongest cuss words), sergeant, you didn't come all the way to France to be a truckdriver!" I agreed. Since then he'd been promoted to captain and on August 14, 1918, took command of the company while in combat. The day we were getting ready to move into the combat zone he called me back to headquarters. To my surprise he handed me orders to proceed immediately to Officers' Candidate School at Langres. Throughout the years, while he served as a judge in northern Michigan, whenever I saw him I expressed my gratitude. I was convinced that by sending me there he'd saved my life. On October 9, in the Meuse-Argonne offensive, he was severely wounded and awarded the Croix de Guerre with Palm.

As I proceeded to Langres via Paris, however, I had genuine regret at leaving my buddies. We'd grown up together, and had gone through training and seen our first combat duty together. Tears filled my eyes as they prepared to move forward, and I to leave them, for I knew I would not see some of them again. Within two days several men of G Company were killed in action.

I am proud to have served with the 32nd Division and the brave men of Michigan and Wisconsin. The following quote from "The American Heritage—World War I" shows how justified was General Pershing's decision to retain the 32nd as a combat division:

> On the Ourcq, the tired 3rd was relieved by the fresh 32nd (Michigan and Wisconsin), a powerhouse division, of which Pershing thought so little that he started to break it up.... Then the 32nd with one brigade of the 28th stormed and took a dominant ridge. With that the Germans lost their hold on the Ourcq. The Allied attack northward resumed August 1st.... Best of all was the 32nd, which crushed through the new German resistance line in the first stroke and held what it gained.... East of Bachoches the 4th Division crossed the river and the 32nd on the right of the 4th captured Fismes.... But it cost more than 50,000 American casualties to go from the Marne to Vesle. (A distance of about 50 miles or less.)

En route to Langres I stayed all night at the YMCA in Paris. That beautiful city was completely blacked out. Few people were seen on the streets. It was a desolate and dreary sight. The Germans were within 30 miles of the city when they were turned back at the Marne a few days previously, but the "Big Berthas" were still blasting sections of the city.*

In Paris I ran into Master Sergeant Reg Hollister of Houghton, originally of G Company (transferred to the headquarters company of our regiment), now also assigned to OCS and on his way to Langres. Some 200 men attended the school, all noncommissioned officers, most of whom had been in combat as platoon sergeants and had considerable battle experience.

There were more bayonet and gas drills. We had to crawl through barbed wire and demonstrate familiarity with all types of offensive weapons. The thrust of the course was based mainly on platoon leadership; it was known that we were to join combat units then being reinforced for the coming all-American offensive on the Meuse-Argonne front. The schedule was rough, the training intense, but few failed to make the grade. On September 25, 1918, we were commissioned as 2nd lieutenants of Infantry and assigned to combat divisions, mine being G Company, 6th Infantry Regiment, 5th Division (Red Diamond). I had just turned 21. Reg Hollister was sent to H Company of the same regiment.

Training seven days a week, few of us found time to visit the town of Langres, less than a mile away, but on our last evening several of us got together in our quarters to celebrate. One buddy had a few bottles of Benedictine which we polished off and had hangovers the next morning.

The 5th Division had just participated in the St. Mihiel offensive and were on their way to join the Meuse-Argonne battle which commenced September 26. When I joined the outfit on October 5, it was camped in the woods outside Nixeville and was in the process of being reequipped and receiving replacements to bring it up to full battle strength. Its full complement of six officers consisted of 1st Lieutenant S.M. Bemiss of Virginia commanding, 1st Lieutenant James Casey, a former regular army sergeant, 2nd Lieutenants Maurice Ricker, John E. White, Paul A. Connally and myself.

Within hours orders came to move out. At 2 p.m. the 2nd Battalion commenced the 15-mile hike to the Bois-de-Hesse, during which time we passed through the original no-man's-land and the trenches occupied by French and Germans for four years. Every foot of ground had been shelled; what trees still stood were no higher than fence posts. Looking at the devastation all around us, we paid silent tribute to the French "Poilus" who defended their country so magnificently during 1915 and 1916.

At Bois-de-Hesse we were billeted in a German dugout large enough to shelter 600 men. From October 6 to 11 I barely had time to get acquainted with the noncoms and men of my platoon whom I would soon lead into battle. We had little time to drill, but we found a few fields in which we could go through the four-wave drill. The regiment was visited by our brigade commander, Brigadier General Paul B.

*"Big Berthas" were manufactured by the Krupp Munitions Works, which, along with its owner and board of directors, was to play such an infamous part in World War II.

Malone, who knew we were about to go into our first rigorous combat. He gave us a great pep talk, praising the conduct of the regiment in all its engagements. Major Courtney Hodges, our battalion commander, was a soft-spoken Georgian and a capable officer. In World War II he was placed in command of our First Army, advancing to the rank of Lieutenant General.

On the afternoon of October 11 we hiked to the Bois-de-Montfaucon; October 13 we moved on to Cote 315 at Montfaucon where we rested two hours. Orders came then to move immediately, as the division was scheduled to attack the next morning on a large front, its four regiments of infantry in line—the 9th Brigade (composed of the 6th and 11th Regiments) on the right.

The order to move forward came at 4 p.m. Lieutenant Bemiss briefed the officers and noncommissioned officers. The 3rd Battalion of the 6th Infantry Regiment under command of Major John Leonard was to be the attacking force. The 2nd Battalion under command of Major Courtney Hodges was to be the reserve mopping-up group.

Our company left Cote 316 at 5 p.m. and started the long hike to the front. As darkness fell and the tramp over the muddy fields had just begun, the Germans began dropping high explosive shells on us. The route led across open fields, the company being in columns of two's with 25-meter intervals between columns. In spite of a heavy rain of gas, shrapnel and shells, the men kept their interval and distance. Lieutenant Bemiss proceeded to the command post of the 38th Regiment at the front where he was briefed by Colonel McAlexander, their commanding officer.

At 4 a.m. on the morning of October 14 we lay in foxholes on the slope of a hill when our guides returned to lead us to our assigned posts. By 6 a.m. all four platoons were slightly in rear of our jumping-off positions. It was still dark, and on our way over shell-pocked terrain we stumbled over the dead bodies of the brave men of the 3rd Division which we were on our way to relieve. One body grasped a new Lewis automatic rifle which we took with us. It was a great improvement over the antiquated French "Chaut-Chaut" automatic we were equipped with.

In addition to the Germans, we now had a new enemy to fight. A virulent type of influenza had attacked the troops. Many men died. Those who survived were left weakened by frequent spells of diarrhea and vomiting from the smell of mustard gas. Nervous and frightened waiting there in the darkness, often we had to go back to relieve ourselves.

When heavy shell fire, which seemed to come from the rear, broke out, we had to seek any cover the valley offered. Day was breaking when the Germans, with the aid of their observation balloons, discovered the battalions forming for the attack and opened up along our front with everything they had—machine guns, 37's, 55's, 88's, 105's and 155's. We called them "whizz-bangs." The enemy had leveled their artillery and were firing at us point-blank. As the shells skimmed over us, we heard the whizz, which flattened us to the ground, then the bang as the shells exploded, either among us or on the hill behind. It was the roughest time we had during the war.

Glancing to the rear, I noticed a reserve battalion, moving across the fields in perfect formation, was getting the brunt of the explosions. Gaps came in the formation, but even as shells burst, the gaps were filled and the men went on.

That hour before 8:30 was hell on earth! The bombardment was so intense, so severe and close that when the zero hour finally came some 10 percent of the company had already been taken to first-aid stations at the rear; more lay dead or wounded in the foxholes, unable to move out when the whistles blew. Some were so terrified they just stayed behind. Some wounded men endeavored to maneuver to a safer place. One man on my left repeatedly tried to get to his feet, only to fall back again. I saw the bright red spot on his forehead where he'd been hit by a machine gun bullet and knew he was mortally wounded.

Now it was time for *me* to blow the whistle!

It is difficult to describe a soldier's feelings during a heavy bombardment just before the zero hour. Scared to death, he thinks of family and loved ones and wonders if he will see them again. He thinks of the wrongs he's done and asks forgiveness. Then he prays for a small machine gun wound rather than have his body blown to bits or mangled by heavy guns or shrapnel. But, as soon as the whistle sounds, he's out of his protective cover, moving ahead; anxiety ceases as action begins.

The intensity of that bombardment is told in the "History of the 5th Division":

> The attack might have been pushed on northward had not the lines been struck by a concentration of fire from three directions.... From the east... the west... and straight ahead... came the steady murderous stream of machine gun and rifle bullets.... Overhead flew the whizz-bangs, and the shrapnel popped. The waves were stopped. Further advance, until the woods on the right and left were cleared, meant disaster, even extinction.

Our objective was the town of Bantheville where we were to take the outskirts, dig in, and protect our position. My direction was 45 degrees on my officer's prismatic compass. As we went over the top, the firing increased, the machine gun fire so intense we moved forward by running from one shell hole to the next. Gas shells exploded, so we had to put on our gas masks, making running difficult. Men were hit and dropped out of the line. When the whizz-bangs came hissing over us, we hugged the earth. Lieutenant Connally in the shell hole next to me was hit by a machine gun bullet and forced to leave his platoon to report to a first aid station. I never saw him again.

Tears from gas necessitated the removal of masks to dry our eyes, then we had to put them on again in that heavily gassed area, a necessary procedure which made our progress slow and arduous. I had no time to think of my compass but felt we were headed in the right direction. We had to press forward and get the enemy at close range. By making short runs at a time we managed the maneuver. Going down a hill, we came to an old cemetery on the outskirts of a town which I assumed was Bantheville. We were out of reach of the machine gun fire, still heavy on the slope behind us, preventing the men from leaving their shell holes and joining us.

We regrouped at the cemetery, and to my surprise I found the only men I had with me were my platoon sergeant, Martin B. Cullen, Private Stephen Baker and two other men of my platoon, plus two men from L Company, part of Major Leonard's assaulting battalion. The seven of us moved toward the town where we learned it was Romagne Sous Montfaucon and not Bantheville! Apparently, while running down the hill, I had veered to my left, and we'd overrun the assaulting battalion which had received the brunt of the enemy shelling. That was when we picked up the two members of L Company. No Americans were nearby, so I told them to stay with us while we reconnoitered the town; I would report to their commanding officer later and tell him who we were. As a safety measure officers were dressed in G.I. uniforms with no insignia of rank. From experience we'd learned the Germans tried to knock off those distinguishable as officers first of all.

The town was not under shell fire. Cautiously, the men in two rows with Sergeant Cullen and myself in the center moved down the street, exploring the deserted houses on both sides. Some must have been occupied until quite recently as tables were set with linen and dishes. Two German soldiers in full military gear dashed out of a doorway just ahead and disappeared round a corner before we could bring our guns into play. We took after them, maintaining our formation. As we turned the same corner, we were confronted with a German officer about 15 feet away. Head down, he didn't see us until we had him covered. "Halt!" I ordered. "Put up your hands!" He obeyed, saying over and over, "Kamarade! Kamarade!" A tall slender blond, he wore a decoration indicating he'd been wounded. While

Sergeant Cullen kept him covered, I unhooked his belt holding his Lugar pistol and holster; the sergeant removed the field glasses hanging around his neck. All the time his hands were shaking as he repeated, "Kamarade!" Then he panicked, jerked away, turned and ran toward a temporary barracks. In a flash Sergeant Cullen pointed his .45 Colt at him, shouted for him to stop but he kept on going. Sergeant Cullen then fired and the German dropped to the ground. Already as we approached, he was dying, his eyes blazing up at us, filled with hate.

Hearing noises ahead, we rounded the barracks and saw a group of German soldiers hurrying up a hill toward a machine gun emplacement. Four of them were carrying a machine gun. Between us we had six rifles and two Colt automatics and should have opened fire; however, we'd been told the Germans were ready to give up so, unwisely, I appared in the open and yelled, "Put up your hands!" They looked at us, then ran on to the top of the hill. "Let them have it," I ordered, "then get to cover inside the barracks." Opening up with our rifles, we picked off a few, but time was short. They'd already reached the top and would soon have their gun in place. We ducked into the barracks and hugged the floor. Firing commenced; we heard burst after burst of bullets, saw them smash into boards above our heads. It was now evident to us the officer whom we'd killed was the commander of the unit and had ordered his men to proceed to their positions while he came to investigate.

The only way out of the barracks faced the gun emplacement. Crouching down inside the 2 × 4 frame of the door, I was barely low enough to escape the bullets. One of my men was hit in the arm, and I cautioned them all to lie flat on the floor while the sergeant rendered first aid as best he could. We had to get out of that building or be shot. The pattern had been a long burst of fire, then a lull, then more fire. I told Cullen that during the next lull I would run out the door and around to the rear, hopefully to safety—about a 12-foot exposed run. He was to follow during the next lull, then each man in turn. Those who'd found cover could then secure the evacuation of our wounded man by diverting the enemy's attention. The plan worked.

We went back through the town just as the 127th Infantry of my old division, the 32nd Red Arrow, came up on our left at the rear and captured the machine gun nest. Luckily the town was not being shelled either by German or American artillery during this time. The Germans were under the impression their troops still held it, and our artillery headquarters knew we were pushing toward it.

Despite the fact I wasn't where I was supposed to be, at least two miles from our objective, Bantheville, I tore a sheet from my official message book informing my Battalion Commander, Major Courtney

Hodges, we had captured Romagne Sous Montfaucon and sent it with one of my men who accompanied our wounded soldier to the rear. My company and regiment were given credit for the capture of that town.

There, in the largest American cemetery, are buried several thousand American soldiers killed during World War I, among them several of my buddies. At the entrance, the National Graves Commission has erected a beautiful large relief map showing the battle lines during the Meuse-Argonne offensive and the names and positions of the divisions involved.

By that time I decided I'd better get back to where I belonged. We worked our way to the right overlooking Bantheville where we regrouped our platoon and company, extending our lines above Bantheville and Cunel. En route I saw several dead Germans in a gravel pit; beside one were his ration tins. After days with only a scant ration of bully beef and hardtack, I was hungry and decided to see what the German had. There was tea in his canteen; in his condiment can I found a quarter loaf of black bread and marmalade. To me that was a feast. The bread was soggy from rain but I peeled that part off, found a dry morsel inside and covered it with marmalade. It sure tasted good washed down with the tea. Wonderful what a bit of food can do.

As a rule I didn't keep a diary but in my old field message book I find the following:

Sun. Oct. 13. Moved from Boise de Hesse. Got heavily shelled and gassed.

Mon. Oct. 14. Went over top. It was hell! Beaucoup souvenirs. Only had four men of my platoon to mop up Romagne.

Tues. Oct. 15. Soaking wet. Raining hard. Slept in an old cave. Have my platoon dug in hillside.

Wed. Oct. 16. Took my platoon on a patrol to 32nd Division on my left. Pretty tough but I succeeded. Fell in the river. Heavily gassed and shelled.

Thurs. Oct. 17. Took a squad and posted on Lieut. Bounds of H Company's right, close to Bantheville. Gassed and shelled by trench mortars.

Sat. Oct. 19. They are shelling us heavily today. It sure gets my nerves. H Co. is attacking Bantheville tonight and I have my platoon standing by in case they are wanted.

Nov. 5. Crossed the Meuse.

Nov. 7. Patrolled Velosnes.

October 22 at 8 p.m. our regiment (6th Infantry) was relieved by the 358th Infantry of the 90th Division. That night we hiked to a wood near Montfaucon where our company remained four days while receiving replacements. We also got new equipment, ammunition and reserve rations. During our stay two men of the company were killed by long range artillery from German batteries, both hit by the same shell, and were buried in the woods with military honors.

October 26 orders came to move to the front lines at once. After a long hike that afternoon the company took over the front lines along the outskirts of Brieulles-sur-Meuse along the banks of the Meuse River. We established outposts on the edge of the town and sent out organized patrols, one of which was cut off from our company for two days without rations. Another three-man patrol succeeded in swimming the river and returned with valuable information.

My platoon was stationed just inside a fringe of woods on high ground overlooking the Meuse and the canal with an excellent view of the river all the way to the city of Velosnes and toward Dun-sur-Meuse. The afternoon of November 2 I led my platoon in single file, the men about five yards apart, down the slopes toward Breuilles. From their position across the river and canal, the enemy had a long range view of us, but we crept along slowly, heads down, trying to hide our movements as best we could. Although a few shells landed close by, we got to the town without casualties and took up our positions near the river, occupying a large dugout recently used by the Germans.

There had been a lot of air activity all during this phase of the Meuse-Argonne offensive on the part of the Germans, French and Americans, and we witnessed several aerial gun fights. We learned to identify enemy planes not only by their insignia but also by the sound of their motors. They had an undulant sound, coming in waves, while ours were constant. On October 14 Count von Richthofen's "flying circus" flew over, and we counted 25 red-nosed planes in one formation.

When an American two-seater pursuit plane ran out of gas and landed near us on our side of the river, the Germans began to shell it at once. We yelled for the two airmen crawling out of the plane to run toward us, which they did, relieved to hear their own language and know they were close to our lines. As they reached us, their plane was blown up by a direct hit. Safely ensconced in our dugout, Lieutenants Grey and Richardson were two happy airmen. They told us that on a sunrise alert they pulled their fur-lined "teddy bear" suits over their pajamas, and after a glass of orange juice and coffee, went off on a patrol of the lines after which they returned for breakfast. We hadn't seen pajamas or orange juice since we left home.

When Major Hodges, commanding the 2nd Battalion, received orders to advance across the river, he selected companies E and G for the mission. Briefing us carefully, he said it was vital we get across and establish a beachhead. The entire army was poised behind us, waiting to cross, and we *must not fail*.

As darkness approached we were ordered to start the advance. In spite of heavy machine gun and artillery fire, we could not be deterred, and somehow by midnight most of the company, wading or swimming, had successfully crossed the river. We still had to cross the canal, some thousand yards beyond. In between was a flat area totally exposed. Intensive machine gun fire from the east bank of the canal was cutting us to pieces, and there were many casualties.

At daybreak the company formed a line of skirmishers and crawled to a position along the west bank of the canal where we remained. The enemy was within hand grenade range on the other side, so rifles and hand grenades were used to good advantage. Stretched out along the bank, peering over the embankment, I felt a piece of shrapnel hit me under the back of my helmet. It was a ricochet, its force spent, and there was little bleeding so I didn't have to go to the rear for first aid.

As the east bank of the canal was strongly fortified, we were forced to wait until the night of November 4 to cross. Meanwhile under both our own and the enemy's shell fire, it looked as if we would suffer complete disaster. Each officer carried Very pistols, and we kept shooting flares in an attempt to tell our artillery their shells were falling short. A French artillery regiment was supporting us, but apparently our signals got crossed up. As a result, they were killing our men.

I was crawling along my platoon front when I heard a shell coming and with no delay jumped into a shell hole occupied by three of my men. Imagine my shock to discover they were all dead from concussion. Not a mark on them.

The signals written in my field message book to indicate "friendly artillery firing short" were: "fire one white star rocket followed by a green parachute rocket." This we did without success. Private Willie Harris, a runner, saved our lives and our mission by managing to recross the river under heavy artillery and machine gun fire and reach our Battalion Command Post in time to stop their artillery fire.

After completing a pontoon bridge across the canal under an incessant barrage of machine guns, a part of the company rushed across and captured many prisoners. Several times the bridge was shot to pieces, thereby dividing the company, but it was finally repaired and the rest of the company crossed in safety.

Here again an account from the "History of the 5th Division":

> It was certain that there had been no withdrawal from the east bank of the Meuse, and the Hun evidently intended to hold on at all costs. The

> orders of the defenders were later captured, stating "the enemy's crossing of the Meuse is to be prevented absolutely! Should he succeed, he is to be thrown back into the Meuse at once. The enemy must not get a foothold on this side of the Meuse under any circumstances."
>
> Nevertheless we had crossed the Meuse but the canal still lay before us. The Meuse was bridged, but the more difficult problem of crossing the canal, a steep-banked unfordable stream, 20 meters wide and five to ten feet deep still remained. Through the day of the 4th (November) this small force of infantry and engineers continued to hug the canal bank where they had been since early on the 3rd. At 5 p.m., just after dusk, the two Infantry Companies (E and G) opened fire with everything they had and rushed the bridges. The lower bridge had been almost shot to pieces by hostile guns but the men waded waist deep over the sections where two pontoons were sunk.... Firing as they advanced, the units deployed and pushed on into the pocket, cleaning up the ground to the front and either flank.... Every trace of the enemy was wiped out.... Nine machine guns and two minenwerfers were taken; 21 Boches were in our hands and several were dead from our rush. We had lost one officer and nineteen men....

Every member of G Company deserves praise and honor for that operation. As a result of this drive we swiftly advanced beyond the bridge to form our bridgehead which extended a mile in all directions. By 4 a.m. November 5 our mission was accomplished; by 8 our entire regiment had passed over the bridges built by our engineers, through our bridgehead to the east of the river and the canal, and were advancing against the enemy, then on the run. Many were killed at the canal, among them Reg Hollister, my OCS buddy, the only man in my outfit from Houghton.

We dug in while the other two battalions leap-frogged over us about daybreak on November 5, leaving us in support until November 9. By the morning of November 7 the entire division had passed over our bridges.

The importance of the crossing of the Meuse and the establishment of the bridgehead is best understood by reading what General Pershing, the Commander-in-Chief, had to say in his letter to General Hanson E. Ely, Commanding General of the Fifth Division ("History of the 5th Division"):

> The feat of arms, however, which marks especially the Division's ability as a fighting unit, was the crossing of the Meuse River and the establishment of a bridgehead on the eastern bank. This operation was one of the most brilliant military feats in the history of the American Army in France.

Later on November 7 I was ordered to select a patrol of 15 men to proceed eight kilometers down the west bank of the river to the town of Velosnes where we were to assist the French "Blue Devil" Division on our right in their crossing.

On our way Brigadier General Paul B. Malone, passing through our bridgehead with his headquarters staff, returned my salute and inquired as to my mission. On being told, he said, "Be careful, Lieutenant. According to our information there's heavy enemy concentration in that area."

We proceeded along a narrow gauge railroad running to Velosnes, always on the alert for the enemy. Six French soldiers guarding a young German captive came toward us along the tracks. Passing at a fast stride, the officer in charge shouted, "Beaucoup Boches labas! Beaucoup Boches labas!" To us, it was a comic situation. A diminutive prisoner escorted by six soldiers speeding to the rear, away from "Beaucoup Boches" while we were on our way to help their comrades cross the Meuse River. C'est la guerre!

Beside the canal we came on a large German dugout, lately abandoned, evidently in haste. A German officer had left his beautiful light blue dress overcoat on the back of a chair. I took it along as a souvenir but had to drop it in a hurry when we were confronted by machine gun fire as we entered Velosnes.

With the help of another patrol from our 3rd Battalion, we cleared the town of the enemy. The French division then crossed the river and entered the town. Our mission was a success. We had outflanked the German machine gunners who were holding the French units pinned to the ground across the canal.

It was for leading this mission I received the Silver Star. It is a great honor and I am proud to have earned it, but behind every medal are the men who helped accomplish the mission. I first learned of it in a letter from one of my former men, Corporal Virgil Mottinger of Akron, Ohio. The letter is dated May 12, 1920, and I quote:

> I am glad you got it (Silver Star) and you certainly deserved it more than any officer in the outfit. I had occasion to observe your actions under both shell and machine gun fire and knew you to be entirely fearless, at least to all outward appearances. When we went up that hill October 14th I was right on your right. When you had charge of those 25 men that were needed to fill in that gap connecting the 32nd Division I was there. When we crossed the river and then the canal I was with you and was your runner when we finally got settled to the right after crossing the canal. I remember one instance in particular about your cool-headedness and that was when we were awaiting to cross the canal and were under our own shell fire. You were standing near the canal bank, whistling.

Now don't think I am imagining any of this because I wasn't. I was there and have a very good memory for details.

A very good memory, indeed, and generous praise!

The citation for the Silver Star reads as follows:

HEADQUARTERS FIFTH DIVISION
AMERICAN EXPEDITIONARY FORCES
A.P.O. #745

GENERAL ORDERS
No. 21

June 27, 1919

"The following officers and enlisted men were cited in orders for distinguished conduct in action.

"Second Lieutenant William J. Wilkins, 6th Infantry.

"For exceptional devotion to duty, energy and initiative. On November 7, 1918, near Breuilles, France, he received command of a patrol which was to proceed to Velosnes to capture, pursue or kill enemy machine gunners who were harassing and delaying the advance of French elements attempting to cross the Meuse River at that point. His patrol in conjunction with another patrol from the 6th Infantry successfully accomplished this mission, thereby aiding the advance of the French at this point. Lieut. Wilkins personally killed two of the enemy and captured six more single handed, thus setting a fine example of aggressiveness and initiative to the men under his command.

By command of Major General Ely
C.A. Trott
Chief of Staff"

Official
David P. Wood
Lieut. Col. Infantry
Division Adjutant

On the night of November 9 the company advanced to the town of Remoiville. Patrols were sent out, routing several enemy machine gunners and snipers. After mopping up the town, we got orders to move on to Jametz, two kilometers east. We proceeded the following morning over an open road, with machine guns firing point blank at us, forcing us to crawl in the ditches along the roadway for protection. We finally reached the town about 2 p.m. November 10, taking cover on the outskirts in a gravel pit alongside the highway, and established our outposts.

Though we were getting heavy machine gun fire from the farm areas east of the town, we proceeded with preparations to go over the top the next morning down a hill into heavily fortified fields. Zero hour was 8 a.m. We posted sentinels and tried to get some rest. It had been a rough day with many deaths and casualties. It was raining; the water in our foxholes was deep, but we found some boards to keep us above water. During the fighting I'd dropped my bedroll so had only my heavy overcoat to put over me.

At 10 p.m., guided by a runner, I was called back to our battalion headquarters in town. We'd been hoping to be relieved; I supposed this was the good news. At headquarters Major Hodges advised the officers assembled that there was supposed to be some kind of armistice signed the next morning at 11 a.m. He stated he was uncertain whether the cease-fire would remain long thereafter. Our jump-off time was temporarily canceled, but we were to have our men "stand to" for the rest of the day.

We were also told to instruct our men not to fraternize with the enemy who might cross our line. If any did cross, we were to require them to leave, showing them bayonets if necessary. Enemy fire continued intermittently until 11 a.m. November 11, when suddenly—all was still!

I have often been asked how I felt when the quiet came. In 1953 Frank Lynch of the *Seattle Post-Intelligencer* asked me to talk about that Armistice Day, 1918. I quote from that interview.

> Somewhere, we heard that Judge Wilkins killed some of a German machine gun crew, captured the rest, and was given a Silver Star for it. When we reminded him his thoughts turned to something else again.
>
> "People think of our armies as 'every man a hero,'" Judge Wilkins said. "In that last battle we were in combat for almost a month. In the first days I think any of us would have settled for a nice clean flesh wound. After that life, death, nothing seemed to matter.
>
> "People think of a victorious army as shining, somehow, marching to music and rousing cheers, enemy heads on pikes, as it were. So, the firing stopped and there we huddled, wet and cold and hungry, our clothing in rags and crawling with lice.
>
> "I can only say that there was a little something of relief, and then a great accumulation of weariness."
>
> And that is how peace came to one man, 35 years ago today.

Had the armistice not come, many of us would never have survived the next day's drive across those broad grain fields where we would be confronted with bristling machine gun emplacements.

The saddest duty remained for my men. They gathered up the bodies of eight buddies killed that morning and the evening before and laid them to rest, covered with O.D. blankets, under a small apple tree in that gravel pit outside the town of Jametz.

Following the lull in the firing at 11 o'clock, we all "stood to," moving around freely but at the same time maintaining our defensive positions.

A long line of soldiers came down the highway from the German lines. They were Italian POW's who had been released by the Germans and were headed back to Italy. We conversed with them as best we could, and our mess-sergeant, Andrew Lovett, fed them from our reserve supply of rations. Feeding 200 hungry men was a problem, but he managed and we helped them on their way. No German soldiers approached our lines.

So there we were! G Company, 6th Infantry, in the very front lines at the end of World War I. It is difficult to describe that scene. To us, it was one of the most beautiful sights in the world. The Americans kept campfires burning brightly all through the night as we sat and talked of our great adventure and the victory that had been so dearly won, grateful to be alive. We celebrated by shooting flares of all kinds of colors into the sky, especially those of red, white and blue.

The next day we moved into more comfortable quarters in Jametz, taking over those used by the Germans during their years of occupation. We remained there until November 13 when we hiked to Liny-et-Dun, where we established a camp, using shelter tents for cover. The company was reequipped with new clothing and replacements. Our personal packs, which had been stored at division headquarters, were returned, and we officers were able to don our tailored uniforms, insignia and Sam Brown belts—without benefit of bath. We just stripped down in an open field, shed our underwear, socks and fatigues—cooties and all—on the ground where we left them and rubbed down with towels. Showers came later.

On November 21 we were inspected by our division commander who complimented us on our neat and soldierly appearance and stated we were to be one of six divisions assigned to the Army of Occupation in Germany. This was welcome news indeed.

It was a long march, however, to Trier, our destination. We made overnight stops in Brandiville and Remoiville, towns we had taken some days before the Armistice, as well as Longuyon and Rehan. Thanksgiving Day was spent at Backarage, Luxembourg, with so much to be thankful for! Our mess-sergeant had scrounged around the neighborhood and found chickens and geese. He gave us dumplings and gravy and a special cake.

After hiking through the towns of Sanweiler, Olingen and Wasserbilly, on December 1 we crossed the Moselle River and the

German border. There we received a warm reception, not with minenwerfers or 88's but smiles and pleasant words and salutes from the people. At last, we reached Trier (known as Treves by the French), where we were quartered in the spacious and comfortable Goebel Barracks with a drill field adjacent.

This ancient historic city, once occupied by Roman legions, afforded many interesting hours of sightseeing among the ruins and environs. I had my first picture taken in my second lieutenant's uniform and proudly sent it home to my family.

In Trier we continued our military exercises, stressing the necessity for continued good military appearance and conduct, as we represented our country to the former enemy. Our interlude in Trier was short, however, for we soon had to give up our comfortable quarters to another division and proceed by truck to the town of Mamer, Luxembourg, where we were billeted in various private homes.

April 6 the regimental commander received orders to have G Company proceed to Luxembourg City for guard duty at the bridges and tunnels to protect supply lines. We served there until May 15 when we left by train for Diekirch, a beautiful city on the Moselle. After duty, late in the day, we sat in a cafe by the river and sipped the wonderful Moselle wine. The people were very kind and entertained us often, a courtesy we reciprocated.

In April I was given a 14-day furlough to visit relatives in England. While passing through Exeter on my way to Cornwall, I bought a pair of leather puttees which I wore at the Officers' Club dancing parties given for the natives, where I came to be known as "the lieutenant with the beautiful leggings!"

I visited with Uncle Jack, the warder at Dartmoor Prison, and at Torquay with Mother's sister, Aunt Janie O'Brien, whose husband had just returned from four years of service in France. Four of her sons were still in service. After a good visit with them and their daughter, Doris, and son, Jim, I went on to Cornwall to visit Father's sister, Aunt Lydia, and her son, Arnold, recently returned from service in the British Army where he served as batman (orderly) to a British General. Imagine my surprise in the mornings to find he'd polished my puttees and Sam Brown belt.

From there I went to St. Austell, the home of the mother of George Hicks who was married to my sister Alice. I arrived in time to be best man at the marriage of her daughter, Emma, to a handsome British soldier. They took me right into the family and promptly called me Cousin Billy. The night before the wedding I took the bridegroom, Harold, and Emma's father to the local pub. This second lieutenant of Infantry, 21, having just received several months back pay before leaving Germany, bought drinks for the marriage celebrants and, as the evening wore on and things livened up, for the house. On returning home, locked arm in arm, swaying from side to side, we encountered Emma's mother, who took one look and blamed me.

"Billy!" she exlaimed. "What you been doin' 'ave?"

Next day the bridal party returned from the church in an early vintage Ford taxi. My hands were itching to get at the wheel of a car after all this time, so the owner let me take it for a short run.

En route I saw a man leading a donkey and cart down the hill, coming my way. Forgetting that in England traffic passed to the left, I moved to the right. The road was narrow with sharp banks on either side; as I swerved back to the left to avoid hitting the donkey and cart, the two left wheels of the taxi went up the steep bank and the car turned over on its side. There I lay in the overturned taxi, the motor still running and the rear wheels spinning. A native Cornishman came over and said, "'ow did it 'appen?" I assured him I didn't know. After reimbursing the taxi owner for the damage, I had considerably less money to spend when we returned to the pub that evening.

Following those terrible months of war, life in Germany was pleasant. Everybody was happy and our esprit de corps was tops. Army headquarters sent entertainment our way. Elsie Janis, so popular for her rendition of the favorite war songs. Marie Louise Roderick from Seattle, a talented sparkling entertainer at the piano with wartime songs, one being:

> Did you see my little Jimmie marching?
> They were all out of step but Jim!

Orders came in early June for me to report to Paris for assignment to the Inter-Allied Games at Pershing Stadium at Joinville, June 22 to July 6, 1919. A friend from OCS days in charge of the stadium had requested I be assigned to the reception and entertainment section of the Games. What a break!

My assignment was to arrange transportation to and from the stadium for the men and women entertainers of the Red Cross and YMCA. I got to see the Allied athletic games *and* Paris, which was just coming back to life after the war years. I stayed at the YMCA at 72 Avenue Montaigne off the Champs Élysée, close to the Place de la Concorde and the Pont Neuf.

Three other second lieutenants and I saw Paris together, attending the Opéra Comique, the Foiles Bergère and the Casino de Paris. One of them was Gene Clare from a small town in the far far West with a strange name. Indian, I supposed. The name of the town was Seattle in the State of Washington.

A favorite drink then being served at the cafes was the "Soixante-Quinze" named after the famous French 75 artillery pieces—three parts champagne and one of cognac. It really packed a wallop! We visited the catacombs, amazed to see the bones of six million people piled like cordwood. On a plate commemorating the visit of Prince Oscar of Sweden on May 7, 1867, the following words were engraved:

Every life has its death;
Every death has its life.

With my jackknife I pried a tooth loose from one of the ancient skulls for a souvenir. During that time we saw a mammoth Victory Parade that stretched from the Place de la Concorde to the Arc de Triomphe. Generals Pershing, Haig, Foch and other Big Stars were there, and all the Allies participated, including an American crack composite regiment.

While walking the streets and sitting at the tables at the Café de la Paix, we had difficulty avoiding the so-called "ladies of the evening." They approached us from doorways or at intermissions, saying quite frankly, "Voulez-vous se coucher avec moi ce soir?" We declined, mindful we would soon be at the Port of Embarkation where those who couldn't pass the physical would be held until cured. It was unthinkable!

July 23, 1919, I received orders to report to Brest for embarkation home. The famous Marine General, Smedley Butler, took time to gather us together at the port and made our stay while waiting for the ship a pleasant one.

Aboard the *Northern Pacific* we heard and sang songs, one being:

Aprés la Guerre fini
Partez Amerique toute suite
Mademoiselle in ze family way
Aprés la Guerre fini.

The ship set a record for crossing of five days and 20 hours. Quite a contrast to the fourteen days we spent on the *Antigone* going over.

After a brief stop at Camp Merritt, New Jersey, then Camp Grant, Illinois, where I was formally discharged, I was at last on my way home!

Reunion of Company G, 125th Infantry 32nd Red Arrow Division

A reunion of G Company, 125th Infantry of the 32nd (Red Arrow) Division was held at Ontonagon in northern Michigan on July 18 and 19, 1959. It was the first time in 41 years I'd been with them as a group since July 19, 1918, during the Battle of the Marne, when they were moving forward into battle and I was headed back to OCS at Langres.

Well-planned by our illustrious commanding officer, Captain Joe Donnelly, some 50 of our original company of 250 attended. A part of the ceremonies was the dedication of a bronze plaque imbedded in a red sandstone boulder in the Porcupine Mountain Park on the shores of Lake Superior. The inscription reads:

> This plaque was erected by their comrades to the memory of those of Company G, 125th Infantry, 32nd Division who died on the Field of Battle in France in World War I.

Listed are the names of 52 of our comrades who were killed in the three major engagements in which our division participated. Many families and friends joined with us in paying tribute to their memory.

Captain Donnelly, for whom we all had great affection, wrote a history of Company G in November, 1973, which contains an article by our comrade, Nick Lukkarila, honorary Mayor of Mass City, entitled: "Adieu, Company G, 125th Infantry." In this article he places credit where credit is due:

> Over 40 years ago a group of young men joined the Army and went off to the big war. Most of my old high school Junior class were in this bunch of recruits. We enlisted to keep the world free; we also added a lot of worry and gray hairs to our parents.
>
> On Saturday and Sunday, July 18-19, 1959, about fifty oldtimers—some pot-bellied, some bald, runts, tall ones, shorties—gathered in Ontonagon to relive the days of 1917-1918 when they belonged to an outfit in Uncle Sam's ledger as Company G, 125th Infantry, 32nd Division.
>
> I may as well mention right here that this reunion was made a reality through the tireless efforts of one man who never gave up in his intentions that Company G should meet once again to renew friendships, perhaps the last occasion. That man—Captain Joseph M. Donnelly.

How prophetic! That was our *only* and *last* reunion. Captain Donnelly, former prosecuting attorney of Ontonagon County, assistant United States attorney for the State of Michigan and Judge of Probate of Houghton County, passed away on St. Patrick's Day, March 17, 1975. What a day to go for a fighting Irishman!

Last Man's Club

In the early 1930's a group of World War I veterans who were active members of the American Legion formed the "Last Man's Club" of Seattle with a membership of 85. The purpose of the club, which met once a year on Armistice Day, November 11, was to preserve our ties and share experiences of the Great War.

A bottle of Cognac was brought from France, wound with red, white and blue satin ribbons, and kept in a bank vault throughout the year. At each meeting it is conspicuously displayed on the table. According to our by-laws, the last surviving member is to open it and toast those who have moved up to the last *Front*. The question has been asked if the last man will be able to raise his glass to his lips, let alone drink the toast!

Through the years we have all looked forward with pleasure to these meetings where we join enthusiastically in singing World War I songs. Roy Rosenthal, former publisher of the *University Herald* of Seattle, is the sparkplug. His antics while leading us in "Alouette," "Tipperary,"

> We don't want the bacon, we don't want the bacon,
> All we want is a piece of the Rhine.
> We'll crown Bill the Kaiser with a bottle of Budweiser,
> We'll have a wonderful time—
> Old Wilhelm the gross will shout "Vas iss Los"
> When we hit that Hindenberg line, Fine!
> We don't want the bacon, we don't want the bacon,
> What we want is a piece of the Rhine!

and other songs are a fun part of the evening. Attorney Joe Sweeney, business man Art Lee, architect Bill Bain and I now comprise the quartet. Steve Chadwick, past national commander of the American Legion, was a respected member until his death in 1975.

Membership in this club means a great deal; except for the years away during World War II and a year in Nuremberg, I have missed only one meeting. When last we met in 1980 to celebrate the 62nd anniversary of the Armistice, only nine of the 17 original members surviving were able to be present.

At Mt. Clemens, Michigan, July 1917. Seated left to right: Cudahy, Colenso, Bowden, Born, Messner, Penberthy, LaPointe. Standing: Bilger, Ingram, Wilkins. Colenso and Ingram killed in action. Born, Bowden, Messner, Penberthy wounded in action.

Private, 1917 Fort Wayne, Detroit.

Camp MacArthur, Waco, Texas, 1917.

Promoted to Corporal, August, 1917.

Brother Chris, 1917

Second Lieutenant of Infantry, Trier, Germany Army of Occupation, 1919

Memorial Day, May 30, 1918 at Massevaux, Alsace, in area occupied by 125th Infantry. Girls in native Alsatian costume.

General Haan and party leaving church at Massevaux on Memorial Day.

Captain Merritt Lamb was one of nine Company men who were killed in action on Aug. 29, 1918.

Capt. Joseph M. Donnelly

"Les Terribles" Doughboys, Co. "G"

Hommes 48–Chevaux 8

It was a wonderful feeling not to have always to be watching for a Boche machine gun and to be able to hunt out the cooties.

Moving up a "forward 75" by hand for direct fire on visible targets.

One foot-bridge across the canal, at the site of the old bridge destroyed by the Boche, was completed by the Engineers shortly after midnight of November 3-4, but so intense was the German machine-gun resistance that Companies E and G of the Sixth Infantry could not cross to the eastern side until nightfall of November 4. (Engineer No. 7.)

It was only on the 20th that the rolling kitchens could be gotten up close enough to give the front-line doughboys a feed of hot "Corned Willie" and coffee.

No wonder the men in the front lines had occasionally to subsist on cold chow when it had to be carried up over shell-swept roads in this fashion.

When news came that the Armistice would go into effect at 11 o'clock of November 11 the regiments were forced to call off their attack on the heights of the Loison River.

More than six hundred of the Red Diamond men had fallen in ten days' fighting that finally won the Bois des Rappes. Many of our soldiers were buried here in the orchard cemetery south of Nantillois.

Company "G" 6th Infantry entering Trier, Germany, December 1st, 1918.

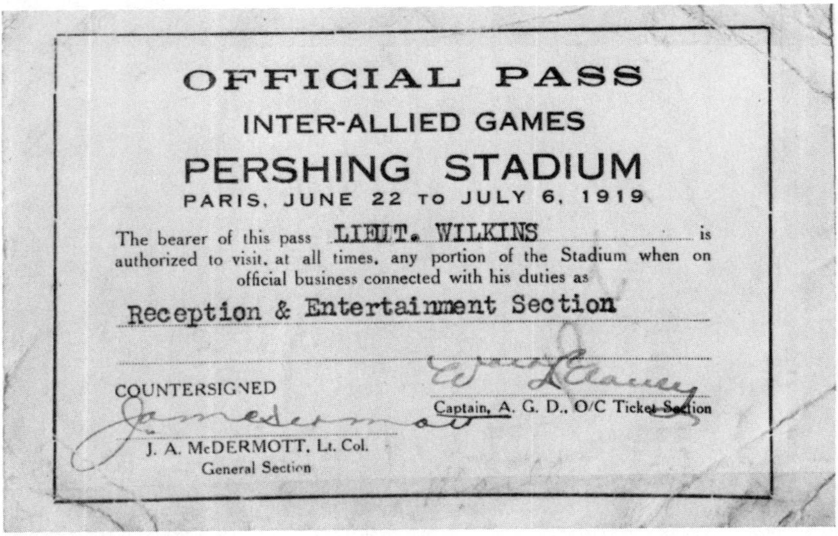

OFFICIAL PASS

INTER-ALLIED GAMES

PERSHING STADIUM

PARIS, JUNE 22 TO JULY 6, 1919

The bearer of this pass LIEUT. WILKINS is authorized to visit, at all times, any portion of the Stadium when on official business connected with his duties as

Reception & Entertainment Section

COUNTERSIGNED

J. A. McDERMOTT, Lt. Col.
General Section

Captain, A. G. D., O/C Ticket Section

Official Pass, inter-allied Games. Pershing Stadium.

When the Army of Occupation marched into Germany the Sixth Infantry had the honor of entering just behind the advance guards of the First Division to become the garrison of Treves.

Cousin Emma and Bridegroom, Harold, with attendants. St. Austell, April, 1919.

On leave to England, at LeHavre, France. Two buddies.

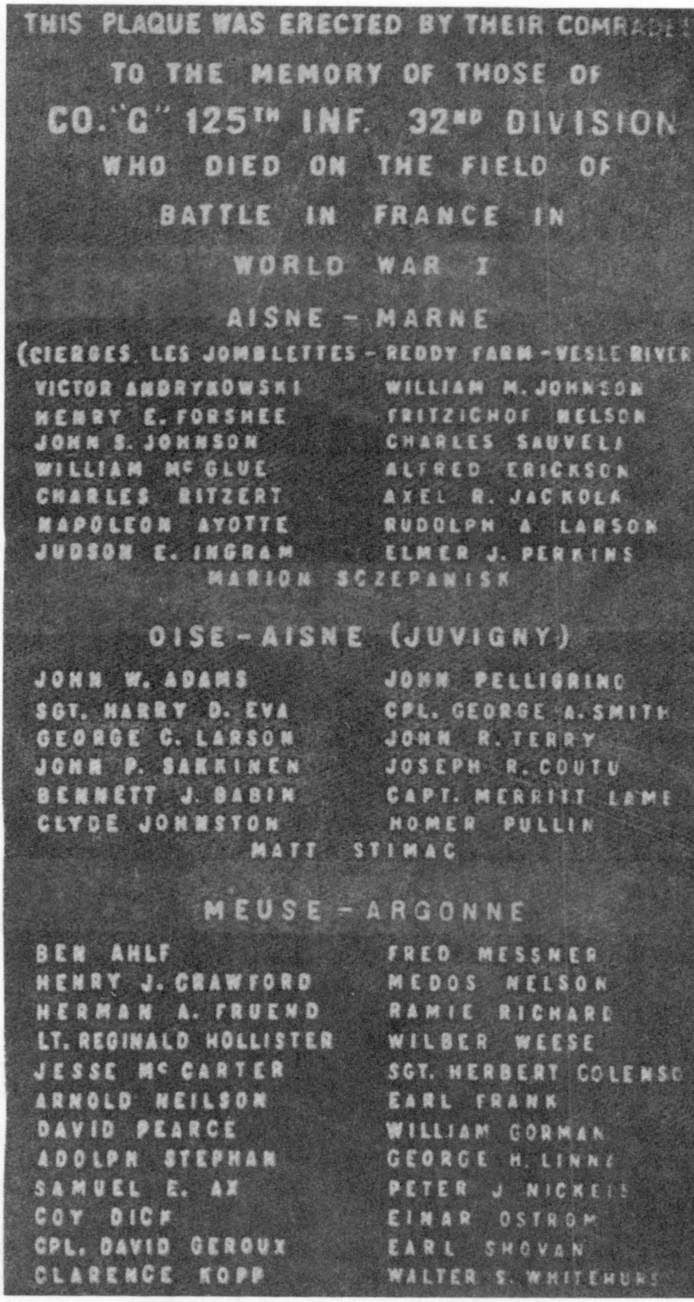

This plaque was erected by their comrades to the memory of those of Co. "G" 125th Inf. 32nd Division who died on the field of battle in France in World War I. Aisne - Marne

The quartet, Last Man's Club, 1974. Roy Rosenthal, director, Steve Chadwick, Joe Sweeney, Wilkins, Art Lee.

The quartet, 1975. Joe Sweeney, Bill Bain, Wilkins, Art Lee.

CHAPTER III

New Horizons

(1920-1929)

Only a soldier who has been in fierce combat can fully appreciate the wonderful joy of "coming home." The reunion with family and friends in northern Michigan was all I had anticipated—love and laughter and tears. Like all life experiences, however, it had to come to an end. For me, the war was over; now another horizon beckoned: the task of getting an education.

After an honorable discharge from the army in 1919, there were three choices: remain in the Regular Army with the grade of second lieutenant of Infantry, sign up for service in the Reserve, or sever all connections with the service. To remain in the Regular Army meant competing with many second lieutenants who were West Point graduates. In the fall of 1919 I attended a conference of Michigan National Guard officers at Lansing, called for the purpose of reestablishing Guard units, and decided not to sign up. After 2½ years of army life I'd had enough and chose to leave the service.

It had been a long way since that conversation between a 10-year-old boy and his mother when I'd said I wanted to be a judge, but my experiences along the way had not only strengthened my intent but motivated it. The training and discipline received in the service probably saved my life many times. The justice I saw administered illustrated the importance of punishment as a deterrent to offenders and a protection for the innocent. So, the law it was. At that point it seemed a long long road to travel, but once having set my feet on the road, I never turned aside.

Post-war America was experiencing one of the longest business booms yet in its history. The technology learned during the war years had an almost unbelievable influence on all industries, the automobile business in particular. Before the war the automobile had primarily been a luxury enjoyed by the rich. By 1920, however, cars began to roll off the assembly lines in large numbers which made the price less, and by 1930 approximately thirty million cars were registered in the United States. In 1920 my brother Chris was living in Detroit where he worked in the accounting division of the Ford Motor Company and suggested I share his room in a boarding house there that summer. I had no trouble getting a job on the assembly line of Graham-Paige Motor Company and, living with Chris, was able to put most of my money away for school. In addition, thanks to Howard's good stewardship, I had been able to sell the Oakland for exactly what I paid for it.

The fall of 1920 I enrolled at Ferris Institute (later Ferris State College) at Big Rapids, Michigan. The school was started in 1884 by Woodbridge N. Ferris (later to be governor of Michigan, 1915-17; and U.S. Senator 1922-28) and his wife with 15 enrollees in the back rooms of an office building on Main Street. Today it is one of Michigan's leading educational institutions with a student body of ten thousand.

I found a room which I shared with another student and got a job dishwashing at Mrs. Goltz's boarding house for which I received three meals a day. My sister Elsie attended Ferris that year, lived across the street, and we had many good times together. She had worked as a secretary, saved her money and was now taking an advanced secretarial course, which enhanced her business career. She was a beautiful girl and resembled our mother, as well as being endowed with her disposition. Subsequently she married and reared three children.

Captain Frank Shaw, a former prosecuting attorney from Grand Rapids, was then in charge of the ROTC unit at Ferris and needed an assistant. He approached me about reenlisting in the regular army for a one-year stretch with the promise of the rank of sergeant-instructor, assuring me I would be able to carry on with my classes while doing full time army duty. This was the real break, though—I was to receive $112 a month! So I gave up the dishwashing job and became Captain Shaw's chief assistant.

Governor Ferris himself conducted the morning assembly of the entire student body at 8:30. He also taught psychology, philosophy and logic. A handsome silver-haired educator, he was an inspiring leader but had an acid tongue frequently directed at wayward students. One of the things he disapproved of and resented the most was the time wasted by students in pool halls, and he would not tolerate the breaking of rules. He kept a taut rein; examples of this stand out in my memory.

At a January assembly in 1921 he announced the names of three students to be expelled for violation of rules, stating that they could go to an attorney if they wished, but they were *out* of Ferris for all time. That same morning he also told of the discharge of a piano instructor who had broken a rule. She had gone to Hadden's—a nightclub of that era—and been seen dancing cheek-to-cheek, an offense Mr. Ferris had warned would bring discharge. "Such disloyalty," he said, "will destroy any school or community. I will not have it, even if I have to close this school."

Governor Ferris was interested in phrenology; in fact, he taught a course in it. One of his visiting professors in this field was Dr. J. W. Fitzgerald, a medical doctor and phrenologist from Chicago who gave a series of lectures and interviewed students. A six-page typewritten copy of his analysis of me dated February, 1922, cost me $5, a hard sum to come by. At the top of the report Governor Ferris wrote: "Most excellent advice. See below how he describes your temperament." I quote a sentence from the report.

> You can become a competent attorney... I would recommend the legal profession as a work that would be highly satisfactory to you.

Being a music lover, Governor Ferris brought Grand Opera singers from Chicago and New York; sometimes male quartets which he told me he personally enjoyed very much.

We had a fine ROTC unit; some of our men served with distinction in World War II. Setting-up exercises, close order and rifle drill were a part of the everyday curriculum with frequent sessions on the rifle range and overnight encampments on weekends. Those 30-minute morning military exercises were the highlight of the day. Unfortunately that year Congress eliminated many ROTC units; Ferris ROTC was closed the following year, and it was my duty to supervise that operation. I was then and am now an ardent supporter of compulsory military training for senior high and university students.

My grades at Ferris were high, and by attending summer school, I was able to graduate at the end of the term and get my high school diploma. However, I remained at Ferris for the rest of the school year to phase out the ROTC, studying long hours to complete credits which made it possible to enroll as a sophomore at the University of Michigan in 1922 in the College of Literature, Science and The Arts. Referred to by students as the Lit school, it was the largest and considered the most important department at the University.

Before he became president of the University of Washington, Dr. Charles E. Odegaard was the dean of this college at Michigan. Seattleites will agree that Charles Odegaard was one of the ablest and most personable presidents the University has ever had and is admired by all Washington grads and Michiganders.

I am grateful to Ferris for what it did for me and the Honorary Doctor of Laws Degree awarded me in 1964. Dr. Victor F. Spathelf was then president and a great inspiration to the students of that later generation.

The summer of 1922 I landed a job as bellhop at The Inn at Charlevoix, Michigan, a summer resort near Petosky. Uniforms were modeled after those of cadets at West Point, soft gray with black braid, and I wore mine proudly. Nickels and dimes received as tips were saved, my largest being the $5 received from a Mrs. Garland of Kansas City. By September I had saved $350.

The greatest dividend was meeting an insurance man from Ann Arbor, Harold P. Trosper. On learning I was going to Michigan and had plans to study law, he arranged for me to live at the Delta Theta Phi law fraternity house; through him I met many of the members and while in Lit school was accepted as a member. "Pete" Trosper also introduced me to Ted Brown, manager of the Michigan Union, who gave me the job usually held by a football player—"The Desk"—where I took care of lodgers and customers. Thanks to him I kept the job throughout my stay at Michigan. The work schedule—four to six hours a day at 50 cents an hour—carried me through school, though there were times I had difficulty making ends meet and feared I'd have to drop out and go back to the assembly line. With the help of brother Chris and his dear wife Imoe, I managed to pull through.

Our football coach, the famous Fielding H. "Hurry-up" Yost, was a grand old man loved by all. He often stopped by the desk to, as he put it, "Visit with my boys." The present football stadium, seating 106,000, bears his name.

It was at Charlevoix I met Dick Loeb of the infamous murder partnership of Loeb-Leopold. Dick's parents, who owned Sears Roebuck, had a summer home at Charlevoix, and he often came to The Inn to play poker with our manager, Mr. McDonald, and guests. When I brought them refreshments, their tips were liberal, and Dick and I often discussed Michigan, where he was in his third year. That fall he and I were enrolled in a public speaking course in which we took turns delivering short speeches without notes. When Dick spoke, he stood with his weight on one leg, a peculiar droop to the corner of his mouth which gave it a sarcastic or sinister look albeit he was a handsome young man, friendly and personable. Who would dream that one day, with his fraternity brother, Nathan Leopold, Jr., he would commit the dastardly crime of killing his cousin Bobby Franks, 14 years old?

I saw Dick for the last time in front of the Michigan Union in June,

1923. He had graduated from the University at 17, the youngest ever to graduate, and was leaving for their summer home with plans to go to Harvard for his master's degree in history. Leopold, 18, returned to the University of Chicago in the fall of 1923.

The Loeb-Leopold case became known as the crime of the century. Both men, sons of multi-millionaires, were defended by Clarence Darrow, who was clever enough to waive a jury and have the case tried by a judge, knowing full well he was before a judge opposed to capital punishment. Darrow's eloquent pleas resulted in sentences of life, plus 99 years for each of the defendants. Loeb was subsequently knifed by a fellow prisoner at Joliet Prison and died at the age of 30. Leopold was paroled in March, 1958, after serving 33 years in prison; on his release he went to Puerto Rico where he worked as a laboratory technician in a missionary hospital until his death in August, 1971.

At Ferris I had often sat in on faculty meetings as a member of the Military Science Department in the absence of Captain Shaw (and later when president of my class) and became personally acquainted with Governor Ferris. The fall of 1922 he filed as a Democrat against U.S. Senator Townsend, a long time Republican incumbent. His son, Phelps Ferris, called to ask if I would arrange a meeting of former Ferris students when his father came to Ann Arbor for a campaign address.

We organized a Ferris-for-Senator club, and 500 turned out to greet the candidate. It was my privilege to present Governor Ferris, who seemed pleased with the enthusiastic reception. During the opening ceremonies I noticed he'd pull out his watch, look at it, wind it a bit, put it on the table. Finally, turning to me, he said:

"Wilkins, pay no attention to my eccentricities. I'm always nervous as a cat before giving a talk, but once on my feet the tension ceases."

I smiled. "Something like waiting in the trenches for zero hour. Once the whistle blows, though, you're going over the top and there's no time to worry."

"Exactly," he said. "Both the same."

Not exactly, but similar.

He won the election, and I was to meet him again in Washington, DC when he was in the Senate. He was recognized nationwide as an outstanding speaker and Michigan's most noted educator.

My job at The Desk in The Union gave me an opportunity to renew old acquaintances and make new ones; H.B. Rust, president of The Koppers Company, a Mellon corporation in Pittsburgh, was one of the latter. Mrs. Rust was not well, and he'd brought her to the University of Michigan hospital for treatment; during her hospital confinement he stayed at The Union and we became good friends. Later I was to be in his debt for his courtesy and the opportunities he gave me.

The war had put me back a number of years, and in my impatience to get my degree and get on with the job, I took every chance I could to make up for lost time. By attending summer school in 1923, I earned enough credits to enter law school that fall and learned that law and politics go hand in hand when I was elected president of the freshman law class.

Michigan had one of the best law faculties in the country. Dean Henry M. Bates, a strict but just disciplinarian, taught constitutional law in addition to his duties as dean of a large outstanding law school. Noted professors were Grover Griswold, Ralph Aigler, Edson Sunderland and John B. Waite, grandson of a former Justice of the Supreme Court of the United States. Professors Wilgus, Lane, Durfee and Shartell were experts in their specialized fields. All these men contributed to the superior reputation that Michigan law school enjoyed nationally.

My first year tuition was $110 as an in-state student. In 1977 tuition was $1316 for in-state students, $3,000 for non-residents.

Classes started at 8 in the morning and ran six days a week. The fraternity house was a mile from the campus, so the day began with a brisk morning walk. Many students were working their way through school—fraternity brothers Carl Weinman played the trumpet and Paul Wilson the piano, leading the orchestra at Union dances. After practicing law for several years, Carl was elected to the Court of Common Pleas in his home town of Steubenville, Ohio, later promoted to the Federal District Court at Dayton. He was the federal judge who granted the writ of habeas corpus in the celebrated Dr. Shepard case, holding it was impossible for Dr. Shepard to receive a fair trial in Cleveland due to the overpowering adverse publicity generated in the newspapers. Dr. Shepard had been convicted of murdering his wife. Carl's scholarly opinion was affirmed by the Supreme Court of the United States and resulted in Dr. Shepard's release from prison.

Distinguished members and guests were often entertained at the fraternity house with formal dinners. One evening we were to have Sir Paul Vinogradoff, a Russian count and honorary member of our fraternity. After briefing sessions on etiquette, dressed in dinner jackets, we were amused to see Sir Paul tuck his napkin under his chin. At the post-mortem Carl Weinman said: "Well, that's the Russian custom."

While at Michigan, alumni members helped us finance a new house on Washtenau Avenue. At that time Delta Theta Phi had 52 branches called "Senates" at universities throughout the country.

Ours was named "Christiancy after an early Michigan judge. I believe professional fraternities, operated as ours was, contribute to a well-rounded education for its members and add zest to college life.

First-year law was a period of maturing; that summer I took two additional courses to lighten the workload the coming year. Earlier that spring I was elected president of the Michigan Union, an activity involving the whole male student body and requiring a lot of time. It was a strictly male organization, and in those days we had a uniformed doorman at the front entrance who directed all women, even when accompanied by men members, to the ladies' entrance.

Michigan women then were working on plans for building the Women's League building; while I was still at Michigan, the new League building was completed and *men* were not permitted to enter via the front entrance. A fair retaliation!

The job as president of the Union was a nonpaying job and demanded many hours in addition to my work at the desk and second-year law classes. I soon found I wasn't spending enough time on my studies; a fact reflected in my grades. One day Dean Bates called me to his office and gave me some good advice. During our conversation he asked: "Wilkins, did you come to Michigan to be a lawyer or a cheerleader?" At first I was indignant, for I believed the office of president of the Michigan Union was a more elevated position than cheerleader. However, I held my tongue, knowing he was genuinely interested in my welfare.

As a result of that conference I resigned as president of the Union. A wise decision, for my grades improved.

Another incident occurred that spring which was to have an important influence on my life. Mr. Rust invited me to Pittsburgh to meet members of the law department of the Koppers Company. Mr. Rust generously paid my expenses, and Easter vacation was spent as a guest in the Rust home on Murray Hill Avenue. The head of the law department was John Ste. Clair Brooks; his chief assistant was Hugh Smith, son of Addison T. Smith, congressman from Idaho. The many kindnesses extended to me by Mr. and Mrs. Rust will never be forgotten.

After completing second-year law, Mr. Rust invited me to spend the summer working in the law offices of the Koppers Company at a salary of $150 a month. As graduates were being hired at $50 a month, this was being overpaid, but I didn't turn down the job!

Life was pleasant. I boarded at a large house on Dithridge Street once owned by "Diamond Lil" Russell. From carefully hoarded funds, money was taken for an occasional golf game, and I saw my first professional golf match—the U.S. Open at Oakmont Golf Club.

Among the top players were Chick Evans, Gene Sarazen and Bobby Jones. Bobby won.

Mr. Brooks and Mr. Smith were pleasant and helpful men to work for, and occasionally Mr. Rust looked in to see how I was doing. When a telegram came with news of the death of my sister Alice at Lansing, Mr. Brooks reached into his own pocket to advance me $150 to go to the services. At the family gathering after the funeral I noticed my father did not look well; he had great difficulty breathing and confided to me he knew his days were numbered, which they were. He died November 25 that same year, 1925.

In September when due to return to Ann Arbor for my final year of law, I was in debt to the firm. Mr. Brooks and Mr. Smith, both graduates of George Washington Law School at Washington, DC suggested that I stay on with the firm until the following February. Then when the second semester started at George Washington, I could apply for admittance and also seek a job with the government. The university had an afternoon school which started after government offices closed at 4. So with great regret, I did not return to Ann Arbor that fall but went to Washington, DC in February and enrolled in the law school at GWU with classes from 4 to 8. From Mr. Brooks I had a letter of introduction to Senator David Reed of Pennsylvania, and one from Hugh Smith to his father, the congressman from Idaho. It was then I called on Senator Ferris; he had two more years to serve but seemed quite frail.

The office of the Alien Property Custodian, a branch of the Department of Justice, gave me a job as law clerk at $1,800 a year. On the outbreak of World War I the United States had confiscated property in this country owned by German citizens residing abroad. The office had many files which contained claims by these German citizens or their heirs for return of their properties. Our job was to determine heirship, one which required a review of wills executed in German and supporting papers in the files.

It was an interesting study, as German wills were different from those drawn in America. Typically, the testator reviewed his life and, in awarding his property, sprinkled through the will advice as to how his survivors should properly conduct themselves during their lifetime.

Some law clerks were students at the university; others were graduates and now practicing lawyers in the department. It was a relaxed organization, thanks to our supervisor, Harmon Acuff, a lawyer from Kentucky.

George Washington had an excellent faculty and many mature older students who like myself worked for the government while going to school part time. I affiliated with Wilson Senate of Delta Theta Phi fraternity and was often invited to visit and play bridge at the White Senate house at Georgetown University. Delta Theta Phi had a lively group and gave many social events at downtown hotels. Several members were sons or brothers of congressmen and served as their secretaries. One of my best friends was Hugh Colton, brother of the congressman from Utah.

That fall my fraternity brothers nominated me for president of the senior law class. Pitted against me was Clyde Tolson, a member of Phi Delta Phi law fraternity and secretary to Hanford McNider, secretary of war under President Coolidge. McNider, from Iowa, was one of the first national commanders of the American Legion, an active member of the administration and strong politically, which strength spilled over to his able assistant, Clyde Tolson, for whom I have always had a high regard. After graduation Clyde joined the FBI and became J. Edgar Hoover's chief assistant.

On counting the ballots, the secretary of the law school declared the vote a tie. My committee filed objections to her findings when it learned she'd thrown out five ballots which it was believed had been cast for me. The committee found that the five students who cast the ballots in question lived across the river in Virginia and had voted according to their custom, drawing a line through the name of the person for whom they were not voting. This left my name clear on all five ballots with Clyde's name crossed out. The secretary maintained an "X" should have been placed before the name of the person for whom they were voting.

The dispute lasted for weeks. Finally it was agreed the case be argued in moot court before three law professors. Clyde and I each selected two senior law students from the class to represent us. I picked two fraternity brothers, Hugh Colton and Willard Hansen, both from Utah. By their able briefs and arguments they won the case and I became president of the senior law class of 1927.

Washington, DC was exciting. As often as I could, I went to the Hill to hear the debates. I had a pass to the Senate from Senator Borah and for the House from Congressman Smith. I heard all my favorites: Senators Borah, Hiram Johnson of California, Norris of Nebraska and LaFollette of Wisconsin.

One Sunday morning on my way to church I met four men walking two abreast; recognizing President Coolidge, I tipped my hat and said, "Good morning, Mr. President." He smiled and waved in return. Another day, while crossing the Connecticut Avenue bridge, I passed jovial Chief Justice Taft, who smiled at me and said "Hello, son." Walking near the Capitol, I passed Charles Evans Hughes, secretary of state; he too spoke graciously to me. He was a very handsome man.

It was a real thrill for the boy from Greenland, Michigan, to have that close a contact with those staunch leaders of our nation.

Law school completed, I received a Doctor of Laws degree and moved up to become a lawyer on the staff of the Alien Property Custodian department.

Late in the fall of 1927 a letter came from Weldon G. "Betts" Bettens, classmate and fraternity brother from Hancock, Michigan, then practicing in Seattle, in which he said he was coming to Washington, DC to do some research at the Supreme Court. He stayed with me for four days and did a good job of selling Seattle. The outcome of his visit was a decision to apply to take the Washington State Bar examination in January. My chief arranged for me to transact some business in Seattle with the understanding, if I passed the Bar and decided to stay, I could return the documents with recommendations to the office.

I arrived in Seattle in January, 1928, two days before the examinations, fortified with letters from the chief of our law department to three of his friends: Richard Munter of Spokane, Dix Rowland of Tacoma and Ralph Williams of Portland, all established attorneys and active in the Republican party. Betts met my train; with him was Warren G. Magnuson, then a law student at the University of Washington. "Maggie" became our distinguished senator.

On presenting my letter to Dix Rowland, chairman of the Board of Bar Examiners, I told him I was worried about not having had any special courses in Washington State laws, especially community property. He suggested I read a case recently decided by the Washington Supreme Court relating to community property and familiarize myself with the probate code.

Examinations were given in the old Capitol building in Olympia on Thursday and Friday; those who passed were sworn in before the Supreme Court on Saturday morning. That year *everyone* passed, including "Radio Speaker" John C. Stevenson, a controversial political figure. At that time he was a barker for "Painless Parker," advertising dentists on Third Avenue in Seattle. A dentist's chair had been installed in the entrance to the building, and John, in a white jacket, would stand in the street and entice people to witness a wonder of the world—the painless extraction of a tooth. The patient was usually a "skid road" bum. After extracting his tooth, the dentist would ask him, "Did that hurt?" The patient would then shake his head and reply, "No, not at all."

George Boldt, who in time was appointed a federal judge by President Eisenhower, came from Montana to take the exam. We've often laughed about John Stevenson. Once George said jokingly, "It just so happened, Bill, that a dental examination was being given in

Olympia at the same time and John got into the wrong room.'' In fact, John went to California to practice law, became counsel for the Western Conference of Teamsters and later for the national organization. Many who were sworn in before the Supreme Court that memorable Saturday became leading members of the Washington Bar, and eight became judges.

By then the decision was definitely made to stay in Seattle, so there I was—a full-fledged lawyer without a job. Betts had told me he'd pounded the pavements for three months before he finally landed a job with the firm of Caldwell and Lycette at $50 a month. Knowing he was number two in our law class and had had a letter of recommendation from Dean Bates, I started out on my own with some trepidation, but my luck still held.

The first place I called on was the admiralty firm of Huffer, Hayden, Merritt, Summers and Bucey. Mr. Summers, the managing partner and son-in-law of Dean Effinger of the Lit school at Michigan, hired me for the munificent sum of $100 a month. I sent off my papers to Washington, DC with a successful collection record, got off the public payroll and went to work for the firm.

On his first visit to Seattle, Richard S. Munter of Spokane, who had a letter of introduction to me from my former chief, called and invited me to luncheon at the Olympic Hotel, where I found myself in the august company of Frank Hull (the hotel manager) and Governor Roland Hartley, the latter a feisty man, but he treated me cordially and told of his coming to the Pacific Northwest from Minnesota. Dick a Michigan law graduate, and his wife Helen became very good friends, and my wife and I were happy to be present when he was installed as president of the Washington State Bar Association some years later.

Then I met Lucille.

Up to that time life had been primarily one of survival. Whether peddling papers with brother Howard, hard-rock mining at 16, fighting a war, working on the assembly line or washing dishes—every step had been one to survive. Motivation had been just one desire—to be a lawyer, and the best lawyer it was in me to be. To that end dedication of all time was entirely to work and study; not much was left for frivolity. Oh, there were dances at The Union, and I did my share of dancing, but that was usually "stag." A steady girl friend meant time and money, two commodities in short supply.

Actually, my situation in Seattle at that time was pretty much the same except I had my foot on the ladder, but it was still the bottom of the ladder. A serious romantic involvement was not in my carefully planned scheme of things, much less marriage. But Fate is no respecter of plans or people or problems. And Wilkins was a willing victim.

I will always remember the night I met Lucille. A mutual friend of Betts and mine gave a dinner party for him and his gal, Eddys Reynolds, and her houseguest from Yakima, Lucille Schreiner. As in all fairytales, it was an enchanted evening. Over the Cascades the harvest moon rose to cast before it a shimmering golden path across the waters of Lake Washington. The sky was full of stars. A soft breeze lifted the branches in the garden, carrying with it all the scents of Arcady.

Into this enchanted garden came Lucille—blithe and willowy, her head crowned with naturally curly brown hair, her large long-lashed blue eyes filled with merriment, her sun-tanned skin, burnished golden bronze by the Yakima sun, all aglow. And Wilkins was a gone goose.

I don't remember much of what went on that evening except I was bewitched. When we parted, thoughts of Lucille swirled through my mind the better part of the night, the foremost one—when would we meet again?

And again Fate stepped in. The next day, while I was having lunch in a downtown restaurant, in she walked! Some days before, she'd taken a job as secretary to Raymond G. Wright, the senior member of his law firm, and commenced work that morning. Later we both admitted our hearts were pounding.

She is the daughter of pioneers. Her father, Joseph F. Schreiner, was of German descent, his grandfather having come from Trier and settled in Yakima in the 1850s when irrigation came to the valley. "Dad" was tall, slender, handsome and charming with twinkling brown eyes and a wonderful disposition.

He'd worked hard to develop his homestead of 160 acres, now grown to 500, into a productive diversified ranch—orchards, wheat and alfalfa fields, and a large dairy herd of purebred Holstein cows. When I met him, he'd retired early and we had grand times together, fishing on the lakes and streams in the Cascade foothills west of the Yakima Valley. Sometimes we camped overnight. Always he found time for his favorite sports—hunting and fishing.

Lucille's mother, née Marie Louise LaBisonniere, was of French descent. The first ancestor in America, Jules Trotier, arrived from Perche, France with a land grant from King Louis XIII at Trois Rivières, Province of Quebec in 1630. Vast herds of buffalo (bison) roamed the great tract of land and soon the family was known as "les Trotiers de la Bisonniere," endowed with the titles, "Sieur de Beaulieu, Seigneur (Lord) de la Rivière de Love de Trois-Rivières" and Sieur Desruisseaux, Seigneur de L'Ile Perrot." Some generations later the Trotier was dropped and the name became LaBisonniere. Lucille is of the 12th generation in America. Her grandfather, Grandpère Georges LaBisonniere, "went west" and took a homestead in the Yakima Valley (now part of the town of Yakima) in 1893.

Soprano Marie Louise LaBisonniere and baritone Joseph Francis Schreiner met the year of 1895 while singing in the choir. They told us they walked hand in hand as they left the church, Joseph leading his horse. When they reached the outskirts of town on the way to the family home, they rode together and talked of their dream, a ranch home in the valley, which was fulfilled. They had a bounty of six healthy robust curly-headed children; Lucille was the youngest of the brood.

Courting on a shoestring can be far more glamorous and exciting than people might believe.

Lucille first shared a room with her cousin, Celestine "Sis" Curry, at St. Theresa's Catholic home, a setup similar to the YWCA, near St. James Cathedral. A sister of the order greeted late house-guests, and doors closed at 11 p.m. We made many a dash to meet the deadline.

When her friend, Eddys Reynolds, took an apartment, she invited Lucille to share: this arrangement gave me a few more hours in which to pursue the cause of Cupid. In those days the cinema was good entertainment and reasonable—about 25 cents. We enjoyed wonderful evenings at the movies and saw the change from silent to talking pictures.

Sunday was our day to splurge. Blanc's, the famous old gourmet restaurant on Marion Street, served a delicious seven course Sunday dinner for $1.50.

With Lucille, a whole new world of sights and sounds was opened to me. Her keen perception and all-seeing eyes brought the beauty of ever green Puget Sound country to life. For her Seattle was a never ending thrill. After the small farming town of Yakima, surrounded by low rolling hills which were brown most of the year, the contrast was overwhelming. The big city with its busyness, was stimulating. She especially liked the city lights. Often we took the streetcar to Beacon Hill where there was a lookout over the city and Puget Sound. There we sat and watched the lights come on as the golden glow of sunset faded behind the Olympic mountains.

During her late 'teens, she'd belonged to The Cascadians, a mountaineering club, and climbed many of the peaks near the Yakima Valley, including Mt. Adams. She both appreciated and respected those heights. The power and grandeur of the volcanic thrust that had created those giants of the universe never ceased to fill her with awe. With her beside me it was a real thrill to see Mt. Rainier, that grand old mountain that dominates our city, reflect the sun's rays in all its glory.

The tall evergreens took on new meaning, with their soft velvet tips and various-shaped cones, speaking a special language when the wind tossed their branches. The flowering trees, the endless varieties of grasses heavy with seeds—all spoke Lucille's language.

Coming from a dry climate where every drop of water was cherished, to be surrounded by water on all sides was to her unbelievable. Her swimming had been in the Yakima River or the city pools. In Seattle we could swim in a real lake! There was also a large natatorium on Alki Point with a high diving board at one end. She dove off it with ease and grace; *I* didn't even dare *jump* off! A cable car took us from the foot of Madison Street up the steep hills and down to Lake Washington where we could picnic and swim.

The evenings we double-dated with Betts and his girl were great fun. Betts was gifted with a fine bass voice and had sung in the Michigan Glee Club; a part of those evenings was spent in song—Betts and I harmonizing through the old favorites. Sometimes the girls joined in but more often they listened, nodding with approval. Those were happy days!

Then there were the times we just sat and talked. Lucille, a naturally alert and enthusiastic listener, drew from me the highlights of my life. Our first Armistice Day together we celebrated by cooking a steak and having wine. After dinner she quizzed me about my World War I experiences and what Armistice Day meant to me. Once she blurted out, "I wish the Allies had gone all the way to Berlin!"

For the first time since 1918 I talked of those last days and my position at the time of the Armistice. "So, you see," I said when I finished, "if we'd pushed on the next day, I wouldn't be here now to talk about it."

In turn, she told many interesting stories about her life on a big ranch. One thing, she never gossiped. Her father's creed had become her creed. "If you can't say something *good* about another person, don't say anything."

Alas, every Eden has its serpent, and Fate is not always kind. Late that fall an infection which broke out on my hands and feet sent me to St. Luke's Hospital. The dermatologist whom I found in the yellow pages admitted he'd used the wrong medication on a rash! Faithful Lucille visited me every evening, bringing a blue and white luncheon set to embroider as we talked—her first venture into domesticity. Afterwards she said she'd never felt that way, especially *any* inclination toward domesticity.

A change of doctors turned the tide but, swathed in bandages, I appeared with my roommate, Betts, before a luncheon meeting of the King County Bar Association where I argued the affirmative and he the negative in a debate: "Resolved: that capital punishment should be retained." The State of Washington had had capital punishment since territorial days until 1909 when it was abolished; in 1919, after the senseless murder of a judge, it was reinstated by a vote of the people.

In time finances afforded the purchase of a secondhand Chrysler 70 roadster with a rumble seat. The speedometer was on its second round, but it ran like a top. Those wheels enabled us to explore the many beauties of the Puget Sound country and eastern Washington. Our first drive was to Snoqualmie Falls—nothing like that in Yakima! I was continuously impressed with Lucille's appreciation of nature's bounty. She was ecstatic over a small flower thrusting its bloom above the grasses, rain sparkling on a branch, a gnarled old tree, a stump covered with moss and tiny flowers and huckleberry bushes. Through her loving artistic eyes I too learned to appreciate beauty.

Thanksgiving, 1928, found us on our way to Yakima to visit Lucille's family. Unaware how anxious she was to get home, I drove cautiously. "Speed it up!" she urged. "Would you like to drive?" I asked, and drive she did. She gave me a real thrill with a speedy ride over the mountain roads she knew so well.

Her family's welcome to me was so warm and gracious I fell in love with them at once. After we'd visited for a while, her mother said, "Bill, won't you please come to us for Christmas?" I hoped this meant I was in. At least, I was making progress, and I'd found no evidence of competition on "the other side of the mountain."

At Thanksgiving and again at Christmas a heavy snowfall had turned the valley into a fairyland, and the days were filled with fun and laughter and a deep and abiding happiness. Soon after, we made a visit to Lucille's Aunt Helen and Uncle Joe Monte in Chehalis. Sensing Lucille and I were deeply in love, Aunt Helen put in a pitch for me to join the Catholic Church, but my reservations were strong and resistance stubborn.

After Christmas, when we talked of marriage, Lucille's mother wanted us to come to Yakima for a church wedding but the hurdle of getting a dispensation from the bishop was too great. Lucille resolved the problem, using the depression, which had already hit and bankrupted many farmers, as an excuse.

"Can it really have any effect on our ultimate happiness?" she asked. "Let's just keep it simple."

So, on January 19, 1929 we were in Everett before the county auditor chatting with a University of Michigan lawyer friend, Frank Mansfield, and his wife while we applied for our marriage license. The county auditor raised the issue of Lucille's legal age; legally, the Mansfields couldn't vouch for it so we called our mutual friend, Percy

Thomas, the King County auditor, also a Michigan man, who satisfied the Snohomish County auditor.

Frank suggested his Presbyterian minister rather than a civil ceremony and we agreed. It was a simple charming wedding and, as in all fairytales, we've "lived happily ever after."

We'd planned to go to Vancouver, BC for the weekend, but when we counted our money in Bellingham Lucille said, "This is a lovely city; why not here?" The Leopold Hotel, 50 years younger than now, was most hospitable. From there we called Lucille's parents and told them our news; they gave us their blessing and wished us much happiness.

When we returned to Seattle, I had $2.50 in my pocket—my sole monetary worth—but I *had Lucille!*

Fate, chance, luck—call it what you wish—continued to smile on us. Within a few months we were the proud owners of a home. The first of three log houses which started us on that long long trail of new, old, antique, remodeled and moved, early American homes. Owning property, much less a house, had been the farthest thing from our minds; it was all we could do to keep ourselves afloat. In April, however, while visiting friends at their summer home on Lake Lucerne about 25 miles south of Seattle, they showed us a large rustic log house on the lake nearby.

The story was that it had been built by a sea captain who lost it to the mortgage company when he got mixed up with a scheme to smuggle Chinese workers into the country. He had installed a pair of large portholes on either side of the huge fireplace that took up most of one wall, and left a fine ship's model on the mantel, also several old brass ship's lanterns on the walls. A wide balcony ran around three sides of the large living room which opened up to the thrust of the roof of hand-split cedar shakes. In dry weather we could see slithers of daylight between them but when rain came, the shakes swelled and sealed the roof tight, and we loved to listen to the music of the pitter patter of the raindrops.

Two wide porches—one on the lake side and one at the back—tempted one to idle slothfulness on a balmy summer day. A kitchen with a wood-burning stove, a bathroom and three small bedrooms were tucked in the rear of the house under the wide sloping roof.

Lake Lucerne was a small gem of emerald green water surrounded by tall virgin fir and cedar. At that time there weren't many homes there.

The ground was covered with moss and a cushion of old needles; everywhere were clumps of wildflowers, salal and huckleberry. We fell in love with it at first sight; visions of actually living in a log house during the summer drowned out the voices of common sense. Going contrary to the usual procedure of acquiring a house in town before the luxury of a summer place, we bought it on a loan sufficient to pay off the mortgage against it with small monthly payments. So we had ourselves a quaint charming house on a nice piece of waterfront property.

A lot of finishing work was needed, which led to the role of carpenter on weekends. The rustic construction of the house fortunately tolerated my early blunderings with saw and hammer. In addition, there was always wood to be cut and sawed and split for the fireplace and stove which kept me in good physical trim.

Furniture for our hideaway had to be scrounged. By then we were in the throes of the depression and secondhand stores and antique shops were filled with bargains—better than the poorly made new things. Lucille spent hours either taking off layers of old paint to expose really fine wood or painting over the poorer wood. The bright oranges and yellows used throughout the house were a cheerful note against the soft patina of the dark logs. Our first dishes were the old Blue Willow pattern; glassware was odds and ends of various patterns, some of which turned out to be real treasures during the heyday of the early American pressed glass craze.

Groceries were bought at Sawyer's Country Store; there we heard all the valley gossip, for most everyone traded there. Jacob's Farm provided fresh eggs and farm-grown chickens. Most Sundays there was a chicken in the pot, though we preferred it fried in the big old iron frying pan on the cookstove. I always associate the aroma of chickens frying with that log house by the lake along with the woodsy fragrance of the trees mingled with the woodsmoke from the chimney.

Summers the lake was warm enough to swim in, and the sylvan retreat became a popular gathering place for family, friends and various organizations to which we belonged. The Fourth of July was a family celebration, a custom that continued for many years in other homes. Lucille's parents, her two brothers and three sisters came from Yakima with all their children for fun, food and fireworks. At night the overflow of people was taken care of with various and sundry couches on the balcony where guests could enjoy the last glowing embers of a cozy fire below. On one occasion Lucille's brother arrived with two cases of "home brew" fastened to the running boards of his car. Fine thing! I was then a deputy prosecuting attorney trying cases involving the unlawful possession of liquor!

The University of Michigan Club held its annual picnics at a nearby resort, and many gathered at the log house in the evening, some practically hanging from the balcony, while Lucille played the old square grand Rosewood piano we'd bought for $30, accompanied by talent on banjos and guitars with everybody singing Michigan songs.

Much the same program was established by the Associated Clubs of the South End, the Seattle Post of the American Legion, the New Order of Cincinnatus, picnics for the prosecuting attorney's office and many others.

From early spring to late fall I commuted the 25 miles to the courthouse every day. That was a long drive in those days but it was well worth it. We took a small apartment on Capitol Hill in winter, but every weekend possible we spent at the log house enjoying the peace and quiet of the woods.

Necessity, however, prompted some purchases for the apartment. Frederick & Nelson had imported hand-hooked rugs from Quebec which supplemented those made by Lucille. Before I could rescue it, she'd put my World War I uniform in one; that would have been a real antique by now! A New England hand-wrought iron floor lamp with a spun brass shade was decorative but *not* a good reading lamp and eventually ended up beside the organ. A secondhand sofa and chair were slipcovered to match draperies and valances, a lovely old chintz pattern, by a friend who owned a wholesale drapery establishment. We found an 18th century walnut secretary fronted by a skilled cabinet-maker with a beautiful piece of burled walnut; the antique dealer called it "bastard walnut." Doug Welch, with characteristic humor, described it as "a cross between a walnut and wild cherry." We paid $150 for it but a recent appraisal put it astonishingly higher.

The Victorian bedroom set that one of Lucille's ancestors had brought across the plains in a covered wagon had an old-fashioned three-quarter bed which was converted to twin beds by a decorator specializing in antiques. He used the same sized head and footboards for a headboard for each bed and turned a pair of perfectly matched footboards on his lathe.

In 1933 King County went broke, and my salary which had risen to $260 was reduced to $240; the county warrants were accepted by the banks at a discount. Frederick & Nelson, The Bon and Augustine & Kyer's grocery store accepted the warrants on purchases. To help meet pledged obligations and living costs, Lucille got her old job back with Raymond Wright for a year.

Our idyl ended when fire destroyed the log house in 1935. We had just returned to the apartment in town one Sunday when neighbors called to say it was on fire. We rushed back to see the last log fall inward as flames devoured what was left. Lucille burst into tears; I was numb. Everything was lost except the heirloom Victorian bedroom set, as that winter we'd decided to use it in the apartment. Apparently the wiring, which a neighbor and I had installed, was faulty. A good example of what *not* to do yourself.

But, as Mother used to say: "The Lord always provides." A settlement came from the insurance company which had insured the house for one-half its appraised value. Later the three waterfront lots on which the log house stood were sold and added to the nest egg for a Seattle house.

Sergeant-Instructor of R.O.T.C., 1921.

Delta Theta Phi fraternity house at Ann Arbor, 1922.

Mrs. Goltz's three waiters–Fairbanks, Beauchamp, Wilkins, 1920.

Sister Elsie at Ferris, 1921.

1853-1928 Our President–Mr. Ferris.

The Class of Twenty-One Welcomes you to their Exercises June 31, 1921, Ferris Institute. (Class officers named following)

The Class of Twenty-One

Welcomes You to

Their Exercises

June 30

1921

Ferris Institute

Class Officers

President.......................................William Wilkins

Vice-President.......................................Glenn H. Parker

Secretary.......................................Ruth Travis

Treasurer....................................... Gilbert Johnson

Patron ....Gerrit Masselink

Patroness....................................... Miss Mary McNerney

Honorary Doctor of Laws degree, 1964 Ferris State College, Big Rapids, Michigan.

WILKINS, CONNABLE, HAYDEN TRIUMPH IN CAMPUS ELECTION; RECORD VOTE SHOWN AS MORE THAN 2,400 BALLOTS ARE CAST

BROMLEY, MERRIAM, SMITH HYDE, BEUKMA WIN; HIGLEY SUCCESSFUL

ROBERTSON SELECTED RECORDING SECRETARY

New Union Head Leads Field With 622 Margin Over Nearest Competitor

In what is believed to have been the heaviest campus vote on record, W. J. Wilkins, '26L, was elected president of the Union and Perry Hayden, '25, of the Students' Christian association, for the next college year. Karl Robertson, '25 was chosen recording secretary of the Union, J. P. Bromley, '25, literary vice president, C. W. Merriam, '25E, engineering vice president, A. M. Smith, '25L, law vice president, B. E. Hyde, '25M, and J. P. Beukema, '25D, combined vice president. Charles Higley, '26, was elected secretary of the S. C. A.

When the count had been completed at an early hour this morning, the following individual scores were announced:

President Union: W. J. Wilkins, '26L, 1144; C. D. Livingstone, '25, 482; Thomas Cavanaugh, '24, 361; W. W. Spanagel, '25, 247; R. J. Hummer, '25, 115; and F. J. Dickman, '25E, 62.

Recording secretary Union: Karl Robertson, '25, 1100; Milton Peterson, '25, 1009.

Literary vice president Union: J. B. Bromley, '25, 316; F. R. Smith, '25, 310; Harry W. McCobb, '25, 280; Robert Halsey, '25, 233. Engineering vice president: C. W. Merriam, '25,

THE WINNERS

WILKINS

CONNABLE

HAYDEN

PRYOR

GLASGOW TO LEAD CHEERING SQUAD

MERRIAM, KERR, SABO, COLEMAN KELLAR, FINN ELECTED TO COUNCIL

PRYOR WILL DIRECT ORATORICAL ACTIVITY

Haggerty, Brooker, Rice Hayden, Sabo Garlinghouse Chosen For Boards In Control

Alfred B. Connable, '25, was named president of the student council for next year by a 280 vote majority in the largest ballot ever cast on the campus here yesterday. Other officers named in election were the boards in control of athletics and publications; Millard H. Pryor, '25, president of the Oratorical association, and junior and senior representatives on the student council.

The record vote cast yesterday will easily exceed 2,400, although no definite count has been made. This exceeds by 400 the vote recorded in last year's election, and eclipses any previous election on the campus.

In winning the presidency of the Student Council, Connable received a total of 1,228 votes, while his opponent, Edward M. Fox, '25, totalled 948. The men named as senior representatives to the council and their votes were Charles W. Merriam, 1166; William W. Kerr, 1107; John Sabo, 1044. The defeated candidates and their votes were Irwin Deister, 777; Eugene L. Dunne, 991; and John Garlinghouse, 950. The junior representatives elected were Kenneth Kellar, 1019; William Coleman, 980; and Joseph Finn, 934. The defeated men

Wilkins, Connable, Hayden triumph in campus election; record vote shown as more than 2,400 ballots are cast.

Glancing Back...

George Johnson

It doesn't seem possible in this day, but for years and years, the Michigan Union had a doorman whose principal duty was to make sure that no women entered the building by the front door.

This intrepid fellow was George J. Johnson and he protected the bastion for 26 years before he died in the fall of 1946 at the age of 86.

George was known to thousands of Michigan alumni, many of whom may remember stopping to chat with George as, cigar in hand, he reminisced about his earlier days when he used to drive in harness races.

Normally genial, George could become politely stern when women would attempt to violate the tradition of being excluded from the use of the Union's front entrance. There is the story – largely unsubstantiated – that George once stopped Mrs. Sergei Rachmaninoff, wife of the famous composer, from entering the Union's front door. When Rachmaninoff explained who she was, George was reported to have replied: "I know, I know. Side entrance."

Johnson's two daughters still live in the Ann Arbor area.

Glancing back.

Delta Theta Phi dinner meeting honoring initiates, Ann Arbor, 1922.

Lucille, 1929

Lucille's parents 1898

Log house–Lake Lucerne

"Sharp"

Lucille and "Sharp"

CHAPTER IV

Public Service and Private Practice (1929-1940)

When I came to Seattle, my old friend from Paris days, Gene Clare, commander of Rainier-Noble Post of the American Legion, invited me to join. At a Legion meeting I met Ewing D. Colvin, prosecuting attorney of King County. Cap, as everyone called him, and I discovered we'd been in the same division during World War I, fought in the Meuse-Argonne battle, and our paths had crossed in the vicinity of Remoiville and Jametz in the closing days of the war, although we never met "over there." He was in the 11th and I in the 6th Infantry of the 10th Brigade of the 5th Division. Often, after Legion meetings, Cap and I would reminisce and fight those battles all over again. Gene Clare and I had some good laughs over our "battle of Paris" too.

In April, 1929, Cap told me he had a vacancy on his staff and asked if I would be interested in being a deputy prosecuting attorney in the criminal division with a salary of $240 a month. Then a married man of three months, the raise in pay was an important consideration. Also, though I would be sorry to leave the admiralty firm after just one year, this was an opportunity to gain experience as a trial lawyer. And that I certainly did!

The first cases I prosecuted were in the justice courts (now known as district courts), where I earned my spurs. In court day after day, I became a workaholic, working Saturdays and often on Sundays. Prohibition was in effect, and my daily trial calendar contained up to a dozen or more cases involving the illegal sale of liquor. There was big money in the liquor business, and the defendants could well afford to hire shrewd counsel.

Cap Colvin was a superb prosecuting attorney—a scrapper, a man of high integrity and morals, kind at heart. His instructions to his deputies were, when in court to exercise compassion but ask no quarter nor give any, and he always backed up our decisions. He detested graft. Realizing the difficulty of obtaining evidence of police graft, he felt the best and only ultimate way was to send undercover men into gambling and liquor joints to get evidence, then at the appropriate time, obtain secret search warrants and raid those places. Accompanied by deputy sheriffs and federal prohibition agents, I was in charge of most of those raids. We arrested the operators and called the police department to come down with the "black marias" to pick up the patrons of the joint who were released on $10 bail. Owners and operators were held on higher bail, charged with the felony offense of operating a gambling or liquor joint. This was striking at the source of the graft, as we were confident the owners were paying protection money either to the "cops" on the beat or to the Inspector or Captain of Police.

The Tony Matson Case

Next came assignment to trials by jury in the superior court. The first case in which my name appears as counsel in our Supreme Court Reports, heard before Judge Edwin Gruber visiting from Bellingham, was State vs. Tony Matson, Fred Elo and Dick Talo, alleged to be operating a joint for the sale of intoxicating liquor, a felony offense. My witnesses, federal prohibition agents, testified they had purchased liquor there on seven or eight occasions between August 27 and September 27, 1929. Convictions of the three defendants were affirmed unanimously by our Supreme Court March 6, 1931, and they paid heavy fines and spent time in jail. Presumably this was a deterrent and took them out of the business of illegal sale of intoxicating liquors.

The Trenchell Jointist Case

In the months following I tried so many felony liquor and gambling cases with success I thought I'd become an expert, but I got my comeuppance in the Trenchell case, heard by Judge William J. Steinert, one of our ablest trial judges.

The defendant and his wife were charged with operating places for the illegal sale of intoxicating liquor, and our federal prohibition agents testified of many purchases. When the testimony was concluded by both sides, the evidence was so strong I decided to address the court, "If it please the court, the prosecution waives its opening argument." I assumed Henry Clay Agnew, the experienced lawyer for the defense, would argue the case and there would be an opportunity for rebuttal, but Mr. Agnew thereupon ceremoniously addressed the court, "The prosecuting attorney having waived argument, the defense will likewise waive argument."

Realizing my faux pas, I asked the judge for permission to address the jury, but as Agnew had made no argument, there was nothing to rebut. Judge Steinert denied my request and instructed the jury to retire and deliberate on the verdict. It was a good lesson, and I had it coming to me for being overconfident. However, the evidence was strong and the jury found the defendants guilty.

By the time Prohibition was repealed and the trial of liquor cases phased out, I had become chief trial lawyer for the prosecutor's office. Assignments were for the prosecution of more serious offenses such as murder, robbery, burglary, rape and assault, as well as lesser crimes.

Dedicated, working arduously in the preparation and presentation of every case, the opportunities came to address juries sincerely on my views of the evidence. On September 19, 1932, primary election day, a rather unusual turn came in a case as a result of my prosecution. Unusual enough for the editor of *The Seattle Times* to put it on the editorial page.

> Yet at the very height of primary day excitement Seattle was given an example of the convincing power of eloquence in a field apart from politics. It was last Tuesday that William J. Wilkins, deputy prosecutor of King County, summed up in court the state's case against four young men on trial for assault and robbery. All four had pleaded not guilty, firmly protesting their utter innocence of the offense for which they had been brought to bar.
>
> But as Mr. Wilkins talked on, two of the arraigned quartet began to undergo conversion. It was as if they didn't know what they had done until they heard the prosecutor's graphic portrayal of the crime. Gradually, it seems, the force of his presentation convinced even them and they interrupted his discourse to enter pleas of guilty. The instance is almost without parallel. Eloquence apparently still has its uses as a device of justice, if not of politics.

In the fall of 1930 Cap Colvin decided to go into private practice, and chief deputy Robert M. Burgunder, a capable and experienced man in the field of law, filed for the office of prosecuting attorney. He was opposed by John F. "Johnnie" Dore, noted criminal lawyer and old-fashioned spellbinder who campaigned on the slogan that he would serve without pay.

One evening I was sent to the south end of the county to speak at a large community gathering on Bob's behalf. I made the joking remark that Johnnie couldn't possibly win because all his clients were in the state penitentiary and not able to vote. Johnnie, chafing at the bit to reply, said, "An elephant running through the jungle can't be bothered by a few monkeys throwing coconuts." It brought down the house. Bob won, but Johnnie was later elected mayor of Seattle.

I prosecuted many murder cases but will cite only three of the outstanding ones.

The Thanksgiving Day Massacre

On Thanksgiving Day, 1932, Julian Marcelino, a Filipino part-time farm laborer, ran amok. Without warning, he turned on his roommate, Tito Qualti, and killed him by a knife stab over the heart. He then took a swing at Tito's nephew, cut his finger and stabbed him in the chest but the victim survived. Marcelino then walked down the hall of the Midway Hotel to another room where he stabbed a third Filipino. In the course of 20 minutes and within four city blocks he ran along the streets, fatally stabbing five other victims and wounding 12 others. Four Filipinos and two Caucasians were killed. Among the 12 wounded were Japanese, Caucasians, Filipinos and blacks.

Finally he was confronted by a courageous police officer, Gordon Jensen. As Marcelino made a lunge toward him, grazing his sleeve, Jensen grabbed the killer and disarmed him. Other police officers soon arrived and brought the murder orgy to an end.

I filed first degree murder charges based on the death of Tito Qualti. The court appointed two competent defense counsel who filed a plea of "not guilty by reason of insanity or mental irresponsibility"; also two alienists to examine Marcelino, who both testified at the trial in the defendant's behalf.

The statement made by the accused to Seattle detectives and to our alienists was that after leaving Qualti, he left to go to a show. While walking down Sixth Avenue, he was assaulted by two blacks, knocked to the pavement and robbed of $200; that he'd left $100 in a bag in the room and when he returned, it was gone. When he saw the knife on the table, he "felt funny" and remembered nothing thereafter.

The defendant's psychiatric witnesses diagnosed his condition as "dementia praecox—catatonic type" and testified that Marcelino was insane at the time of the murders. Our psychiatric witnesses disputed this and gave the opinion, based on all the evidence, that Marcelino was sane at the time of the incidents and at the time of trial, which was before Judge Malcolm Douglas.

The jury had been out for more than 48 hours when Judge Douglas called counsel to his chambers and advised us the jury was deadlocked at 11 to one for the death penalty. He suggested the prosecution withdraw its demand for the death penalty, which I was reluctant to do, as I felt Marcelino would be a menace to human life unless he was permanently put away but acquiesced to the judge's suggestion with Mr. Burgunder's approval. Judge Douglas then gave this additional instruction by agreement of counsel:

> Counsel for the state withdraw their demand for the imposition of the death penalty, but still insist on a verdict of guilty of murder in the first degree, carrying the penalty of life imprisonment.

A few hours later the jury returned with a verdict, finding the defendant guilty of murder in the first degree and replying in the negative to the special interrogatory as to whether the death penalty should be inflicted.

Judge Douglas sentenced Marcelino to serve the rest of his natural life in the penitentiary at Walla Walla. We also jointly recommended that consideration be given to deporting Marcelino to the Philippines contingent on his serving the sentence in a penal institution there. Later this recommendation was carried out.

The Carter Murder Case

Richard Carter was charged with killing his stepmother, Sadie Carter, in May, 1932. The evidence showed that he shot her with his .32 caliber pistol after a heated argument. He admitted the killing to detective Captain Ernest Yoris and me and identified the gun. He was ably represented by counsel, and a plea of not guilty by reason of insanity or mental irresponsibility was entered. A psychiatrist testified on behalf of the defendant.

The jury found Carter guilty of murder in the first degree but voted not to impose the death penalty. The jury also made the following recommendation: "We, the jury, recommend that the defendant, Richard Carter, shall at no time be granted a pardon or parole," and he was so sentenced by Judge Chester A. Batchelor.

In 1939, while chairman of the Parole Board, I interviewed Carter at the penitentiary. The assumption must be that since then, he has been released on parole despite the recommendation of the jury as an inquiry to the warden of the penitentiary in 1977 remains unanswered.

The Ted Bradley Murder Case

On March 5, 10 and 15, 1932, Ted Bradley, a tough ex-convict, had committed armed robberies on Mr. G. Ikeda and his wife at their neighborhood grocery store, obtaining small amounts of money each time.

At noon of March 17, on his fourth appearance at a holdup attempt, he tried to open the cash register without success following which the Ikedas asked for police protection. The captain of the detective force assigned two officers, Sands and Rehmke, to the job. Although they were instructed to carry a sawed-off shotgun and take no chances, to shoot if necessary, they carried only their ordinary police .38 caliber automatics. Arriving at the store shortly before 6 p.m., they suggested that Mr. Ikeda leave the outer door open to allow free entrance.

Because, in previous holdups, the robber had forced the Ikedas into the back room where he emptied their pockets of any money they had, the two officers decided to place themselves there. Soon after, Bradley was spotted about a block from the store. Mr. Ikeda and his 16-year-old assistant Tommy remained in the front of the store while the officers, with the landlord of the building and Mrs. Ikeda, were in the back room, all alerted to Bradley's approach.

Immediately on entering the store Bradley, gun in hand, told Ikeda and Tommy to "stick 'em up" and drove them ahead of him to the back room. As they crossed the threshold, Bradley saw the officers and blazed away, shooting twice at officer Sands. Taken by surprise, Sands crouched to protect himself; aiming low, he fired twice, forcing the bandit back. The shooting was fast.

Officer Rehmke, who had stationed himself behind the door, swaying it to attract attention, was shot in the wrist. Taking careful aim, he fired at the robber who fell to the floor. Rehmke held his fire, thinking his man was wounded and would give up and desist. Such was not the case. The robber rolled over, raised himself enough to shoot at Rehmke. It was then Ikeda was seen lying on the floor.

Now recognized as Ted Bradley, the robber, though wounded, was able to get up and leave the store pursued by Sands. As he ran up the street, he fired two more times at Sands who returned the fire.

Bradley was seen to enter a large black sedan pulled up to the curb on the wrong side of the street. No longer able to see him, Sands withheld his fire. The car was the same one employed by Bradley in other robberies and was driven by a man named Preston. He testified at the trial that, as Bradley got in the car, he said: "I got in a beef and he plugged me."

Bradley directed Preston to take him to his home on Seventh Avenue in Seattle, which he did, and there Ethel French, with whom Bradley was living, came down and had the driver help her take him to their apartment. Asked by her if he'd been hurt, Bradley replied: "Hell no. Drunk again." Preston was asked by Ethel French to call a doctor whose name she had written on a slip of paper.

Mr. Ikeda, who had been shot in the stomach, was taken to the hospital where he died at one o'clock the following morning. An x-ray was taken, the bullet located and removed by the autopsy surgeon, marked for identification and turned over to Luke S. May for examination. A noted criminologist, Mr. May was an expert on guns and bullets and had performed numerous tests and research at his experimental Northwest Laboratories. Many experiments there were based on determining whether a particular bullet came from a particular gun. At the first degree murder trial no challenge was made of May's expertise in this field.

Detectives searched Bradley's premises, where they found a .32 caliber revolver. The bullet that killed Ikeda was a .32 caliber bullet. May's testimony was positive it came from Bradley's gun. The officers had used .38 caliber special police guns. The defense had attempted to convince the jury that Ikeda was killed by police bullets, hence the importance of May's testimony.

Bradley was taken to the city hospital. Questioned by Captain Yorris about his business, he blatantly stated he was a stickup man. Laughing, he also said he'd "made" the Ikeda place several times before and knew it was a "plant" as soon as he got in there that day. The day after that session, while talking to his half-sister and a detective who accompained her, he said, "I got that son-of-a-bitch I was after." She remonstrated with him about his language and he replied: "If I'd had a .45 I'd have got away. If I get out of this, I'll carry a gun with wheels on it."

While confined to the county jail, Bradley wrote a letter which he gave to a trusty to deliver. It read:

Seattle, Washington July 7, 1932

Claude Hoover

I am a friend of Dinks and when I left him he gave me a kite for you, but I never got as far as Spokane. He said if I needed anything you would help me. I need help now in the worst way. I was on a stickup job here in Seattle and had a little argument with the law. When the smoke cleared away there was one guy dead and a cop had a bum wing. So I am in jail on a First D murder charge. I was in the hospital for eight weeks and just got out of the hospital. I am not singing the blues to you. I am just trying to tell you the fix I am in. The guns around here are afraid of their own shadow so if you can get me four (4) Humming Bird Royal hacksaw blades, size 5, I would appreciate it and you wouldn't lose anything by it. I am out of money and everything else but if you want to take a chance on helping me I will see you don't lose anything by it. I know it is not right to ask that much of a stranger but I am just down to rock bottom. I have as much chance of beating the rap as a snowball in hell. The kid wrote to you a few days ago. If you can and will get those blades, send them to my sister in Tacoma, Washington. . .(name and address deleted) and she will see that I get them, or if things are slow up your way bring them yourself and go to see my sister and she will bring you up to see me. If you come by yourself the bulls won't let you see me as I am in "sol." Just my folks and the kid get to see me, I have been in some hot spots but this is the hottest I have been in. Here is hoping you will do something. I am trying to send this out by a trusty. He seems to be good people.

A friend

Ted Bradley
King County Jail, Seattle

P.S. If you answer, answer to my sister's address.

The trusty turned out to be "good people" indeed, for he turned the letter over to the sheriff and it was admitted in evidence.

As prosecuting attorney in the case, I had no hesitancy in asking the jury of eight men and four women to find Bradley guilty and to vote the death penalty be imposed. This they had the right to do and they did, to their credit. The case was appealed to our Supreme Court where the conviction and sentence to death were affirmed. The court stated:

> Had any other verdict than conviction of murder in the first degree been rendered by the jury. . .it would have been a travesty on justice. We can find nothing in the record justifying reversal of the verdict and special finding of the jury and the judgment of the trial court pronounced thereon.

With another police officer, Captain Yoris went to the penitentiary in Walla Walla to witness the hanging of Ted Bradley. As Bradley stood on the gallows, he was asked if he had any last words. Looking at the two officers, he waved and said, "To hell with the cops. Let her go!"

Two minutes later he was pronounced dead. Thus ended the career of a proudly self-proclaimed stickup man. Never again would society have to pay for his crimes.

In 1934 I returned to private practice of corporate law as the partner of Jay C. Allen; Charles R. Carey and Edgar Rombauer were then associates of the firm. A rugged individualist and recognized as an astute and resourceful lawyer, Jay was thinking of retirement and arranged for me to take over a good number of his clients, several of whom were in the theatre business: Jensen & vonHerberg; the Motion Picture Theater Owners' Association, of which John Hamrick of

Hamrick-Evergreen was an active member; and John Danz, owner of the Sterling chain which operated several theatres in the Seattle area. In time these men became good friends, and we often played golf together.

Lucille and I were fond of John Danz and his wife, Jessie. When he came west, he started on a shoe string. His tremendous success in the theater business was due to his drive and energy and, as he told me, "to Jessie's sound head for business." The four of us often got together for dinner and a game of bridge. A part of the evenings at their home was John's performance on the mandolin surrounded by their three children, Dorothy, Bill and Fred.

Our friendship continued through the years, and we were happy to attend John and Jessie's golden wedding anniversary dinner in March, 1961, when hundreds of their friends gathered to pay tribute to that wonderful couple. John died in October of that year, and I was honored to be asked by the family to give the eulogy at the services conducted by Rabbi Levine. John made a bequest to the University of Washington of approximately $300,000 for the purpose of providing a series of lectures based on man's rational view of the world in which we live.

This was a period in which civic affairs and organizations played an important part in our lives. I served two terms as president of the Associated Clubs of the South End, a group of 49 community clubs in King County. Through our joint efforts we were able to interest the federal government and county commissioners in a much needed flood control project for the fertile Kent Valley. The result was construction of the Mud Mountain dam.

The King County Humane Society was another interest, as I'd always loved animals; in return for my work on its board I was given a collie-shepherd dog, much like the famous Lassie, we named Sharp. Lucille taught him a lot of tricks which became the focus for many stunt programs. One night dressed as Mae West, with blond wig and padding, she took Sharp on stage. After putting him through his regular repertoire she asked him, "Would you rather be Roy Allen, (then president of the Associated Clubs) or a dead dog?" With no hesitation Sharp "played dead." Another question was: "Can you do a Mae West?" Sharp lay on his back, feet up, and wiggled around as dogs do when scratching their backs! Needless to say, he got a big hand.

We were active in the Masonic Order of the Amaranth, both of us holding offices which culminated in my serving as Grand Royal Patron of the Order in 1935. Also in the American Legion and the University of Michigan Club.

In 1936, when a Michigan alumnus, John S. Robinson, was

elected to our supreme court, the club, of which I was then president, honored him and three other members of the court—John F. Main, William J. Steinert and Bruce Blake, all Michigan grads. We said then all we needed was one more Michigan graduate to have a majority, which we got some years later when Frank Weaver from Spokane became the fifth Michigander to be elected to the State Supreme Court.

In 1931 I joined the New Order of Cincinnatus, a young men's political organization opting for clean government. Cincinnatus, as you may know, was the old Roman general who left his plow to lead his country when threatened within by corruption and without by war, returning to his fields when the crisis was passed and declining any reward for his unselfish patriotic service. Lawyer Ralph Potts was the vigorous leader of Cincinnatus. To keep out the "old politicians," membership was limited to those under 35, and no donations were accepted in excess of $50. Some 400 active young men from the Seattle area joined. Campaign literature was run off on mimeograph machines operated by the wives and girlfriends. In due course Cincinnatus elected Dave Lockwood and Arthur Langlie to the Seattle City Council. Lockwood served faithfully and well for several years before his retirement; Langlie went on to become mayor of Seattle and one of the most outstanding governors of our state.

Encouraged by our accomplishments and the favorable way the program was received by the citizens, in the fall of 1934 we decided to branch out into state elections. A special nominating convention was held, and candidates for several state and county offices were put on the ballot. I was nominated for United States Senator and Cecil Fuller for Congress from the first district. John Day, an active young lawyer, was our candidate for prosecuting attorney; several were nominated for the state legislature.

The campaign was rough going. There was little organization outside Seattle. One member, the late Mel Voorhees, a reporter for the *Seattle Star,* took time off to help me organize units in various cities. In Aberdeen there was a good nucleus, "Frosty" Richardson among them, with similar groups in Spokane and Yakima. Mel and I went to Boise, Idaho, in an attempt to persuade Senator Borah to come to Seattle for a major address at a mass rally to wind up the campaign. He wasn't able to come but expressed approval of our organization and encouraged us to carry on. Senator Borah was a kind, ruggedly handsome man with massive eyebrows and blessed with a polite and pleasant demeanor. He told us how much he enjoyed campaigning when he was our age and seemed pleased that we had come to invite him.

An old clipping at that time expresses so well the wishes of the American people today. Our goals stated:

> We cannot more graphically set forth the Cincinnatus program than by saying we seek a more efficient, a less expensive and a more honest government.
>
> We firmly believe that these qualities must be imparted to our American government if it is to be preserved as the democracy we have cherished and progressed under.
>
> The American people, today, yearn most of all for a government that will function, for a government that will be administrated in the best interests of all the people—not in the interest of cliques or classes.
>
> We of Cincinnatus are convinced that a "new man" must be injected, must be given authority in our government. He must be thoroughly honest. He must be intelligent. He must be industrious. He must be willing to tell the people what they should hear, not solely what he thinks will attract votes.
>
> He must be firmly of the belief that his reward for his public work will not be material—that it will be the gratitude, esteem and admiration of his fellow citizens.
>
> His state of mind must be foreign to that which is now all too prevalent in governmental circles, in that he must seek less government, less expensive government, and therefore a more truly helpful and protective government.
>
> There must be a thorough and thoughtful governmental reorganization from the top of the federal heap down thru the smallest school or port district.

In the end Lew Schwellenbach, the Democratic nominee for senator, took me as well as my friend, Reno Odlin, the Republican nominee, to the cleaners. The Seattle *Argus* published the accompanying cartoon and invited the comment that I was the only one of the three candidates shown with his feet on the ground.

With private practice my income had increased, and we began to think of a house in town. The log house was gone, but the insurance and money from the sale of the lots on Lake Lucerne enabled us to pay cash—$2,200—for a lot in Broadmoor. I mention this to show what has happened to property values over the years. John L. Scott, a well-known realtor, told me he sold a lot in Broadmoor a year ago for $35,000. If a choice lot were available today, he said, the price would be $50,000.

At that time Broadmoor was a comparatively new residential district built around a championship 18-hole golf course and clubhouse, surrounded by a brick wall with two entrances, the front one on Madison near Lake Washington, the back one at the edge of our beautiful Arboretum, both gates manned by guards. Friends often referred to them as the Pearly Gates. It was and is, of course, a matter of security. For men, the two great attractions were the short drive to the downtown area and a golf course at their back door. This was my first opportunity to play golf since days at Michigan where my fraternity brother Donald Duncanson loaned me an old set of clubs and we played at the Washtenau Country Club.

By this time Lucille had joined the Seattle Antiquarian Society and the Early American Glass Club and collecting was her absorbing hobby. We both had developed a strong interest in the finding and restoration of early American antique furniture, so for us the only way to go was to place it in the right frame. Since in the West there were no old houses of early New England vintage for restoration, we decided to duplicate as near as possible an early New England house and found an architect and builder who were compatible.

Lucille researched the subject, keeping voluminous files on all the details of such houses, so when we were ready to build, we had it all there on paper. She made patterns of the hardware used in the old houses and took them to the blacksmith near Lake Lucerne who used to shoe her horse. He did a wonderful job of handcrafting rat-tailed latches, dog-eared bolts and "H and L" hinges. In colonial days they signified "Holy Lords" with the power to keep out evil witches. In fact, the blacksmith made all the hardware for the house.

During the years we had the log house at Lake Lucerne Lucille had proved her talent for making much out of little. "Frugally French," I called it, but when we spent a year in bombed-out Germany, while observing this trait at work, I suspected her German ancestry also contributed to her ability to scrounge. Whatever it was, she scoured the second-hand stores and antique shops and with her trained eye spotted real finds, brought them home and worked them over into beautiful pieces. One early buy was another square rosewood piano to replace the one lost in the fire. She paid only $50 for it but had to strip and refinish it.

Mrs. Murphy advertised as wanting to make hand-braided rugs—little did she dream she would end up making rugs for the whole house! Every week Lucille went to the Goodwill, where she searched through large bins of clean wool rags, took them to the lady who cut and braided them into beautiful rugs to go with the solid oak plank floors, some as large as 11 × 12.

The most fun room was the "barn," the recreation room in the basement. Antique circular sawn 1 × 12 ceiling boards were set one inch apart with handfuls of hay hanging down between—from the "loft." A "box stall" and "manger" served as a bar, and Lucille painted barnyard animals on the whitewashed walls.

The house was a background for the collection of beautiful colored pressed glass and old blue china. It received a write-up in *Ameri-*

can Home magazine because of the unusual design of such a house in a western city. At the end Lucille was asked to make a statement about it, and she said, ". . . It is not an elegant one, but we have tried to build it true to type and hope it will have at least a degree of homespun charm." Being traditional, it is in good classic style today.

Some people may not have thought it elegant, but they sure liked to come there and we had a lot of fun in that house. I remember one Gay Nineties party when guests came dressed in that period, and our neighbor asked to come over and take pictures.

Later, following my induction to the Superior Court Bench, all the judges were invited to a stag dinner—a custom for a new judge, and plans were made for a dinner in the barn. Lucille made a huge kettle of bouillabaisse from a recipe given us by Doug Welch. That was a wonderful evening of relaxation and laughter. The judges told stories on each other, and the dinner was especially enjoyed. The punch line to the evening, though, is that the next morning we discovered someone had added a missing functional part to the billy goat Lucille had painted on the wall!

Earlier, in March of 1938 Governer Clarence D. Martin appointed me to the position of chairman of the State Board of Prison Terms and Paroles. With the assurance I could participate in certain litigation then pending in our law firm if it did not conflict with duties on the Parole Board, and after long and careful consideration, I accepted.

Here was a new challenge. This board created in 1935 supplanted a haphazard politically oriented parole organization; Governor Martin was sincere when he said he wanted the new system to work effectively. The other two members of the board were William I. Daley, former sheriff of Whitman County, and Thomas R. Waters, a Bellingham lawyer. As a team, the board made a giant step forward in developing a good parole system.

Under the provisions of the act which created the State Board of Prison Terms and Paroles, the sentencing judges were obliged to set *maximum* terms for those committed to the reformatory or penitentiary. The board set the *minimum* terms within six months after the prisoner was committed. This afforded the board ample time to compile all data pertinent to the individual, the reports of the prosecuting attorney and the sentencing judge, and their recommendations for minimum terms, as well as the reports of the FBI on criminal records, if any. Also the board was able to interview friends, relatives and other interested persons at its headquarters in Olympia before interviewing the prisoner at the institutions. Once the minimum term was set, he could earn one-third off for "good time," depending on the warden's recommendation. This law made for a uniform system of sentencing.

Lack of uniformity in criminal sentencing is the great tragedy in many jurisdictions today.

In 1935 my late humanitarian friend, Henry Broderick, well known and much admired realtor in Seattle, gave me his book, *The Commandment Breakers of Walla Walla,* which was most helpful. The penal system was one of his hobbies, and he'd attended many sessions of the former Parole Board.

The board met on the first week of each month, alternating between reformatory and penitentiary. Our calendar took two to three days a month at Monroe Reformatory and about five days at Walla Walla Penitentiary. It was a great study in human nature.

The board members joined the National Probation Association and the Western Parole and Probation Association, of which I became president in 1939. Sanford Bates, Austin McCormick of New York, and James Bennett, head of the U.S. Bureau of Prisons, all well-recognized authorities on penology, were active participants in the field of probation and parole. All on the board benefited from their advice and experience. With Governor Martin's help, the board succeeded in getting two very important acts passed by our legislature. The first related to deferment of imposition of sentence and probation which served as a forerunner and has been adopted by several other states. (Session laws of 1939, Chapter 125, page 353.)

This act made it possible for a judge to defer imposition of sentence on first offenders during the period he set for probation. At the end of that time (generally two years), if the probationer had lived up to the terms of probation, the judge could set aside the verdict or plea of guilty and dismiss the case. This way there would no longer be a criminal record against the defendant. Subsequently, if ever asked the question, "Have you ever been convicted of a crime?" *as to that offense* the defendant could truthfully answer, "No." The act did not apply to more serious offenses such as murder, manslaughter, rape, robbery or a felony offense while armed with a deadly weapon, but only to first offenders for less serious felony offenses.

The second act related to "honor camps." We had learned from experience that the transition period from strict confinement in an institution to civilian life was difficult and traumatic. One recidivist whom we had released on parole was back in a month for grand larceny. In talking with him we expressed our disappointment and asked how he accounted for it.

He pondered a while then said, "Well, you know how it is. You turn a fellow loose with a new suit of clothes and $5. After he buys a bottle of whiskey and gets a piece of tail, he's back in again."

The new act provided for and effected the establishment of trusty honor camps to which certain inmates of both institutions were to be transferred. It was anticipated the appropriate length of time for a prisoner to serve there would be about six months. The camps were to be located on the state- or county-owned land and the inmates employed in clearing and reforestation. Here they were paid 25 cents for each day they worked (how about that?), one-half of which was paid to them at the end of the month, the balance on release.

This act also provided that during their stay at the honor camps, inmates could be furloughed to their homes for short periods. Only those who had served a third of their sentence and were recommended by the superintendent of the institution would be eligible for honor camps. The purpose of these camps was to help inmates make a more tranquil transition from strict confinement to ordinary civilian life.

On our first scheduled trip to the penitentiary, Warden McCauley told me there were many long-term prisoners not scheduled to appear before the board who would like to write or visit with us and suggested we initiate such a program. I agreed, and the warden and I set up an interview office inside the walls for 7:30 evening sessions when we met individually with inmates who had requested an interview.

It was hard work, consuming long hours, but the warden assured me it paid off in the maintenance of discipline and morale in the prison. I was amazed to learn that many of those interviewed had serious mental health problems.

The associates on the board were knowledgeable, helpful and cooperative. We had a staff of 12 probation officers throughout the state who effectively supervised those released on parole. Thanks to the two acts we helped implement, we had saved first offenders from the stigma of a criminal record, offering them the inducement not to become repeaters, and helped those making the transition from prison to civilian life to stay *out* of prison.

Shortly after my appointment by Governor Martin, the following editorial appeared in a Seattle paper:

> NOT A JOYFUL JOB—His many friends are said to have been congratulating William J. Wilkins on his appointment as chairman of the State Parole Board. That is the natural thing to do. It is an honor to be entrusted with duties of such vital importance to erring individuals and the public at large. Readily agreeing that Governor Martin has chosen wisely, we still permit outselves to question any predication of congratulations upon the idea that Mr. Wilkins is going to find a lot of pleasure in the job. Dealing with offenders against the law and their importunate relatives and friends is a sad line of business. Though there need be no lack of understanding, the office, after all, is one to be sternly administered.

All things considered, though it was not exactly a "joyful job," it was a rewarding one.

The two years' experience as chairman of the State Board of Prison Terms and Paroles served me well during the years as a judge of the superior court. Also, the five years as a deputy prosecuting attorney gave me a better understanding and appreciation of the problems arising in the trial and sentencing of law violators. I sympathize with those judges appointed or elected to the trial and appellate courts who have had little or no experience in criminal cases.

Today there are a few judges in our various states whom most judges refer to as "bleeding hearts." Thank God they are well in the minority, but the unfortunate result is that when "bleeding hearts" go overboard in their desire to be compassionate toward the defendant and merely slap him on the wrist, and ignore the rights of the victims, the news media play it up to the fullest, thereby resulting in severe criticism of all judges and the entire judicial system. In this sense it is unfair to those judges who also do not approve of the result.

The purpose of criminal law is for the protection of society. If a citizen violates the law, depending on the seriousness of the offense, he must be punished, and the punishment must fit the crime. While other factors enter into consideration, *punishment must be uppermost.* Things to consider are: What is the nature of the offense? How about the victim? Has he sustained injury to himself and family or suffered loss of property? Should restitution be awarded to the victim as a part of the punishment? What is the defendant's criminal record, if any, his family background and work record?

Last come the questions of incarceration in a penal institution, the period of confinement necessary to fit the crime, and the assurance that the criminal defendant, when released, will not violate the law again. This involves the matter of his reformation and rehabilitation.

Most penologists will agree that the great problem today in many of our penal institutions is a lack of proper classification and segregation. I am speaking of separation of the dangerous con-wise hardened prisoners for whom there is little hope of rehabilitation from those convicted of lesser offenses who can and wish to be reformed.

Experience on the parole board, interviewing thousands of inmates, taught me the importance of the classification of the prisoner through a thorough study of his record and the facts of his case. We transferred to the reformatory at Monroe younger defendants sentenced on lesser offenses, and to the penitentiary at Walla Walla those whom we determined to be the more hardened criminal recidivistic type.

I admit that in our desire to be understanding and helpful, we made mistakes and released some inmates before they were ready. "Acts speak louder than words" and "By his acts ye shall know him" were kept constantly in mind as we listened to promises made by inmates seeking release. But we were also careful to review the inmate's criminal record and the facts of his crime in order to determine his chances of making good on the outside. In fairness to the general public, whose protection was our primary concern, our question was: *could we accept his word that he would cease and desist in his prior criminal activity?* His conduct at the institution was carefully studied and classified, and the recommendation of the warden carried great weight. That was one reason why we included provisions in the Act of 1939 which created "honor camps" that only those recommended by the warden would be eligible. Experience further taught us that, having in mind the protection of the public, there were some in confinement who should never be released.

On December 17, 1939, Governor Martin appointed me to a vacancy on the Superior Court Bench of King County in Seattle, effective January 2, 1940. I recalled with emotion that conversation had with my mother 32 years before and wished she could be there to see my childhood dream come true. How proud she would have been and how happy I would have been to have her there. After all, it was she who had given me the chance and the incentive to dream.

WILLIAM J. WILKINS, deputy prosecutor, grilling Richard Carter in his relentless cross examination of the youth in yesterday's murder trial. Note Carter's grin as he is the target for Wilkins' fire.—(Post-Intelligencer Photo.)

Slayer and His Nemesis.

Murderers all. Carter, Bradley, Zerfass, Marcelino.

Steeple Chase.

WILKINS, A FIGHTER FOR YOUNGER IDEALS

Cincinnatus Candidate Realizes He Has Uphill Fight Against Old Parties

Editor's Note: This is the last of a series of three articles about the candidates for United States senator. Previous articles discussed Lewis Schwellenbach, Democratic candidate, and Rene Odlin, Republican candidate.

* * *

BY BILL GRAY

In an uphill fight it's wise to know the hillside.

"Bill" Wilkins does. He's been on life's hillside for 36 years now, digging new footholds in the slippery sod, always battling his way to a higher spot. He knows what it is to fight.

That's why, when the Cincinnatus party chose its candidate for United States senator this year it chose William J. ("Bill") Wilkins.

W. J. Wilkins, Cincinnatus candidate for the United States senate. —Walters photo

The Cincinnatus party did not go into this race blindly confident because it elected one Seattle councilman by a tremendous majority that it would win without a struggle this time.

The young men of the Cincinnatus knew that if they were to win this time it would be against the "well-oiled, well-greased, well-financed political machines of the two old parties," as Wilkins himself puts it.

So they entered their fight with a fighter.

They picked Wilkins, the country doctor's assistant, the copper miner, the blacksmith's assistant, the grocery clerk, the soldier, the student, the lawyer — for those were the milestones in his own life's battle.

Into the late afternoon's shadowed sunlight one day 36 years ago, a miner emerged from the dusty shaft of a northwestern Michigan copper mine. He hurried home to see his wife and their new-born second child. It

(Page 14, Col. 4, Please)

YOUTH VERSUS OLD GROUPS IS THE ISSUE, SAYS WILKINS

BY WM. J. WILKINS
Cincinnatus Candidate for United States Senator

We cannot more graphically set forth the Cincinnatus program than by saying we seek a more efficient, a less expensive and a more honest government.

We firmly believe that these qualities must be imparted to our American government if it is to be preserved as the democracy we have cherished and progressed under.

The American people, today, yearn most of all for a government that will function, for a government that will be administrated in the best interests of all the people — not in the interest of cliques or classes.

We of Cincinnatus are convinced that a "new man" must be injected, must be given authority in our government.

Honesty First Need

He must be thoroly honest. He must be intelligent. He must be industrious. He must be willing to tell the people what they should hear, not solely what he thinks will attract votes.

Wilkins, a fighter for younger ideals.

Swearing in by Judge Robinson, with Governor Martin.

Members of the Board of Prison Terms and Paroles.

Broadmoor house

Broadmoor house

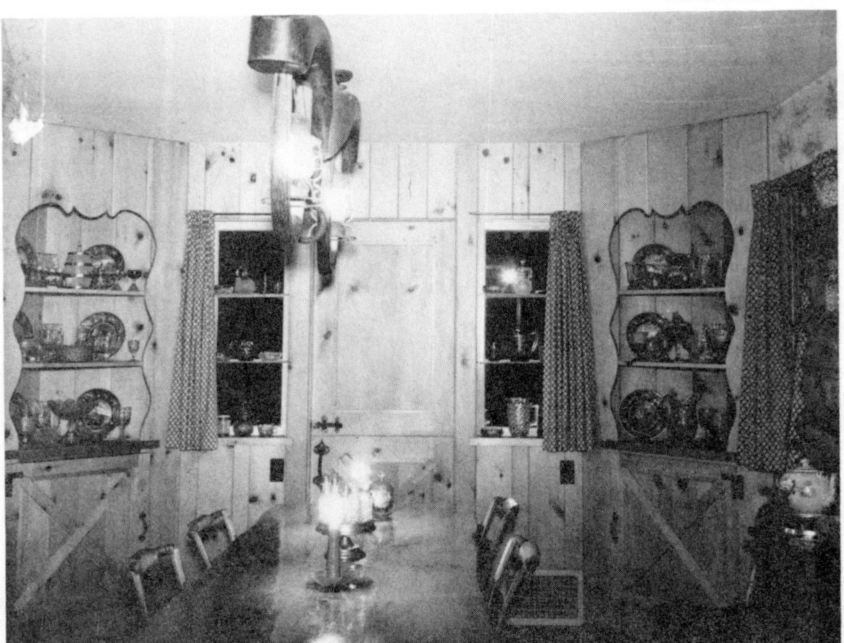

Broadmoor house

Broadmoor house

Broadmoor house

Broadmoor house

Gay Nineties party

Gay Nineties party

Gay Nineties party

CHAPTER V

On The Bench

(1940-1942)

> I, William J. Wilkins, do solemnly swear that I will faithfully and impartially perform the duties of Superior Court Judge as prescribed by law and to the best of my ability, and that I will support and maintain the Constitution of the State of Washington and the United States. So help me God.
>
> January 2, 1940

On the morning of January 2, 1940, the 14 judges of the Superior Court of King County in the State of Washington were seated en banc for the purpose of swearing in their newest member. The ceremony took place in the large Presiding Judge's courtroom, which was packed with jurors, lawyers and litigants, all waiting to be sent to other courtrooms. Friends were seated or standing in the aisles and at the rear. It was a solemn gathering. To enter a courtroom and see one black-robed judge on the bench is impressive, but to stand before 15 black-robed judges, the feeling is awesome indeed; I say 15, for my good friend, Federal Judge Lloyd Black, was seated with them. After the administration of the oath by Presiding Judge James T. Lawler, a graduate of Michigan law school, Judge Howard M. Findley, also a fellow Michigander, gave a warm and inspirational welcoming address.

In part, Judge Findley stated: "An occasion such as this—a swearing-in ceremony of a new judge—is always a pleasant one for the new judge, his family and his friends, for it means the fulfillment of a long-time dream and aspiration on the part of the new judge stretching over a period of many years. For us, it brings back pleasant memories;

we look back with nostalgia to the time when we were standing in the same position being welcomed to this bench, and it seems but yesterday.

"So, Judge Wilkins, this occasion should afford you a great sense of pride and gratification. I am sure I voice the sentiments of my colleagues and of your many friends here assembled when I say that we too share the pride and gratification in seeing you thus honored today...

"It hardly seems necessary to remind you that the work of a judge of the superior court is not easy. But the problems and the challenges are such that a judge is inspired to do his best. It is his task to do justice between his fellow men—to hear courteously, to consider wisely, to decide impartially, to act independently and courageously, to bear no grudge, to play no favorites, and to have but one desire, *the desire to do right*. These are the ideals that characterize a good judge."

Later he told me: "Bill, decide what is the right thing to do and do it, regardless of pressure or criticism. Then you will be able to live with yourself." I was fond of Judge Findley, cherish his memory and consider him the ablest of all.

Following the ceremony in the Presiding Judge's courtroom Lucille and I went to the courtroom assigned to me, which was banked with flowers sent by our many friends, to greet lawyers and friends gathered for a reception. Among them were my former law partner, Jay C. Allen, Ewing D. Colvin and Robert M. Burgunder, my former bosses in the prosecuting attorney's office, Tom Waters and Sheriff Bill Daley, my associates on the State Board of Prison Terms and Paroles.

The dean of the bench was J.T. Ronald—84 and just twice my age—a judge possessed of great human understanding and beloved by all. His mind and memory were keen and alert though he was frail physically, having sustained a broken hip, and had to hobble to court on a crutch and cane. His comments to me were: "The only anxiety a judge has is the anxiety to be right. A judge must conduct himself at all times, both on and off the bench, so that his personal conduct and integrity must be beyond question." Advice I believe in implicitly. He also believed a judge should give freely of his time to civic endeavors.

Here I would like to give my feelings about the conduct of a judge. Certainly he has to recognize his responsibility for conduct beyond reproach and he's not in the same position as everyone else, but at the same time a judge is human. He doesn't have to be a sour old puss who takes himself off to an ivory tower. I have heard more downright joviality and humor among a group of judges many times than at other social functions I've attended.

In April 1946 the judges held a birthday party for Judge Ronald at the Rainier Club. At 91 he became the oldest judge in service in the United States. He retired March 31, 1949. At his party Judge Ronald told us we were also celebrating the 37th anniversary of his election to the Superior Court Bench. It was April 1, 1909, when he took over the job, he said, then with a chuckle, "I was a sort of April fool's joke." His record of 40 years on our Bench will never be equalled. He passed away December 27, 1950.

Next in seniority was Calvin S. Hall, a well-known after-dinner speaker and capable judge. Appearing before him as a prosecutor several times, I always found him kind and helpful. His suggestion on one occasion prompted me to draft the act passed by our legislature in 1939 relating to probation. I had brought before him a young man, 18, charged with the theft of an automobile, a charge referred to in those days as "joy-riding." The young man pleaded guilty, and Judge Hall suggested, rather than sentence him at that time, with my cooperation he would defer the imposition of sentence for two years. During that time the defendant would be required to report personally to Judge Hall and to me once a month. If the young man did as directed and "kept his nose clean," at the end of the two years Judge Hall would dismiss the charge, and it would no longer be a criminal record against him. The young man kept his word and Judge Hall dismissed the case. This incident demonstrated Judge Hall's compassion and advanced thinking in penology.

Before he retired at 77, Judge Hall was in good physical condition, but it was the talk among lawyers he was apt to doze off at times, especially during afternoon sessions. When this happened, lawyers would drop a book on the floor, supposedly accidentally, whereupon, so the story goes, the judge would immediately spring into action and say, "The objection is overruled."

Following Judges Ronald's and Hall's retirement, a mandatory retirement act was passed by our legislature requiring all judges to retire at the end of the year in which they reached the age of 75. I favored this legislation and voted for it. Many judges are mentally alert at that age, but it may well be that their thinking and philosophy are not attuned to that of the younger generation, and they should give way to younger men. I believe that all judges—state, federal, as well as members of Congress and the United States Supreme Court—should be required to step down at 75.

Malcolm Douglas had served with distinction as a captain of artillery in France during World War I and was often referred to by lawyers and friends as "the colonel on horseback" because of his military bearing. He was decorated with the French Croix-de-Guerre, loved to speak French and of French wines, and was a devotee of all the creative arts. We became warm friends and were both granted military leaves of absence in early 1942 to serve in World War II.

Bob Jones, a Virginian, formerly active in the Republican party, with a dry sense of humor, was not an ardent supporter of Franklin Roosevelt's "New Deal." When a newspaper article appeared saying Justice William O. Douglas of the United States Supreme Court had been thrown from his horse while riding on his ranch at Goose Prairie and suffered a broken leg, Bob inquired at our judges' meeting: "I wonder if anyone remembered to give that horse an extra bucket of oats."

Judge Donald McDonald was one of my favorites—a man of common sense and humor. One day a lawyer was arguing before him, diligently trying to put his point across when Judge McDonald finally interrupted him to say: "Counsel, don't labor under the misapprehension that I just came in from the country this morning on a load of hay!"

Many such incidents illustrate my point—that judges are not stiff-necked, stern or aloof but possessed of great human understanding and able to see the humorous side of life despite the serious nature of litigation before them.

Judges of the superior court come up for election every four years, the same years as the Presidential election. As I had been appointed by Governor Martin to fill out one term, I came up for election the following September in the primaries and the final election that November. My opposition was a man named Sweeney, a Democratic constable and member of the Bar but not practicing at the time. He tried to benefit from having the same name as a popular Police Judge, Joe Sweeney, but Joe went on the radio with me in my behalf and I won, three to one. Thereafter I never had any opposition, even when I was in military service in 1944 and in Nuremberg in 1948, when a column appeared in the *Post-Intelligencer,* July 2, headed:

> JUDGE WILKINS' OLD COMRADES FILE FOR HIM ... A group of his former army comrades, now all Seattle attorneys, took care of that (filing for election) for him. Headed by Deputy Prosecutor Herbert L. Davis, eight other attorneys went to the office of County Auditor Robert A. Morris and filed their old army chief's candidacy for reelection to Department No. 11...All served in the judge advocate general's department of the army in which Judge Wilkins was a colonel. Judge Wilkins is in Germany presiding at war crimes trials.

The work of a trial judge is varied, stimulating, exciting, interesting and rewarding. It affords one the opportunity to be of real service to nkind and is, in itself, a tremendous study in human nature. During s on the bench I heard all types of cases: civil, criminal, jury ury, domestic relations, contracts, custody of children—the amut of litigation in a court of record and of unlimited jurisdiction. The custody of children is the most difficult and heartrending of all.

Naturally, the change to the other side of the bar is quite a transitional adjustment. It involves not only crossing over from one side of the courtroom to the other, but an adjustment in mind and emotions. Being an ardent advocate for one party to litigation was quite different from sitting impartially on cases to decide which party under the law was entitled to judgment.

My first case, involving a bit of humor, helped ease me over that transitional period. A man by the name of George Baxter, whom I recognized as one I'd interviewed at Walla Walla some months before and released on parole, was charged with burglarizing an apartment. The evidence against him was not strong, the police having found in his possession only a tapestry and davenport cover claimed by the victim. Standing alone, the possession of recently stolen property during a burglary is not sufficient to sustain a charge of burglary, which is a felony offense. It is, however, sufficient for the charge of possession of stolen property, which is a misdemeanor, depending on its value.

I assume because Baxter had a long burglary record, the prosecutor filed the more serious charge. The defendant did not take the witness stand, and the jury, unaware of his criminal record, acquitted him on the evidence, and rightly so. The deputy sheriff, standing beside Baxter before the bar, addressed me then and asked what should be done now that the prisoner was acquitted. A hold had been placed on him by the parole department. I saw Baxter look over the stolen exhibits on the clerk's desk and expected him to ask, as in the old story, "Now that I've been acquitted, Your Honor, who's going to get those things that I stole?" He didn't, but he did wink at me. Doubtless he had in mind the advice we'd given him when we released him on parole.

During the noon hour of that same day, on entering the elevator the operator addressed me with my new title, judge. A pretty young blonde looked me over and said, "Are you a judge?" I smiled back and answered, "Yes, I am." Her eyebrows raised, she exclaimed, "My God! You sure don't look like one!" Forty-two, the youngest judge on the superior court, apparently I looked it.

During the time on the Bench I sentenced four men to hang.

The Denzel Davis Murder Case.

On March 18, 1940, Denzel Davis, alias W.A. Redding, was charged with murder in the first degree, it being alleged that on that date he caused the death of his mother, Harriet Redding, by beating, stabbing, strangling and wounding by the use of certain deadly weapons, namely a hammer, ice pick, cord and chains. The case came on for trial on May 6, 1940.

The court appointed counsel to defend Davis, who was without funds, and he entered a plea of guilty to the crime of first degree murder; his counsel entered a written plea in behalf of his client of "not guilty be reason of insanity and mental irresponsibility."

The evidence established that for some time prior to March, Davis had been living with his mother in her house in Seattle after separating from his wife. He was not employed and had no income except what his mother gave him. On March 1 Davis cashed a check for $20 to which he had forged his mother's name. She later made the check good but told her son she would not help him out of such a situation again.

The evidence produced showed that the evening of March 17 Davis and his mother had an argument which continued over to the following morning when Davis picked up a hammer and struck her a hard blow on the back of the head. She fell on her back, groaning. When she continued to groan, Davis stabbed her with an ice pick. Still she groaned; he stabbed her again and again—17 times in all—then tied two wire cords and a chain around her neck, placed her in a recess under a drainboard and nailed the door shut. All this Davis freely admitted. After cleaning up the blood on the floor, he put the clothes in a basket in the bedroom closet and left the apartment. Before leaving, he took money from his mother's purse, a watch and ring from her finger. During the day he pawned the watch and ring.

Later that day he and his wife engaged a room at a downtown hotel, went to a movie and a beer parlor after. The following day he told his wife he'd killed his mother and was going to surrender to the police. The murder had been discovered, and he knew he was wanted as a suspect. He did not go to the police, however, but hid himself away. The following Saturday morning he was found by the police, hiding in a closet in the apartment of a friend.

In due course a jury was empaneled. As the defendant had entered a plea of guilty to the charge of murder in the first degree, I held that it was necessary for the jury to determine the degree of murder under appropriate instructions notwithstanding defendant's guilty plea. The law is that where the killing of a human being is admitted, the killing is presumed to constitute the crime of murder in the second degree, giving the jury the right to determine the degree of the crime.

The defendant did not take the witness stand in his own defense. The jury rejected the plea of insanity and found the defendant guilty of murder in the first degree and voted for the imposition of the death penalty. The verdict was filed May 10, 1940, and on June 1, 1940, I sentenced the defendant to be hanged by the neck until dead (the statutory language).

An appeal was filed on June 6, 1940, by defendant's counsel *in forma pauperis* (claiming defendant to be without funds), so a free transcript was supplied by the county, which stayed the execution. The Supreme Court of Washington affirmed the verdict on December 30, 1940, Mr. Justice Walter Beals speaking for the court (6 Wash. 2nd, 696.). Thereafter it became my duty to issue the death warrant and set the date for the execution at the penitentiary at Walla Walla. The order was signed setting the date of execution to be March 24, 1941. Later I received a notarized return on the death warrant as follows:

> Now therefore this is to advise you that the mandate of the court as set forth in the death warrant, has been complied with and that Denzel Davis between the hours of 12 o'clock midnight on the 23rd day of March, 1941, and one o'clock in the morning of the 24th day of March, 1941, was hanged by the neck until he was dead.

It was signed by P.E. Mahoney, superintendent of the Washington State Penitentiary at Walla Walla.

Thus ended my first duty as judge in a death sentence case. The defendant lived just one year and six days after the death of his mother.

With the completion of the Mercer Island Floating Bridge—now the Lacey Murrow Memorial Bridge—large tracts of land on the east side of Lake Washington came on the market. The happy days spent at Lake Lucerne, combined with my early life in a small community where outdoor activities prevailed and Lucille's on a large ranch, had imbued us with a deep love for and appreciation of the land and the wide open spaces. Often we took a picnic lunch and tramped across meadows and through woods with a burning desire to again own a piece of the land—a *big* piece. When a 40-acre deserted farm was advertised for $2,300, we decided to look it over. The directions were: turn left at the turkey farm (now the Eastgate shopping area) and go ½ mile north on 148th Street.

After driving over narrow graveled county roads and through a heavily wooded area, a long deserted lane opened to reveal a vista of yesteryear. A dilapidated old farmhouse was surrounded by fruit trees going wild. A large log barn was connected by a breezeway to a small log cabin nestled under a giant cherry tree white with bloom. All around the buildings were what seemed endless meadows, high split-rail cedar fences, a lovely quiet pond, all framed by majestic firs and cedars. To the east we could see the rugged snowcapped Cascade mountains.

How could you miss on that beautiful property, if only as an investment. So, we bought it.

Instead of golf clothes, the next week found us in boots and jeans investigating our acquisition. Although the exterior of the farmhouse was shingles and clapboard siding, the interior plywood paneled, we were curious about the exceptionally wide windowsills. Some boards were loosened to find the answer. Imagine our astonishment to discover we'd bought *another log house!* Not all but a good share of the house had been constructed with large cedar logs, hand-trimmed with an adze from 2-foot thick trees into 8-inch thick logs.

Before we came home, we stopped at our nearest neighbors—a mile away—to introduce ourselves. They told us the farm had been homesteaded in the 1880s by a family from Denmark by the name of Miller. The small log cabin, later used as the milkhouse, was built first. Their first child was born there, and they lived in it while they cleared the land, using the cedar logs to build the first two large rooms and part of the upstairs of the farmhouse as well as the barn. This time we owned a piece of real Americana—a house that had had its place in settling the West.

As months passed, the feeling for the country lane, the quiet serenity of meadows and woods, the satisfaction in having our own piece of the good earth lured us into saving the old house and living in it ourselves.

It must have been inherent in us to enjoy working creatively with our hands, no matter how hard, as well as a feeling of having earned a good night's sleep as the result of our labor. The anticipation of turning that old derelict house into something beautiful was sheer joy. We had long discussions with Miles Wilson, a builder and neighbor at Lake Lucerne in whom we had complete confidence. Weeks were spent on research and planning.

First we needed more wheels. A small secondhand pickup truck was purchased for Lucille, who drove in and out of the Pearly Gates of Broadmoor every day on her way to the job, loaded with small building necessities, radiantly happy "doing her thing," with never a concern about what the "Joneses" might think.

There were problems. On sound advice most of the old house was torn down except the log structure. Realizing practically all our spare time was spent on The Forty, as we called it, or going and coming, eventually we decided to sell the Broadmoor house and rent a small one temporarily in Bellevue. Our little maid, Marie, to whom we paid the magnificent sum of $40 a month—the going wage at that time—was happy to come along. That left Lucille free to spend her time on the house. She became architect, contractor and interior designer and saved us a great deal of money. More than that, by our mutual planning and physical labor, we had the feeling the house was peculiarly our own. Very much like the first Millers must have felt, I imagine. But, as Lucille said, you have to give to get. We were the original "do-it-yourselfers."

"Any woman can plan and supervise her own house if she has a true interest in it and is willing to give the time it requires," she said in a newspaper interview. "When you do all the work yourself, the house is just the way you want it—and you've saved professional fees too. But it means giving up some bridge parties and luncheons if you are going to be on hand when you are needed."

About that time the book, *Mr. Blanding Builds His Dream House* was published. When friends laughed over our building problems and likened them to Mr. Blanding's, we insisted we were one up on him.

Our experience in building the Broadmoor house was invaluable as, naturally, we wanted another 17th or 18th century New England farmhouse where hand-braided rugs, Hitchcock chairs, pine trestle tables and the much traveled bedroom set would fit in, as well as wide oak plank floors and wood paneling. Before we went too far with the building, it was decided we must have a new well. The abandoned one was out near the pond, too far for practical purposes. A "well witcher" came with his forked stick and, after exploring the slope above the house, pointed where his stick dropped and said, "There."

Ike Stewart, a well driller in the community was hired. Thinking water would be found near the surface, he suggested a dug well with the sides cemented instead of a driven well. Tension mounted as they got to a 50-foot depth and found no water. Bets were made by the crew as to how far they'd have to go, but no one bet over 100 feet. They hit water on the Fourth of July. Clear and sparkling like champagne, it immediately bubbled up to 30 feet. The thought came to me it would probably cost as much as champagne too! The final figure in *depth* was 110 feet. The celebration which followed couldn't have been gayer or more enthusiastic if we'd struck oil. A few extra squared logs lying around inspired me to build a rustic pumphouse.

The next step was to get down to the logs. First, the plywood paneling was ripped off, then layers and layers of wallpaper, layers and layers of newspapers—an apple box full of 1880 and 1890 clippings, ads and literary "gems" were saved—then finally a layer of burlap was removed. After that, we had to pull out thousands of small nails and tacks and dig out the moss chinking between the logs. You can see where our leisure time went!

In a chance conversation with an architect, he suggested Fels Naphtha soap for the logs, applied with a scrub brush and a great deal of elbow grease, which was the process we used. The reward was a beautiful patina of silver gray. The space between the logs was first filled with cement; over that went a coating of plaster which was painted white and given an antique glaze to match the logs.

Mr. Keskull, the blacksmith at Lake Lucerne, was glad to handcraft all the hardware as he'd done for the town house. He'd learned a great deal about door pulls and latches with rat-tails, dog-eared bolts and "H and L" hinges with long straps. Lucille made many trips to his forge with her designs and patterns. He also made a large crane on which to hang an antique iron kettle in the fireplace.

The andirons had survived the Lake Lucerne fire and were the only mementos of the years there. They'd been made from old streetcar tracks torn out about 1929 and presented to us as a wedding present by Albert E. Pierce, then superintendent of street railways and a fellow Legionnaire. Workmen tearing out the brick paving on Madison Street were only too happy to load them into Lucille's truck simply to be rid of them. She spent hours cleaning them with acid and a steel brush. They made a lovely mellow brick facing for the fireplace.

More of Lucille's finds were old coal oil lamps, hobnail glass hanging lamps for the bedrooms, hand-hammered brass sconces for side lights, all of which were electrified. And this time I did not do any of the wiring myself! A pair of antique windows found on First Avenue with diamond-shaped leaded and beveled glass cast rainbow hues across the master bedroom—the only Victorian room in the house, designed for the old bedroom set.

A good friend, Charlie Fisher, who was a cattleman and owned and operated the farmers' auction in the Kent Valley, came by one day to look over the project. "Bill," he said, "what you need is cattle to eat up all this grass." Several days later he returned with six young heifers. Breeding had no part in our plans. Six was enough, but to our amazement one heifer presented us with a beautiful little calf. That made another problem—milking mama.

We attacked the problem with our usual vigor and, at first, it was fun. Each took a side (our cow didn't know we weren't professional), and the job was soon over with plenty of milk for the calf, the cats and Brownie, our German shepherd. When several social engagements came in a row, though, the business of milking on schedule, showering after (oh! that cowbarn smell!) and getting to the party on time got to be too much. We put an ad in the paper and parted, then and there, with our little wayward heifer turned mother.

The fall of 1941 found us comfortably ensconced in the homestead. Here was the perfect hobby—an absorbing interest with a creative background. We could see ourselves busy for years to come—

gardening, planting and pruning and harvesting the crops, tending the animals or just puttering about. Ducks came to our pond, and when the hunting season came, I was pleasantly surprised to find Brownie was also a retriever. The peaches and pears and prunes and apples all ripened, and we had enough to share with friends and still fill our canning cupboard.

There were many unfinished projects, repairs to be made, but we relaxed with the comforting thought: "The land will keep." The house was finished, beautiful to behold. So, in that fall of 1941, we had our first fire in our brick fireplace, drank a toast to the Millers and surveyed our calloused hands with utter content. All was well with our world, or so we thought, until that fateful Sunday, December 7th, 1941. A day that was to change many lives, ours among them.

Judicial youth, age.

Judicial robes. (newspaper)

With Ewing D. Colvin, Jim Bailey, Elizabeth Wesley and Robert M. Burgunder.

Back row, L to R: McDonald, Lawler, Long, Batchelor, Allen, Todd, Meakim, Wilkins; Front row, L to R: Findley, Jones, Ronald, Douglas, Hall, Frater, Kinne.

Reward!

Newspaper artist's conception of the principals in the trial.

Seattle school children visiting court, 1941.

Owner-architect-contractor

Remodeling job–"The Forty"

Remodeling job–"The Forty"
Remodeling job–"The Forty"

"The Forty"

The finished house

The finished house

The finished house

"The Forty"

Tea in Pioneer's Log House. (Newspaper)

TEA IN PIONEER'S LOG HOUSE

CHAPTER VI

Retread

(1942-1945)

By 1940 the United States was increasingly confronted with the choice between guns and butter. With the ever-burgeoning war in Europe, however, the American people were having to be more realistic and face the fact our choice had really been made for us. So it was guns—and planes and tanks and tons of shipping. As the days of 1941 spun themselves out and the year inevitably moved to a close, we were, so to speak, preparing for the dive but not yet ready to take the plunge. Here again our choice was made for us.

On December 7, 1941—"a date that will live in infamy"—the Japanese bombed Pearl Harbor. That was the date Lucille and I had set for a gala housewarming party to show off the product of our year's hard work on The Forty. By evening the feverish excitement, and fear for the days ahead, had taken precedence over our own personal accomplishments. Guests were buzzing with questions, speculations, predictions. All ears were glued to the radio. The news was ominous. The next day, December 8, the United States declared war on Japan and, on December 11, war on Germany and Italy. So, once again, the world was in flames for freedom's sake.

Like the old fire horse, "I'd had the smell of smoke and wanted to go to the fire." It was hard to fasten attention to the litigation before me, and my mind wandered as we were making preparations for an all-out war. Soon after December 7 I applied to Major General Myron C. Cramer, judge advocate general of the army, for a commission and in April, 1942, received a temporary appointment as major in the Army of the United States. Orders followed for me to report for duty May 10 in Washington, DC, where I was to attend the third class of the Judge Advocate General's School. Governor Langlie granted me a military leave of absence, appointing James W. Hodson to serve in my position for the duration.

The other half of the team insisted she was going to the fire with me, at least, as far as she could. Neither of us knew how far that would be but, for the present, we decided to stay together. We leased the house and Forty to a naval officer, packed our bags and went to Washington.

There was time to drive across the country, stopping to see friends and relatives along the way. An accident while driving through Montana made me a war casualty before I'd even seen service. The car skidded on an oil slick, and we rolled over, landing on the top, the wheels spinning aimlessly in the air. When we'd recovered from the shock, we managed to roll down the windows, crawl out and up the embankment to the road and flag down a driver who contacted a garage in the next town to send a tow truck.

Lucille was uninjured, but my cheekbone had hit the side window, resulting in an ugly bruise. The car was considerably damaged, but with the necessary repairs made for safety, we got an OK from our Seattle insurance man to proceed to Washington, DC, and complete repairs there. A doctor treated my cheek, covering it with a large white patch, and refused pay, as he too was waiting for orders from the army. So with bruised car and driver, we went on our way. It was wonderful to see all the old familiar faces and places in Michigan—to be with family and friends after so many years.

So in May of 1942 we came to Washington, DC.

The capital in wartime was quite different from the city I had lived and worked in 14 years before, and the first hurdle was finding a place to live. By camping at the *Washington Star* building when the paper came off the press, we finally located a comfortable apartment on 39th Street N.W. on Rock Creek near the Connecticut Avenue bridge.

You couldn't describe the apartment as de luxe, but it had the necessary amenities and a screened deck over Rock Creek where the rippling water made the air seem cool whether it was or not. There was room, too, for us to entertain Seattle friends we found in Washington as well as new ones we made while there.

Fellow officers told me how lucky I was to have my wife with me; the truth was they envied my home-cooked meals. Lucille was often referred to as "the little corporal," and on more than one occasion in steaming Washington, DC, she pressed our "summer light" pants when, on short notice, we were expected to attend a reception for a visiting VIP.

JAG class, conducted by Colonel Hamilton Young, was a

difficult, concentrated crash course, and we worked hard. We knew we'd soon be at camps and bases where we'd be expected to have all the answers to problems in military law that were bound to arise. One hot day in June while we were, literally, sweating it out writing a tough plus-minus exam, Judge Dolph Barnet from Yakima, Washington, said to me:

"Bill how foolish can we be? Just think, right now our associates back home are getting ready to take their summer vacation!"

Graduation was July 5, and we gave a reception for Colonel "Ham" Young and his staff. We'd composed a song to the tune of "Hinky Dinky Parlez Vous" and dedicated it to them.

> Colonel Young is the dean of the school, parlez vous,
> He's plenty smart, he's nobody's fool, parlez vous,
> We often make him want to cuss—
> What's your answer, minus or plus?
> Hinky Dinky Parlez Vous.
>
> And now we bid you au revoir, parlez vous,
> We'll keep our heads in this man's war, parlez vous,
> And when it's over, back we'll go
> To practice law and make some dough,
> Hinky Dinky Parlez Vous.

Ours was the last class held at Washington, DC. Soon after, the school was moved to the beautiful law quadrangle at my alma mater, the University of Michigan at Ann Arbor, where I was later invited to address a subsequent class on "Military Justice in the Air Force."

All those years I'd remembered the two World War I flyers telling us infantrymen about pulling their fur-lined teddy bear jumpsuits over their pajamas and *after* they'd had orange juice and coffee, taking off on morning reconnaisance. To us guys who'd slogged through the mud, lived in trenches and hadn't seen pajamas or tasted orange juice since we left home, that sounded pretty good so, in 1942, I opted for the Air Force.

My first assignment was to the Second Air Force headquarters at Fort George Wright, Spokane, Washington, which brought us close to home. That fort was very much like Fort Wayne with its parade ground surrounded by red brick buildings. Cub planes were used for short flights to Geiger Field on the west side of town. This was one of several large bases where the four-engine bombers, the Flying Fortresses, were used for training purposes. We were proud of what our people in Seattle were doing for the war effort, building the B-17's and later the B-29's—the Super-Fortresses.

Spokane was not then a large city and totally unprepared for the sudden influx of military personnel, and quarters were hard to find, but while Lucille and I were at the Davenport Hotel (an old landmark in Spokane), we met old friend Colonel Lacey Murrow and his wife Marge. He had been ordered to Washington, DC, and suggested we take over their apartment.

Lacey had been director of highways in Washington State and was the engineer who designed the first floating bridge over Lake Washington. His brother Edward R. Murrow, like Lacey a graduate of Washington State University, was at that time broadcasting on radio from England under the famous by-line, "This Is London."

The commanding general was Major General Robert Olds, one of Billy Mitchell's boys who led the group which pioneered and established the route from Brazil to Dakar in Africa. He and his wife Nina were a wonderful couple, kind and considerate of us "juniors." The chief of staff was Brigadier General Nathan Bedford Forrest, grandson of the famous Confederate cavalry general whose key to victory was "to get there fustest with the mostest." Nate, a West Point graduate and the youngest brigadier general in the army, was a fighter pilot but had transferred to the heavy bombardment aircraft. My immediate boss was Lieutenant Colonel Stewart S. Maxey, judge advocate of the Second Air Force.

About 25 officers were assigned to our headquarters for training. Most of them had been commissioned in the Army Air Corps (Signal Corps in World War I) and like myself were "retreads" from civilian life. Many held the rank of major and were there for instruction to become base commanders. My first job was instructing a class in courts-martial, and I made many friends in the group. They often called me for advice during the years we were together in the Second Air Force.

Among them were a few officers from the Intelligence School at Harrisburg, one of whom was Captain Donald Oenslager, an eminent stage designer of New York and a professor at Yale University, assigned to Camouflage.

He and his attractive wife Zorka became two of our dearest friends, a friendship that has lasted through the years. When we returned from Nuremberg in 1948, we visited with them in New York. Don wrote several books about the theatre and in 1974 sent us an autographed copy of "Stage Design—Four Centuries of Scenic Invention." His collection of Old Master Drawings together with many of his own scenic designs have been on tour in shows at major art museums throughout the country. Recently Zorka sent us his last book, "The Theatre of Donald Oenslager," published posthumously in 1978. Don had written the text, and the book included many illustrations of his impressive coverage of American stage productions.

Early in 1943 General Olds was unable to accept an invitation to address a noonday rally in Seattle for the sale of war bonds and sent me in his place, asking particularly that the people of Seattle be told to keep turning out the Flying Fortresses because they were going to win the war. I went to Seattle and gave them the message, loud and clear. The glamor of the day was provided by Joan Leslie, a popular movie star of that day. Lucille accompanied me, and we had an all too brief visit with friends.

Considering the damage wrought to the enemy by Major General Curtis B. LeMay and his Eighth Air Force, General Olds' message was most prophetic. The B-17's and B-29's produced by Boeing were major factors in our winning the war against Germany and Japan.

One evening Dave Williams, a former associate in the prosecuting attorney's office, called to say Cap Colvin had been recalled to duty at an army training base in Pennsylvania and would be on a train passing through Spokane the next morning at 7. He gave me the numbers of Cap's car and berth where, still in his pajamas, Cap was surprised to see me, and for 30 minutes we "retread" warriors had a wonderful reunion.

In April, 1943 my sister Ada's 18-year-old twin sons, both University of Michigan football players, John J. and James L. Lehman from Sault Ste. Marie, came to visit us. They'd just completed their basic training at Farragut Naval Training Station in Idaho and were now full-fledged second class seamen on their way to Norman, Oklahoma, to begin training as aviation machinists mates.

Today Dr. Jim is president of Lake Michigan College at Benton Harbor after a successful teaching career. Jack is a chaplain in the United States Air Force with the rank of lieutenant colonel, stationed in Louisiana. He served overseas in England and in Okinawa and is now executive assistant to the president of Delgado College. Both are recognized as noted lecturers and scholars. They were able to be together at Oxford in the summer session in 1978 while on sabbatical leaves. We are proud of our two nephews.

In the spring of 1943 General Olds was taken ill and sent to one of our southern bases at Tucson where he would still be in command of what we called the forward echelon. He took with him the top members of his staff, including Lieutenant Colonel Maxey, leaving me in charge of the judge advocate section of the rear echelon at Fort George Wright. The general's illness was terminal, and he never returned to our headquarters, nor did Maxey. He was promoted to full colonel and went to Australia to become judge advocate for the Fifth Air Force.

Major General Davenport Johnson succeeded General Olds and in May 1943 appointed me judge advocate to succeed Colonel Maxey; in June came a promotion to lieutenant colonel. At that time our headquarters were moved to Colorado Springs, the center of the web reaching out to the many bases in our command.

Meanwhile "back at The Forty" the naval officer who'd leased our house had been sent to San Diego and written he'd left the keys with a neighbor—a mile away! Lucille went to Bellevue to find another renter, but with gas rationing there weren't any takers. She was not disposed to baby-sit a house for the duration, whenever that would be—all she wanted was to accompany me to Colorado Springs, so we decided to sell the house. We'd put $12,000 into it, not counting the hours of research and hard labor; it sold for $17,500—a top price at that time—and we felt fortunate not to have taken a loss.

The new owners talked Lucille into selling many things that fit so well into the decor—braided rugs, dining table and chairs, lamps—a mistake, of course, because those things could never be replaced. What was kept was put into storage, and we were on our way.

The end of the story, though, is that in 1975 the last owner of The Forty sold it to the City of Bellevue for $850,000. (Today there would be another digit). It is now Robinswood Park, across 148th Street from the Bellevue Community College. C'est la guerre!

The acreage is more beautiful than ever but the house—well, unfortunately someone oiled the cedar with the result it turned dark, dark brown and all those lovely knots turned black! The plaster chinking between the logs is painted dark brown. The heirloom antique lamps and fixtures are all gone, replaced by globes. The leaded windows in the bedroom are gone too. The contemporary business furniture is a sad anachronism. The house is a kind of community house used for many city functions as well as weddings and receptions. Happiness comes to us, knowing the Miller family did not work in vain. Their old home is saved for posterity, and maybe some day it will again be furnished in the proper style for the period it represents.

The Second Air Force was rapidly expanding, acquiring additional bases located in 19 states from the Canadian to Mexican borders and the Pacific Ocean to the Mississippi. Personnel had increased two-fold to approximately 200,000. The commanding general exercised sole general courts-martial jurisdiction, and it was a great challenge to be his legal advisor.

With this mushrooming organization came longer hours and more responsibility. However, so far as our personal life was concerned I can't say it was a hardship tour. Our first home was a hillside cabin near the Garden of the Gods at Manitou Springs where thunder and lightning storms slammed back and forth against those mountain walls. In time a comfortably furnished house near headquarters was found, and Lucille went back to scouring antique shops for "collectables" to give the house a personal touch. Rental controls were on so there was no price gouging. Food, of course, was rationed. Once, when our meat stamps got low, for a buffet supper Lucille prepared a casserole made with rabbit, plentiful in the market. She guarded her secret well, and the guests complimented her on the delicious chicken dish.

The wives were kept busy. Nina Olds had organized the Officers Wives Club which met each week for Red Cross work. Lucille was on the "spotters" committee, so-called because it was the task of the members to locate and call on the new wives, give any assistance they could and, of course, sign them up for membership in the club.

Nearby Colorado College presented the opportunity to at long last indulge in a hobby she had always yearned for—painting! With my encouragement she enrolled in art classes there conducted by Boardman Robinson, a well-known artist.

Colorado Springs, at 6,200 feet, ecjoyed unusually clear air. The establishment of the Second Air Force there was the beginning of emergence from a charming health resort to a large city. Many people from the East had come there for years for relief of respiratory ailments such as tuberculosis and asthma. Civilian residents we called "the cave dwellers" were hospitable to army personnel. At a reception I overheard two well-dressed dowagers chatting. Looking at Lucille, one woman said, "Isn't she attractive? I wonder if she's army or TB."

Often the judge advocate staff had dinner together at the Officers Club, after which all went ice skating at the ice pavilion adjoining the Broadmoor Hotel. For exercise we played tennis and softball. Colonel Wallace of the Inspector General's Department said once: "The esprit de corps of you fellows in the JAG section is the envy of all the other departments at headquarters." And it was true. We worked and played as a team, and no one was ever too busy to listen or help if need be.

Enlisted personnel too were tireless in their dedication to the job. On special occasions we all went to chuck wagon dinners at the Garden of The Gods where, in that clear atmosphere, moon and stars shining on the weird rock formations created a never-never land.

Picnics were held for the entire staff on the high plateau overlooking the city. Lieutenant Colonel Ben Connally, my chief assistant, brought tubs of fresh corn on the cob which we boiled over the bonfire we had made to roast hot dogs and marshmallows. Christmas Day Lucille prepared brunch for the 23 men and WACS of the enlisted staff, baking the wonderful comice pears sent us from Yakima, filled with raisins and other goodies for dessert. The staff said they'd never forget that treat.

Through all this the business of military law ground inexorably on. Our headquarters was responsible for all courts-martial matters arising in that large command comprising 75 bases including lesser bases called satellites. To expedite cases, on each base a Courts and Boards Department was established, staffed with qualified lawyers to take care of all disciplinary matters arising at that base.

Under the military system of jurisprudence there are three grades of courts: summary, special and general. In a summary court the commanding officer of the unit to which the airman is assigned hears the case and imposes the punishment if any. Offenses are usually minor infractions such as AWOL for a few days. In a special court the commanding officer of the base appoints the members, and it decides on the sentence to be imposed if there is a finding of guilt. The general type of case before that court is a misdemeanor. The commanding officer may approve or disapprove the findings and sentence, if any. Both these courts have limited jurisdiction; all records were reviewed at our headquarters.

The more serious cases such as felony offenses were tried by a general court, its personnel appointed by the commanding general, which duty was relegated to my office where written reviews were prepared of all general courts-martial cases and submitted to the commanding general together with our recommendations. Following his decision, the entire file was then forwarded to the air judge advocate general. We had an outstanding law firm—12 officers and 15 noncommissioned officers, all lawyers, and 10 WACS, all excellent legal secretaries headed by Staff-Sergeant Mary Dunnigan, a real soldier. In addition to Ben Connally and his fellow Texan, Dorsey Hardeman, there were many men from the State of Washington on our legal staff.*

When General Johnson was sent to Alaska to assume command of the 11th Air Force, his wife Manon bought a house in Colorado Springs. Educated in Paris, where she met Davenport during World War I, her gallic wit and uninhibited personality was a match for Lucille and Zorka Oenslager. We all became good friends, and those three gals certainly kept Don and me entertained. Many a good laugh we shared.

Major General Ste. Clair Street, a World War I Air Force veteran, succeeded General Johnson.

The mission of the Second Air Force was a staging and training command for crews, brought together for the first time from their various training schools—pilots and co-pilots, navigators, bombardiers, gunners and crews. Each plane had a crew of 11; together they trained as a unit in their new planes from Boeing which they would fly to the British theater after three months of intensive training in our command. They were admirable young men, most of them in their early twenties. Until the air force developed long-range fighter support, they flew without support into flak and enemy fire; many were shot down over France and Germany.

There were casualties among higher echelons too. When Nate Forrest was transferred to the European theater, he visited Colonel Willie Hatcher of Detroit who had served as A-3 (training) at Fort George Wright, then taken the 361st Bombardment Group to England. General Forrest volunteered to fly as a pilot on the lead plane on a bombing mission, its target the submarine pens at Kiel, Germany. The plane was shot down over the sea off Denmark; Nate's body was recovered months later.

A prominent Seattleite, Major John L. Scott, a lovable Scot with a burr, who served with a Scottish regiment on the British front in World War I, had graduated from the intelligence school at Harrisburg and while stationed at Fort George Wright was asked by Willie Hatcher to be his A-2 (intelligence) in England. Happy to be "an old soldier," John was father confessor and counselor in his briefing to the young officers of the B-17 crews taking off on their missions.

John tells about the end of World War I. On November 12, 1918—the day after the Armistice—which was his birthday, his mother sent him a telegram of congratulation. It arrived that day. His commanding officer personally brought the telegram to the trenches at the front and on delivering it said: "This person is congratulating you. Does she believe *you* won the bloody war singlehanded?"

Colonel Willie Hatcher, who was shot down over Germany where he was a prisoner of war for 16 months, visited us in 1945 at Colorado Springs on his return. Some months later in 1946, while flying over Alamagordo testing rockets, his plane burst into flames with the loss of all on board.

General Street soon left to take command of the 13th Air Force in Australia; Major General U.G. Ent—since West Point days called "P.D." for Pennsylvania Dutch—took his place. He'd led the bombing raids on the Ploesti oil fields, was a fearless flyer and a true gentleman. To him must be given the credit for the great success of the Second Air Force during his stewardship.

While on a mission for General Ent at Salina, Kansas, I saw my first B-29 and I'll never forget it. The plane was under tight security, guards stationed at both ends. Entering the tail section, I was amazed at its immense size; it looked to be a full city block long. Soon after that they were coming to us off the production lines in great numbers and

*Captains Herbert Davis, Stanberry Foster, Glover Patterson, 1st Lieutenant Kenneth Jones and Staff Sergeant Tony Felice.

were used for training at the larger airfields. Eventually the decision was made to send the B-29's to the Pacific theater, the first wing commanded by Maj. General K.B. Wolfe going to the China-Burma-India sector, the second to Saipan and Tinian, as did the third, the latter two under command of Generals Rosie O'Donnell and Tommy Power, both from our headquarters. The 20th Air Force, which included the XXth and XXIst Bombardment Groups in the Pacific, was then being organized in our area. Slated for commanding general of this air force, General Ent asked me to go with him as his judge advocate. Before his final orders arrived, however, tragedy intervened.

After visiting a Texas base, General Ent was taking off for his home base, Peterson Field at Colorado Springs—now known as Ent Field—piloting one of the smaller two-engine planes with a second lieutenant as co-pilot. As he taxied down the runway for take-off, the co-pilot mistook a signal of General Ent's for "wheels up;" as a result, the wheels were raised too soon and the plane skidded along the runway, careening to the left. One of the propellers crashed through the plane, struck the general in the back and severed his spinal cord just below his neck leaving him paralyzed.

He was taken to Brooke Army Hospital in San Antonio where he remained for several months. Confined to a wheelchair, he was eventually released and died later of his injuries.

Lucille went to San Antonio to do what she could for the General's lovely wife, Eleanor. Major Dorsey Hardeman of our staff became General Ent's aide while he was confined in San Antonio and did a great job, for which we were grateful. Without question, General Ent would have become commanding general of the United States Air Force had he lived. I then remained with the Second Air Force.

Early in May of 1944 General Ent granted me a furlough which we spent in Seattle. There at a party in the Olympic "Bowl" a realtor friend told us about a piece of property that had just come on the market—10 acres on Clyde Hill in Bellevue. Clyde Hill was country then. All the houses there were on 5- or 10-acre tracts adjoining the old 80-acre farm that is now the exclusive residential area of Vuecrest. The acreage we looked at sloped west toward Lake Washington. The coves between Evergreen, Hunts and Yarrow Points glistened below us, resembling Norwegian fjords. At night we could see the glimmer of the city lights across the lake. In daylight the whole panorama of the Olympic mountain range was spread out before us. Fruit trees, holly and lilac trees surrounded a small house—we both knew it was for us. Something to come home to and work at and build when we came back from the war, and we bought it then and there.

The realtor rented the house for the duration, and we returned to Colorado Springs full of plans. Lucille kept a file of ideas plus a few of her own and so, when we returned in 1945, we had our work cut out for us.

Until the arrival of Major General Robert B. Williams from the Eighth Air Force in Britain, our chief of staff, Brigadier General Albert "Heggie" Heggenberger assumed command. Heggie and Lester J. Maitland when first lieutenants in the Army Air Force, had pioneered the flight from the mainland to Hawaii in 1926, a feat of precise navigation. Since they had only enough fuel to carry them the 2,400 miles from Oakland Air Field to Hawaii, a mistake of two degrees would have let them hurdle by to a watery grave, as the next landing place was the Solomon Islands, 2,500 miles beyond. Flying at a speed of 100 miles an hour, they began to look for land after the 24-hour mark. Heggie told me the suspense was almost unbearable, for they could so easily overshoot those little green specks in the ocean. Just after the 25-hour mark they spotted the island of Oahu and landed at Wheeler Field. They'd hit the bull's eye and were the blazers of the trans-Pacific air route to Hawaii. Think of the millions of pleasure-seekers who have them to thank for the smooth flights they now enjoy to the Sandwich Isles.

I accompanied Heggie to a meeting held at Mobile of all the commanding generals of the air force units then in the United States, the purpose being to form an Air Force Association. While flying back from Washington, DC, Heggie flew so close to Mt. Rushmore National Memorial I was sure I could have touched Abe Lincoln's nose from the co-pilot's seat.

General Bob Williams was in England in 1940 as an observer and during one of the Nazi raids on London was hit by shrapnel and lost the sight of one eye. However, he stayed in service and had a brilliant career, especially during his command of a wing of the Eighth Air Force in Britain, often flying with his men in the lead plane. A graduate of Texas A and M, he was a loveable Texan as was his wife Amy.

The businessmen and city officials of Colorado Springs extended themselves to make the life of the military pleasant. The city derived its water supply from two large lakes, well stocked with Rocky Mountain trout, and surrounded by high wire fences with locked gates. Knowing General Williams was an ardent fisherman, and anxious he learned the fish of Colorado were bigger than those in Texas, the city manager gave the general a key to the gates. Occasionally the general would call me and say, "Let's go fishing."

One day his sergeant driver and I were flyfishing from a vantage point on the lake when we hear a loud splash from around a bend, followed by a blue streak of very choice swear words. "The general," I said, "must have fallen in. Let's journey over there."

As we came around the bend, we saw him, standing in his birthday suit, still cursing as he hung his clothes on branches to dry. We couldn't help laughing at his predicament; he soon joined in.

Later, the chamber of commerce gave a dinner honoring General Williams. When I was called on for a few remarks, after thanking our hosts for their great hospitality, I related the incident, stating: "And there stood the general, as naked as the day he was born—every inch a general." Everybody roared including General Williams. When the laughter subsided, I said, "To conclude, he should have four stars instead of two!"

On January 6, 1945, came promotion to full colonel. As Lucille pinned the eagles on my shoulders, Colonel Earl Patterson of the air judge advocate's staff reminded her she had the "duty of treating me with the utmost deference, humility and veneration."

Because of the size of our command, we had many violations among airmen, most of them of a military nature — AWOL, low flying or failure to obey an order. We had excellent working arrangements and cooperation with the civil authorities at all bases; in some criminal violations, by agreement, we turned the accused over to them for trial. If, however, we felt the airman should be court-martialed, we retained jurisdiction.

A case of great concern was that of an airman who had been convicted of raping and killing a 12-year-old girl. The serious nature of the crime added to the fact he'd served time in a penal institution for a prior rape offense, resulted in the death sentence by the military court, which they had the right to do. In our review of the record of the trial we recommended the commanding general approve the death sentence, which he did. Some time later the army chief of staff sent us an official document with the seal and ribbons of President Roosevelt approving the sentence and ordering the execution. When the colonel in command of the defendant's base received the dispatch he called and said, "What do I do now?" That had us puzzled too.

We couldn't find anything in our military law books of much help. Since the state in which the offense was committed administered the death penalty by hanging, I suggested the colonel get in touch with the authorities at the penitentiary and use their regular hangman. I also suggested, as a deterrent to the men at the base, he have the scaffold built on the parade ground for all to see and the President's order read prior to the execution. He called me the morning after the execution to say the duty had been carried out.

Another case of rape occurred at a base in Arizona. The airman, of Spanish or Mexican extraction, was so charged and defended by a lawyer from New York, a first lieutenant. Before the trial he went to the guardhouse and made arrangements with the airman to have his buddy, who was of the same race, step forward when the name of the accused airman was called. As a result the buddy was brought into court and falsely gave the name of the accused as directed by the lawyer. As the trial proceeded, the victim and her mother both testified the man on trial resembled the one who attacked the girl. The chief of police got suspicious and uncovered the plot. The guilty man was subsequently tried and convicted.

When the facts of the case came to our attention, we directed the filing of charges against the defense counsel; he was convicted of the charge of "conduct unbecoming an officer" under the 96th Article of War and sentenced to receive a dishonorable discharge from the service, which was approved by the commanding general and the judge advocate general of the air force.

At Salina, Kansas, a WAC was raped on her way to her barracks. She reported the incident immediately, but the culprit was never apprehended. It happened on a dark night, and there were no lights so her description was sketchy. When it was ascertained she was pregnant, she wanted an abortion and consulted with the base surgeon, her parents and the base chaplain. The chief surgeon at our headquarters was called; after a session between him, General Ent and me, it was decided I go to Salina, check the girl's story and talk with others involved. I was convinced of the girl's integrity and impressed with the attitude of her parents and the chaplain. Surgeons at the base and at our headquarters assured me an abortion at her stage of pregnancy involved no danger to her; that, if performed by a capable, experienced surgeon, the operation should be a simple one and result in complete recovery. The base surgeon was acquainted with a reputable civilian physician in the city who, knowing all the facts, was willing to perform the operation without charge. The decision was made, General Ent concurring, this should be done with the understanding the base surgeon take no part. Some time later he called to report all had gone well and the WAC had returned to full duty.

Many offenses were related to low flying, commonly referred to as buzzing. These were difficult cases; in some instances we regretted having to file them. They involved both the younger newly trained pilots and those just returned from combat. However, B-17's weren't Piper Cubs, and buzzing with them was hazardous, causing serious accidents. Not only army lives and property were lost but those of civilians as well. It was imperative we crack down and we did.

On January 25, 1945, upon my advice General Williams sent a letter to all base and wing commanders:

> It is desired that courts-martial cases be held to the...minimum and...the War Department policy be strictly followed, namely, that trial by courts-martial should not be resorted to unless necessary, and when...necessary, trial be held before the lowest court having power to adjudge an appropriate...sentence. While it is true that military personnel who commit certain offenses must...be tried by courts-martial...the demand for manpower is so great that confinement of an airman...and trial by courts-martial is not necessarily the appropriate action to be taken in all cases. Maximum use should be made of the powers granted commanding officers under the 104th Article of War...commanders are expected to take a personal interest in their men and study the case of each offender with the view of redeeming the soldier if possible. Efforts toward rehabilitation...are desired...there is a tendency...to shirk this responsibility and recommend trial by general courts-martial merely to get rid of the offender.

This was an excellent statement of the policies that governed our actions throughout the Second Air Force.

Throughout the war years there were two things which the War Department demanded of a judge advocate: First, that each airman receive a fair trial. Strenuous efforts were made to see this was accomplished. Second, that all trials be conducted as expeditiously as possible. Our figures for the month of January 1945 showed the average length of time from date of confinement to date of trial in general court cases was 23.85 days. In special court cases it was 8.83 days and in summary court cases 3.26 days, a proud record.

Can you imagine any of our civilian courts moving so expeditiously? A speedy trial is the best deterrent. That is the theory of the Canadian courts and should be ours.

During the 3½ years as judge advocate of the Second Air Force, I served under six commanding generals, all outstanding men, skilled in air tactics and strategy, of great human understanding and not at all militaristic. They were a credit to the country, and I was proud to have been associated with them.

My favorite would have to be General Ent under whom I served the longest. He was a warm-hearted man, very energetic and knowledgeable and possessed of an earnest desire to be fair and understanding of the problems confronting his men. This was particularly noticeable as we discussed those against whom we found it necessary to file charges. In air tactics he was brilliant and unsurpassed. We who served under him, without exception, were imbued with the feeling that we were a part of the team and were proud of it.

General Ent recommended me for promotion long before I had sufficient time in grade and also for the Legion of Merit, which was awarded in April 1946 by order of General Carl Spaatz, commanding general of the air force. The presentation was made at Spokane at a meeting of the Judge Advocates' Association of the State of Washington a month later. The citation reads:

> Colonel William J. Wilkins, 0461490, Judge Advocate General's Department, Army of the United States. As Acting Judge Advocate and Judge Advocate, Second Air Force, during the period from April, 1943 to August, 1945, Colonel Wilkins exercised close and careful supervision over the administration of military justice and set a high standard of efficiency, fairness and mercy within that command. His brilliant staff work and organizational ability reflect great credit upon himself and the armed forces of the United States.

It was an honor to be flanked by Justice Walter Beals of the Washington Supreme Court, who was with General Pershing's headquarters at Chaumont in World War I, and Federal Judge Sam Driver, who served in World War II, both longtime friends. Also by the six lawyers from Washington State who served with me.

Prior to leaving the service at Colorado Springs in August 1945 to get back to my job in Seattle, General Bob Williams presented me with the Meritorious Service ribbon, signed by General Henry H. Arnold. Mindful of the many able lawyers with whom I had been associated in the Second Air Force, I sent a farewell letter to all of them:

> Orders have just been issued relieving me from active duty in order that I may again return to my judicial position at Seattle, Washington.
>
> It has been my privilege to be associated with most of you for more than three years and I must confess that it is with considerable regret that our association must be severed at this time.
>
> May I take this opportunity of thanking each of you for the splendid cooperation which you have at all times given to me and my associates, and which I know you will continue to give to my successor, Lieutenant Colonel Ben C. Connally.
>
> My prayer is that all of you may soon be permitted to return to your homes and I know you will then carry with you the feeling, so richly deserved, of a job well done.
>
> Sincerely and gratefully yours,

As a final tribute to the officers and men of the air force and to those wonderful commanding generals who carried out the training mission of the Second Air Force, I quote a letter to General Ent from Major General L.S. Kuter, Assistant Chief of Staff, Plans, Headquarters Army Air Forces, Washington, DC, dated June 25, 1944:

Dear P.D.

On D-Day I had the opportunity to go along with 1864 heavy bombers — watched them cross a short line of departure during a 20 minute time period — the leading airplane was not over 10 seconds early, and the last airplane was not over 15 seconds late. Those 20,000 men crossed the Channel to attack targets which they had never seen for security reasons. They were prepared for either visual or instrument bombing. You and your people deserve a great big orchid for the almost unbelievable fact that no one of these 20,000 men, so recently from the corn fields, released a single bomb or otherwise even scratched a row-boat in the Channel which was literally swarming with ships and small craft.

I am sure that the fact that the target areas were hit by this entire force bombing on instruments without damage to our surface units was a major scientific and training achievement. No one would have believed such an achievement possible, even a year ago. Hats off to Training!

As always, it was hard to say goodbye to the many friends we'd made, particularly to the men I'd worked with so closely for 3½ years, but good to be homeward bound. Lucille and I drove home via the Continental Divide and Yellowstone Park, where there were few tourists because of the gas shortage and we had the animals all to ourselves. We talked about our exciting new project—remodeling the house on "PunkinBill Farm," the name we'd decided for our Clyde Hill property. "Punkin" was a family nickname for Lucille I'd carried on—the Bill made it a full partnership. The first question was: Where to start?

The original house had been built in the 1880s by a doctor. It had had three stories, but a subsequent owner lopped off the top two floors and lowered the roof to simulate a bungalow, the style of that period. Someone said, "Touch a match to it." But it had possibilities; to us it was creative work, not drudgery, and fun. The ceilings were high, the woodwork Victorian with interesting turning, the fireplace quaint, and the floors solid over a large concrete basement. The attic would make a good studio where Lucille, having been inspired by Boardman Robinson to continue painting, eventually was to set up old jugs and bottles and fruit, and did some charming still life paintings reminiscent of Chardin, all of which she gave away!

The first requisition was more wheels. They were found in a surplus army jeep, quite a curiosity on the highway then. This one was a great find, one that hadn't even been "unwrapped." It came ready for battle with a trailer, gun emplacements, machetes, paraphernalia for war wrapped in cosmoline, and *spare parts*. Powerful wheels with a four-wheel drive that would go anywhere, pull anything any time of the year. A best friend that never complained no matter how high its trailer was piled with old boards, rusty barbed wire and miles and miles of pig wire that had once divided the little farm into sections but were then deeply entangled in wild blackberry bushes.

Building materials—especially plumbing fixtures and lumber—were hard to come by, and the jeep did yeoman duty when we had to scrounge. It helped tear down unsightly sheds and hauled debris to the bonfire. When snow came, it transported me to the courthouse and pulled cars, which had attempted the long slippery hill, out of the ditch.

Simplicity was the keynote; housework and groundwork kept to the absolute minimum. We wanted to relax and enjoy our farm, not make it a life's work. When it came to tackling the house, we found a good carpenter who could do everything. We didn't find any logs under paint and paper, but when the partitions were torn out, the house began to look much larger as space opened up. The living room was extended to take in the hall and one small bedroom, leaving one large room with a picture window at the west end to bring the outdoors in—the lake, the city lights, the Olympic mountains—all the things we'd fallen in love with that first day. A pair of studio couches, facing each other over an old pine bench, were guest accommodations, but sometimes we used them ourselves to enjoy a particularly beautiful late night or early morning view.

One bedroom we left as it was; the third became a large dressing room with wardrobes and drawers built in. The bathroom went very patriotic. Red and white striped paper hung horizontally above the white tile, red shower curtains and towels, and blue floor.

The big kitchen became a masterpiece of efficiency. A high counter right down the center—cupboard and drawer space—to divide the cooking space from a cozy dining area by large bay windows framed with ruffled white muslin curtains. The divider also served as a bar when entertaining so guests could visit with the cook while she put the finishing touches on dinner. Then, in Lucille's words, "When the casserole is well-baked and the guests well-boiled, you put the former on the counter and let the latter do the rest." The old lean-to next the kitchen became a utility room with a small bath. That was our house!

There is a revolting story about the well. Soon after we moved in, Lucille's sister Sally came to visit us. On tasting the water she was very upset. "You shouldn't drink that water!" she insisted. "Get your well tested."

The next morning the blackberry vines were cut back to the boarded-up well and planks pried loose so we could look in. What a shocker! The bright light aroused dozens of *snakes* which must have fallen in while in search of water. They writhed and twisted around and over each other, trying to climb up the pipe to get out. *Those* weren't so bad. It was the dead ones on the bottom that had turned white with decay that made us wish we could *undrink* that water! A well man was contacted immediately, and he spent hours cleaning, deepening and sanitizing the well, then finished it up with a cement cap.

As for the decor of the house, we used a plaid paper in chartreuse, red and gray on the 12-foot ceilings with a 2-foot drop to bring them down optically. Walls were papered in a grass cloth of the same soft chartreuse, giving sunshine within and without. A dark red linoleum went on the floors with a few hand-hooked rugs for spice. Lucille got out her paint brushes and livened up the place with peasant designs. On the long panel above the kitchen cupboards she painted the motto: "Be Contente With What Ye Are and What Ye Have and Ye'll Not Seek For Happiness."

The exterior got a face lift with brown cedar shakes, white trim and large white shutters. On these Lucille painted bold peasant designs with a big tree of life. With its wide front porch covered with a canopy of wisteria, the house was an inviting home.

Furniture? The antique pieces we'd saved from The Forty fit well into the country decor as did the collection of early American colored hobnail glass, old blue China, pewter and hand-braided or hooked rugs. The old rosewood grand piano was "gone with the war," so we found a small spinet which Lucille painted ivory and antiqued, with bold designs of flowers and fruit. So one corner of the living room became a music room and got plenty of use along with the rest of the house.

One evening Nané and Jim Brennen and Nané's mother, Mrs. Middleton Borland, came to dinner. In 1946 Jim, who'd been a good friend for some years, asked me to perform the marriage ceremony for him and Nané. She had only recently come from Scotland where she was born and grew up in a real castle. Nané is a lovely Scotswoman, with a soft voice and thick wavy honey-colored hair worn braided and wound on top of her head like a coronet. Her widowed mother made frequent visits to see Nané and Jim, and we all called her "Mummy."

This particular night, as we sat down to our candlelighted table with a simple fruit centerpiece, Mrs. Borland said: "You know, I'd rather have an invitation to this house than to Windsor Castle." And she'd been there!

During those years Jim and Nané entertained each New Year's Eve with a masquerade dinner party and dance at their Woodway Park home. Everyone vied for the prize. One year Morris Graves, Northwest artist and a neighbor of the Brennens, came as Bluebeard, his hands dripping with red paint; another time, as one of the Borgian popes. Lucille and I dressed as famous lovers in history—Napoleon and Josephine, Hitler and Eva Braun, et al. On the 10th anniversary of my tying their knot, Glenn Hughes, director of the School of Drama at the University of Washington, gathered together some of the Brennen's good friends for the rehearsal and staging of the forest scene of "A Midsummer Night's Dream." Elaborate costumes were borrowed from the drama department. There was even a harpist, and the stage was the flood-lighted Brennen garden. Glenn read the prologue he'd written and directed the players. That was some evening!

The attitude at PunkinBill Farm was: Relax. The land will keep. The grass was a problem—from winter through spring it was green and beautiful, but by May it was 3 feet high and going to seed which meant it would be dry and brown all summer. Solution: sheep and cattle. Again Charlie Fisher came to our rescue and found us four beautiful Suffolk ewes and a big old ram, which eventually became a butting problem! Also a pair of black Aberdeen-Angus heifers. They would nurse their own calves in the spring, which meant no milking for the farmer. Two jet black cats that kept the farm free of mice, moles, lizards, snakes and other things they dragged in were named Jack Johnson and Joe Louis.

One day while visiting our neighbor Alma Perron, whose father came from Norway, Lucille heard him say: "Here comes the Yudge in the Yeep with Yack and Yoe!"

Ethel and Jack Naylor gave us a wonderful collie. Bob Burgunder presented us with a pair of geese he'd named Bill and Lucille. They were great watch "dogs." They slept as close to our bedroom window as possible and were very quiet until the alarm clock went off unless a strange animal came near. But when the alarm rang, they let go with a loud honking duet. Ducks came to enjoy the little stream filled with watercress and the small pond. There were bantam chickens too. One little hen sat on three goose eggs, hatched them, and those goslings followed her around as they grew to be several times her size!

The following spring the ewes presented us with *four sets of twins!* One was very weak but a shot of whiskey in hot water and a short "warm-up" in the oven revived him. How those lambs loved to gambol. Their favorite stunt was to dash from the lower part of the farm to the very top where they all jumped straight up in the air, then turned back for a repeat. This show proved to be quite a car-stopper.

At one of our more exuberant parties Jay Allen, Jr. invited our pet lamb into the house to everyone's delight. The ensuing excitement and adulation for the lamb naturally resulted in his leaving his calling cards and being pushed out the door, after which Lucille presented Jay with a broom, dustpan and mop and told him to: "Get busy!"

Near neighbors, Helen and Don Clark, had five riding horses and often on Sundays invited us to ride in Bridle Trails State Park. Lucille rode Kentucky, a beautiful mare the marshal had on occasions ridden in the Rose Bowl parade at Pasadena. One Sunday Kentucky decided to switch paths and follow another group of riders. She balked and reared straight up. Lucille smacked her over the head with the reins, gave her a kick and a scolding and won the argument.

"Good for you!" Don said. "The last time she did that she went clear over backwards and fell on her rider!"

Going home, we crossed a field with a deep narrow drainage ditch. The first four horses jumped neatly across it but my horse, Prince, turned sideways and jumped right in. I extricated myself, but he was wedged in so tight Don had to find a truck with a winch to lift him out. It was October, frost was settling in, and though wet and cold I waited to see the horse freed. A vet was called to give Prince a penicillin shot so he wouldn't catch pneumonia. No one, however, asked, "How about Bill?"

With animals, fences had to be improved and a gate was needed. About that time we saw Gregory Peck in "Duel in the Sun." In the picture he rode up to his ranch fence in a buckboard, grabbed a rope which propelled the gate up and over to the side so he could drive through, then, with another yank, the gate swung back in place.

"That's what we need," Lucille said. "One of our neighbors in Yakima had one like it."

We mentioned it to Ben Shearer who was in the theater equipment business, and on his next trip to Hollywood he was able to get the architect's drawing of that gate-opener. A carpenter built the gate, and it became a neighborhood conversation piece.

The "simple little house" did very well for us until 1952 when we became the parents of *five children!* After that, nothing was simple, but such fun! And the most rewarding experience of our lives.

Leaving King County courthouse for military service, 1942.

Spokane, winter, 1942

Spokane, winter, 1942

Spokane, winter, 1942

Major-General Myron C. Cramer, Judge-Advocate General of the army, on a visit to Spokane. Colonel and Mrs. Maxey, Major and Mrs. Wilkins.

Ada's twin sons, Jack and Jim Lehman, visiting at Spokane.

Major General U.G. Ent, Commanding General Second Air Force, 1944-1945.

On assignment for General Bob Olds at Seattle Victory Square–movie star Joan Leslie.

England. Colonel Willie Hatcher, Commanding officer 361st Heavy Bombardment Wing and Brigadier General Nathan Bedford Forrest.

General Carl Spaatz, Commanding General, U.S. Air Force, 1945-1948.

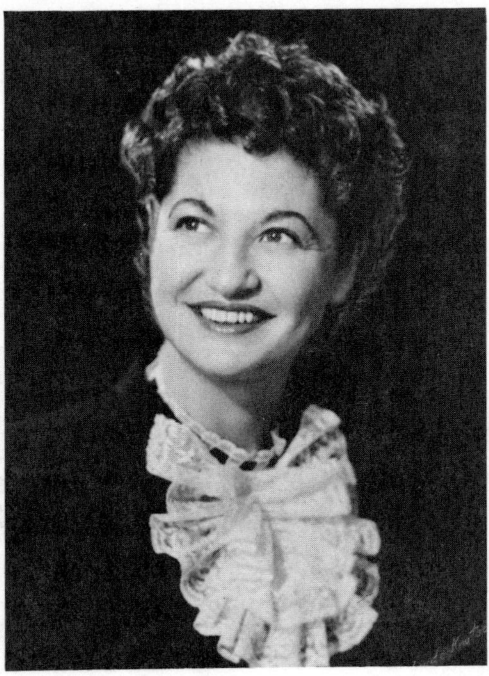

Colorado Springs, 1945

Welcome Home from Judge Hodson

Justice Walter Beals and Federal Judge Sam Driver.

Second Air Force Associates from Washington State, Spokane, 1946.

PunkinBill Farm

PunkinBill Farm

PunkinBill Farm

Good friend Nané Brennen

CHAPTER VII

Nuremberg: Our Coming In

(1947-1948)

In July 1947 a great challenge came in the form of a call from the State Department asking if I would be willing to serve as one of the judges at the War Crimes Trials in Nuremberg. I had been alerted a few days earlier by Justice Walter Beals of our State Supreme Court who had just returned from Nuremberg, giving Lucille and me time to discuss it, pro and con. Actually, there were no cons. It was a great honor, involving terrific responsibility; it also involved some sacrifice on our part, but I knew, from the moment Judge Beals told me, I not only wanted to go but it was my duty to go. So, when the call came I accepted.

On September 30, 1947, notice came from the War Department of my appointment by President Truman with directions to report in Washington, DC, on October 7 for orders and be prepared to sail from New York October 14 for Bremerhaven. Lucille was to accompany me. Again the governor granted a military leave of absence. And again packing operations were in order.

Aside from what we would need for the trip over, we took a large wardrobe trunk. Considering the short notice, we chose well. Electric blankets and a heating pad were mistakes. We'd been told the winters were cold and we might not have enough coal, but eiderdown comforters awaited us. The winter was mild, and the army kept our coal bin full *with* a fireman to tend the furnaces in the American compound.

The decision was made not to rent the house on PunkinBill Farm but close it until our return. A good neighbor, Mr. Walker, who lived on the hill overlooking our place, offered to serve as caretaker. Charlie

Fisher came from Kent with his truck and took all the animals. Suitcases were packed and we were off on a new adventure.

The sensational send-off at King Street Station lives vividly in memory. Among the well-wishers were British Consul Edgar Vaughn, since knighted by the queen and now living in London, and bagpiper Jack Ironside. The crowd in the station was startled when, on our arrival, the assembled company cheered loudly and, led by Ironside, escorted us down the platform to our car, bagpipes at full blast as passengers peered from doors and windows to see what was the cause of the uproar. It was quite an experience to be "piped aboard."

As we entered the lobby of our hotel in Washington, DC about 9:30 a.m., a page called our name. On the phone a pleasant voice with a British accent said: "Lord Inverchapel would like you and Mrs. Wilkins to have luncheon with him at the embassy today." Probably Edgar Vaughn had suggested the invitation though we'd met Lord Inverchapel when he visited Seattle the previous year and been delighted with his sincerity, frankness and personal charm. It was a great privilege to visit again with this exceptional representative of the British people at that historic embassy.

For the occasion Lucille wore her one extravagant purchase—a Nettie Rosenstein suit—chosen for both its elegant cut *and warmth*. It was a heathery wool material in small checks of plum, purple and maroon, topped by a "stovepipe" hat and worn under a plum-colored coat. Her maroon colored alligator bag—sent to her by a friend while on a flight to Brazil in air force days—completed her very snappy outfit.

The country cousins from Northwest Indian country experienced a real thrill as the taxi drove past the beautiful wrought iron gates and swept up to the entrance of that famous embassy at 3100 Massachusetts Avenue. Of lovely soft red brick and stone, it was built in 1928 with Sir Edwin Lutyens as architect.

We were greeted by a smiling butler who took our cards, agreed with our admiration of the splendid portraits of six kings and queens in their coronation robes which lined the main staircase, then ushered us to the rose garden. There Lord Inverchapel and the secretary for labor in the British cabinet made us most welcome as we enjoyed an aperitif together.

With characteristic humor, Lord Inverchapel said his wife was in New York for the day and conjectured as to what color her hair tint would be when she returned from her salon. He told several stories of his years as ambassador to Russia.

"You know," he said, ruminating on those years, "I was really Joseph Stalin's prisoner, but we had some great times together. Exchanged some pretty ribald stories. He was an earthy man."

During luncheon he evinced great interest in the Nuremberg trials, as he knew Sir Hartley Shawcross, the British prosecutor, very well and speculated as to which case might be assigned to me.

Lucille and the old boy had a great chat. When she told him she was apprehensive about getting along in a foreign country we had just conquered, with little knowledge of the language, he said, "Remember, my dear, that a smile is the same in every language. All you have to do is turn that lovely one of yours *on!*"

After returning from service in Colorado Springs in 1945, John L. Scott and I had given considerable time and effort to the British-American Association, formed solely to collect and ship clothing and food to the impoverished people of Britain. Lord Inverchapel again expressed thanks for the vast amount of food and clothing shipped to his country and amazement that a small organization of less than 500 members could collect 45 tons of clothing and $12,000 worth of food in just one year's time. It is a sad commentary that a courageous people, even when victorious, had to suffer such hardships, privation and scarcity of the bare necessities of life.

While we were in Washington, DC the air judge advocate general, Colonel Desmond O'Keefe, and I paid our respects to General Carl "Tooey" Spaatz, commanding general of the air force, who had been the guest of honor at Seattle's Fourth of July celebration the year before. At that time Bill Allen and Wellwood Beall entertained him at luncheon at the Boeing Company when the new B-47 swept-wing plane was displayed for the first time. General Spaatz was tremendously enthused about it. During the visit with him in Washington he told me General LeMay was on his way to take command at Wiesbaden, and he was writing him I would be in Nuremberg. Giving me a big smile, he said, "We have to look after our boys."

Aboard the *Charles A. Stafford,* a converted hospital ship, were Judge Edward J. Daly from Groton, Connecticut, his wife and daughter. A genial Irishman and able judge for whom I had great respect, he was then a superior court judge in that state, later chief justice of the Supreme Court of Connecticut, and was to be a member of Tribunal Number III with Judge Hu C. Anderson and me. The Daly family were among our intimate friends in Nuremberg, and we enjoyed several trips with them.

As a hospital ship, the *Stafford* was equipped for the transport of wounded and sick troops. In deference to our "simulated" rank of major general, the judges had double rooms. That meant a partition had been removed between two hospital rooms so we had *two* sets of iron double-decker bunks, *two* tables, *two* chairs, and *two* bathrooms! We used the upper bunks for our open suitcases. The Daly family had the same accommodations nearby. No VIP treatment this trip. Compared to the troopship crossing in 1918, however, it was deluxe all the way and an altogether pleasant voyage for everyone. The passengers were all army personnel and their dependents.

Time passed quickly. We became well acquainted with our captain who had been with the Norwegian merchant marine for many years and had a host of interesting stories. His hobby was watercolor painting, and he gave Lucille one from a sketch he'd made in Bremerhaven of a blacksmith shop with bombed-out buildings in the background. A forewarning of what to expect at the port of debarkation. Excitement came the second day out when an SOS came from a ship in our vicinity. The *Stafford* went full steam ahead to the rescue and took on several passengers from a freighter having engine trouble.

Aside from a bit of rough weather on the North Sea, it was a smooth crossing. At the White Cliffs of Dover we took on a British pilot to guide us through the channel, though it had been cleared of mines. When we got to the Weser River, a German pilot came out in his little motor launch in a rolling sea and clambered up the side of the ship to take us upriver, recently also cleared of mines—we hoped!

Bremerhaven, we were told, was saved by the Allies for a future port and, therefore, hit by just one raid. On viewing blocks and blocks of rubble, the result of just one raid, we wondered what real business-like destruction would look like. When we arrived in Frankfurt, we saw, firsthand, what absolute devastation could be wrought on a great city by air power. Before that, though, came our train trip from Bremerhaven to Frankfurt.

The second- or third-class train that chugged up to within 50 yards of the ship might have been considered deluxe 30 years before, but the deluxe parts were now missing. Each compartment had a wash basin with hot and cold water (not running) under which was something like our Victorian commodes with a quaint compartment (not furnished) and a pull-down stand on which the German spit-and-polish officer might polish his boots; a ventilating system (not working) and several side lights (not working). We couldn't understand the small sign in German beside the windows, but after the catch slipped a few times and flurries of smoke and cinders invaded the compartment, our German improved to the extent we understood it to mean: "Do Not Open the Windows."

Then there were beds! Mattresses and pillows of straw laid on boards. Each compartment had an upper and lower berth. The upper berth consisted of a sheet of iron topped by a narrow straw mattress. Having two adjoining compartments, we each had a lower berth. The cars chugged and rolled and cavorted along the narrow tracks of a roadbed which had been repaired, after a fashion, from repeated bombings. Train stops came with a hard jolt, and I could picture myself precipitated from the upper berth to the floor, resulting in a smashed skull. The porter told us the Poles stripped the berths of their leather protectors to use in repairing their shoes.

At intervals there were huge bomb craters on the roadside, and all the bridges had, at one time, been bombed out or dynamited by the Germans during their retreat.

Frankfurt was in ruins; the bahnhof (railway station) area and block after city block were leveled. At Frankfurt army cars and drivers met us, thereby sparing us a 12-hour wait for a train which arrived at Nuremberg at 4 a.m. In each city the army had established a rest area with food and amenities for personnel for which we were most grateful. The countryside from Frankfurt to Nuremberg was interesting and beautiful. In the Army of Occupation there was an old saw: "In dividing Germany, the British got the Ruhr, the French got the Saar, and the Americans got the scenery."

Remember, there were hundreds of villages and towns untouched by war. When you got away from the large cities, into the hinterland, things were as they had been through the centuries. Probably in no other place in Europe will you find such a wealth of medieval architecture. Germany remained feudal for some 200 years longer than the rest of Europe, and because they were aware of the tourist attraction, many towns had ordinances that required if a building fell down or was burned or destroyed in any manner, it had to be rebuilt to the old specifications.

On that drive from Frankfurt we passed through several ancient walled medieval cities as well as dozens of old farming villages. The architecture here was Franconian; homes, churches and buildings were made of huge red sandstone blocks, or stucco and heavy timbers. If it had not been painted the olive drab of war camouflage, the stucco might run the gamut of rainbow colors. Roofs were red tile or a reddish slate. The narrow winding streets were paved with cobblestones. We saw examples of the changing of architecture through the centuries. The baroque and rococo periods were well represented as was the German Renaissance with its elegant oriel or chorlein windows enclosed in beautifully carved and decorated overhangs from which the ladies, during the flowering of knighthood, could watch their knights in armor come galloping by.

The farming villages were priceless gems—like pages from a book of fairytales. As in feudal days, the farmers still lived within the confines of their great stone walls, originally built for real protection, going forth every morning with their oxen and carts or plows. Farming here was primitive. We saw flocks of goats and sheep, each with its own tinkling bell, little boys and girls herding geese out for grass. Every animal had its shepherd, as there were no fences.

There wasn't a castle in every village, but the houses clustered together around the center of community life, the church with its tall steeple. The old houses, built of thick stone, were attached to the barn; a few houses in a group formed a dooryard through which we could see the hay lofts, the animals and the inevitable manure pile. And in every window there was a flower box filled with red geraniums. That is the picture we will always remember—the old village in the valley hugging the tall-steepled church or old castle and the rolling fields stretching out in the distance. From one vantage point we counted the spires of six churches, indicating six villages within our sight. Many of those houses had been inhabited by the same family generation after generation.

Thus we came to Nuremberg—another ruined city.

Temporarily we were billeted at the Grand Hotel, one of the two remaining habitable hotels, operated by the army with German personnel. Did I say habitable? All the windows had been blown out; the structure itself damaged by fire, but the army engineers did a fair job of repairing it. In Germany windows, for the most part, had been made of double glass (a custom we recommend for Puget Sound country), but our room in the hotel had only single windowpanes patched in such a manner the wind blew right through. Glass was a scarce item in Germany.

The hotel was for transients only; anyone assigned to Nuremberg was expected to take a house as soon as possible. Most houses in the outlying districts were intact, and the army rented a number of these from the Germans for American families. Because of the hotel shortage, Nuremberg, like Berlin, was a closed city—closed to anyone not having official business there.

Despite the ravages of war the Grand Hotel was colorful and exciting. The dining room was always filled with American army personnel as was the cocktail lounge and dance floor during off-duty hours. So the Americans weren't wearing "hair shirts" and relaxed when they could, and the Grand Hotel was their favorite place.

During the two weeks we stayed there we took frequent walks through the bombed areas. In places we were assailed by a terrible stench; later we were told there were still many bodies which had not been recovered. Deep paths cut into the piles of rubble. We walked along several of those and, to our horror, realized people lived there! Holes had been cut in the rubble and covered with bits of corrugated tin to accommodate makeshift chimneys for little stoves. These were basements still intact. Imagine the bad sanitation, the smells, the poverty, the illness! Heartbreaking. People were living in the upper stories of bombed buildings too, with stairways hanging crazily along the outside. It looked like precarious living, and it was. One night that winter there was a bad windstorm; the next day it was reported that many people had been killed as a result of the crumbling of those partial structures.

As we walked along the streets, the group we felt the sorriest for was that of the crippled and maimed men and boys who had fought in the war. What chance did they have to rebuild their war-weary bodies on a sparse calorie diet? Another sad group was the German soldiers taken prisoners by the Russians and just being released. They resembled those emaciated skeletons of the people our American soldiers released from Buchenwald. And the children! The poor little undernourished children you knew very well were five or six years older than their bodies indicated. Women, bent and wrinkled from the toil of the war years, looked twice their age. The low ebb of suffering for the unfortunate class was probably 1947. Clothes worn out; any fat on the bones or reserves of energy long since used up with no hope of replacement. No yarn to mend rent clothing. No materials to work with. A worker might lose a day while he scrounged for a broken part.

This is the picture of *only one city!* There were others—Berlin, Hamburg, Bremen, Munich, Stuttgart, Dusseldorf, Cologne, all those great manufacturing cities along the Rhine as well as the great Ruhr area (the Pittsburgh of Germany) and the Saar Basin. The story was always the same—75 to 95 percent destroyed by bombs!

Nuremberg was then about the size of Seattle. During the Nazi spoliation program and their retreat, plants and machines for the building of war materiel, airplanes and parts were taken from Alsace and other parts of France and installed in the old toy factories. Consequently, the manufacturing area in Nuremberg became a target of Allied bombers. According to the army paper published while we were there, it was hit by 47 air raids in which some 7,200 planes took part; 18,000 tons of explosives were dropped on it. And 6,120 people were killed, approximately 12,000 injured. Probably it was raided only half as often as, say Munich. But because of the concentration of many old buildings in the manufacturing area, some of them 400 to 800 years old, many of old timber construction, and the fact that on January 2, 1945 there was a heavy wind and sub-zero weather during an air raid, a terrific fire almost completely wiped out that historic old city. Townsmen said it went up in flames like so much paper.

Destruction on such a scale takes the mind a long time to absorb. You have to live with it to believe it. From the old castle of Nuremberg, built on the highest ground and, fortunately, not a bombing target, we looked down on a sea of ruins. With the exception of two Gothic church spires which remained standing, everywhere we looked we saw an endless unbroken brick-scape of jagged walls and rubble.

Now, for comparison, let us reconstruct Nuremberg, "das perle die Deutschland" (the pearl of Germany), claimed to have been their most beautiful city with no town in Europe so medieval in appearance or so suggestive of the wealth, importance and artistic taste of a city of the Empire—the Holy Roman Empire.

Historic records of the castle date back to 1050 A.D. It was an impregnable fortress with a great stone wall some two miles in circumference, 20 feet high and 50 feet thick, with picturesque stone towers at four-block intervals and a moat 50 feet wide. The Pegnitz River winds through the city; fortunately some of the old carved stone bridges are still intact. In early centuries Nuremberg was a chief depot of trade between the West, Venice and the East. Amidst splendor and glory the emperors held a yearly diet there. The crown jewels were kept in the castle. Historic characters you will recognize are: Henry III, emperor of the Holy Roman Empire, Frederick Barbarrossa (the Redbeard) and Richard II, the Lion-hearted, who stopped there for succor and aid on his crusade to the Holy Land. Many bands of crusaders bivouaced there on the journey to Venice. The Albrecht Durer house still stood and was being completely restored; the house of the old philosopher, Hans Sachs, was gone. Perhaps it will help you visualize this "reconstruction" of the past to think of the stage sets of Wagner's "Meistersinger" as the Olde Nuernberg of the 16th century, then called Olde Towne. But now we must go back to 1947.

As we stood there, looking down on the ruined city, I wondered whether, if all the people of all the nations in all the world could have seen what we saw—the utter physical devastation of a people and their land, the result of man's greed and rage and prejudice—it would deter nations from waging aggressive war? Certainly it would make people stop and think and deliberate if it was worth the risk. And certainly nations would not so easily be led into war.

A pleasant contrast to all this dreadful destruction was the old city of Rothenberg. A few kilometers from Nuremberg, we visited it often, climbing many of the winding stairs to the tops of the medieval buildings for a view of the city and visiting the fortifications of the wall.

Rothenberg is called the most perfectly preserved medieval city. It has red-tiled, gabled houses, and the well preserved fortifications with old walls intact are picturesque with their turrets and tall towers. As in Nuremberg, the churches are Gothic, the secular buildings Renaissance. A document of 942 A.D. speaks of Rothenberg. From 1172 to 1803 it was a free city of the Empire. In the 14th and 15th centuries it was an energetic city of the Franconian League, and in 1544 embraced the Reformation. During the Thirty Years' War the city was repeatedly besieged and taken. In its wealth of architectural beauties and its abundance of medieval streets, Rothenberg ranks with any other city in Germany.

The day after we arrived Judge Daly and I went to the Palace of Justice, an immense building at least two city blocks long. One wing had been totally destroyed; it was not repaired, simply boarded up; a continual reminder to us of the terrible war so recently ended. There we met Judge Hu C. Anderson, chief justice of the Court of Appeals of Tennessee, the third member of our tribunal. Judges of the Military Tribunals were appointed by the President and after the arrival at Nuremberg were flown to Berlin to be interviewed and assigned by General Lucius D. Clay, military governor of the American Zone of Occupation.

Together with our wives we flew by army transport across the narrow corridor through the Russian zone—an experience the gals did not care for—and landed at Tempelhof Air Field where, a few months later, was to be enacted that great saga of the "air lift." So, there we were in Berlin, the third largest city in the world, 75 percent destroyed.

The judges were granted the rare opportunity to attend General Clay's weekly Saturday morning staff conference following our assignment to Tribunal number III to try case number 10, the Krupp Munitions case.

We were most impressed with the superior capabilities of the general, his intellect and the deep understanding which he possessed of the problems confronting him there in the occupied zone. He was as well, if not better, posted on all special subjects discussed as members of his excellent staff. The American people can be justly proud of the fact they had such a brilliant commander as General Clay in the European theater. After the conference with him we were given a tour of the ruined city.

One can think of Berlin as a New York and Washington, DC combined, for it had the commercial and financial features of New York in addition to those of a great diplomatic center—the embassies of all the nations. A beautiful city with priceless edifices, monuments and galleries—all gone. We went down the Lindenstrasse—the old "unter den Linden"—and saw the Germans cutting the last of the Linden trees for firewood. As we were under military escort there was no apprehension about going into the Russian zone. There we scrambled through the ruins of the Reichschancellery and walked down that long corridor where the Nazis boot-clicked their way in to see Hitler. Russian workmen were removing the beautiful red marble slabs to send back to Russia. An eerie feeling came as we walked into that room which so many of you have seen in pictures where the little man with the mustache was seated at a long table. From that room we walked out to the garden where began the passage to the famous underground bunkers and apartments where Hitler, Eva Braun and Goebbels spent their last days. We would have liked to go down and see those hide-aways but the passage was filled with water. Two weeks later we read the Russians had dynamited that entire area and leveled it with bulldozers to efface any trace of Hitler's last days.

On Gerfurstandamm Street, known as the Fifth Avenue of Berlin, we saw a few recently built attractive facades—incongrous against their setting of gutted buildings—where enterprising antique dealers had established shops for the American trade. In one we saw people line up five deep to the counter, passing cigarettes over in exchange for priceless old figurines, china, silverware, bibelots and bric-a-brac. Only in Berlin as late as 1947 did this situation exist—a city of about 3,000,000 undernourished people.

As to food, America and Britain furnished supplies to their Armies of Occupation so they did not live off the German economy, but it was with a shrug of despair we conjectured how those poor people in the Russian zone were living with the Russians looting and taking all.

Overcrowding was a natural result of the destroyed city. Bombed out populations rushed to cities which had fared better than they. Some 8,000,000 expellees, or refugees, came from the Sudetenland, Silesia, East Prussia and those parts taken by Poland and Russia, crowding in on an already overcrowded area in the American zone. The displaced persons from Latvia, Estonia, Lithuania and other countries also came. You are all familiar with the stories of the DP camps and their congested conditions.

The educational system had completely broken down. Children had been taught the Nazi ideology for at least 11 years; the teachers were all Nazi-trained. Like everything else, there was a shortage of teachers and now, after a few weeks' course, they were told in so many words, "Go thou now forth and teach Democracy."

As a result of all this devastation and the accompanying upheaval the barter and exchange economy came into being. Here is how it evolved. If, after a bombing, you found yourself with a surplus of rice, rather than sell it for worthless inflated currency, wouldn't you hold it until you could exchange it for a commodity you needed like eggs? After the war the pack of cigarettes turned out to be the most convenient medium of exchange. It met all currency requirements. It was durable, of little weight, compact and internationally marketable. Perhaps it owed its popularity to war hunger and habit. Whatever it was, anyone with a carton of cigarettes found it marketable anywhere for 800 marks. Coffee, tea and cocoa were worth 300 marks. These were luxury items. Rice, powdered milk or eggs, sugar or meat had a value of 50 marks. Marks fluctuated every day and were of uncertain value. People constantly rang American doorbells to ask if there might be anything to sell or trade.

Americans shopped at the commisary, a huge market operated by the Army of Occupation which carried everything necessary—frozen meat and canned foods from America, milk from Denmark, occasionally fresh vegetables from Italy and France. The only thing we could not eat were the eggs. They smelled! One day a farm woman rang our bell and offered to exchange 10 fresh eggs for two bars of laundry soap. Remember, the two bars of soap were worth 80 marks to her; if she sold her eggs at a store, she would receive 2 marks. She was happy with the exchange and so was Lucille.

It was true that right after the war the Army of Occupation was getting priceless heirlooms for practically nothing. The remnants of German wealth were, literally, "going up in smoke." In an effort to break the black market in cigarettes, in May 1947 General Clay forbade the private import of cigarettes and rationed them, one carton a week per person. By 1947 more of a "parallel market" had developed. For example, a Meissen figurine in Berlin which might be priced at 400 marks would be priced at 5,000 marks in the American zone. When you realize a salary for a top German executive was 1,000 marks, this was obviously priced for Americans with their articles to trade.

The antique dealers were the big profiteers. Grocery store shelves were almost bare. Butcher shops had nothing but a few sausages. Department stores were almost nonexistent.

In a further effort to break the black market and help the German people get a better exchange for their possessions, General Clay established six "barter marts" in the American zone. The articles the Germans brought to these marts were appraised by experts, and the Germans were allowed a certain number of points toward the purchase of tea, coffee, cocoa and other scarce food shipped in from America. For these articles they turned in a given number of points. These barter marts were very popular. One day in Frankfurt we noticed a queue of Americans a block long, waiting for the opening.

In June of 1948 the West decided to give Germany a new healthy currency. Shops were empty, factories at a standstill because farmers and businessmen refused to sell their products for worthless reichsmarks. One day a convoy of army trucks pulled into Nuremberg bringing stacks of crisp new deutsche marks. Nurembergers queued all day to exchange their old money for new. The city was transformed!

Farmers glutted the markets with fruit and vegetables; shop windows filled with furniture, cosmetics, shoes. The same was true in all the principal cities.

Imagine our surprise on a return trip from Britain to find all this. But since we were not there during the week the money was exchanged, the marks we had on hand were then worthless.

In view of all those bombed out cities, it was hard to believe the reports of progress in the news during that year. German manufacturing and output had risen to 85 percent of 1936, Germany's peak year. Later, the report was that total German output was 128 percent of 1936! Basically, the answer was a mixture of American aid (four billion dollars!) and German energy and industry. Living there and observing the fortitude, the resilience, the tenacity, the aggressiveness, the rigor of the German people, we could understand why Hitler referred to them, and they believed themselves to be, a superior race.

At that time Germany was a land of paradox. Certainly there was no equal division of wealth. The farmers were the wealthy class. They were building fine homes and barns, buying all the electrical equipment, radios and sewing machines available. And they could smoke! Eventually the small cigarette changed hands until it found its way to the farmer—the source of the real gold. People were smoking in the streets too, which was amazing. Each cigarette was costing them 4 marks apiece. Trains were always crowded. Resort spots like Garmisch and Berchtesgaden were filled with ruddy-cheeked Germans in fancy wool ski togs who made merry on the hillsides. They could travel and were well fed. Even the huge dog population in Nuremberg was an amazement to us—so much so that we inquired of the bureau of records and found that 4,000 dogs were registered in the American zone.

In November Lucille and I were assigned a house about five miles from the courthouse near the village of Dambach, a suburb of Nuremberg and Fuerth. The American homes were located close together for protection. While the architecture was modern, it had a provincial Bavarian flavor we liked. We paid the Army $105 a month; 262 marks ($26.20) went to the owner, a German general then in prison. The balance went to the United States Treasury to help defray expenses of the occupation. We were allowed to spend only $90 a month at the commissary.

Houses were well constructed; walls and partitions were over a foot thick, all windows double glass with heavy storm shutters that closed automatically. Fortunately for the German people without adequate fuel that was the mildest winter in 200 years.

All Americans were requested by the army to employ as many

German servants as possible, wages varying from $14 to $28 a month, to help the German economy. With our house we inherited a cook, a housemaid and a butler! That's right; a butler named Albert. We loved the two dear little maids, Elizabeth and Greta, but a butler! Fresh from the farm ourselves, we felt most uncomfortable having someone at our elbows from morning 'til night, opening doors and waiting on us, so eventually, Albert had to go.

Some American wives did accumulate silver and art objects; many, however, accumulated people. The firemen got their meals in the American homes; the Baltic drivers were part of the displaced personnel, so everyone fed them. The seamstresses who came to sew always arrived at mealtime. Then there were all those worthy people who deserved help. The list kept getting longer and longer until our wives felt like the old woman who lived in a shoe! And always there was a steady stream of bell ringers in spite of the fact all American houses had a sign at the front saying: "Eintritt Verboten." Lucille saw them all, listened to their stories, gave them hand-outs and bought worthless articles out of sympathy. Eventually we had to learn two people couldn't feed all of Germany. Then too, we had to be on guard as to who was deserving against those who might want to "case" a house for burglary, very common in Germany. One judge had all the food and clothing taken from his home.

In our house there was a room in the basement which had windows with steel bars. We kept all our food there and the door locked. Our first night in the house, after hearing the tales of burglaries, Lucille didn't sleep much. When the fireman started grinding out the ashes at 5 a.m., she was up and peeking out the window, sure it was someone filing away at those steel bars. She soon got over that.

Her real cross was the commissary. It was an old barn, never heated, and it usually took three hours to shop. First you lined up to get into the place, then you lined up to get a basket, then you started to shop. Every item you needed was rationed—soap, milk, coffee, tea, canned food, flour, sugar. If it wasn't rationed, there was a sign: "Limit One." The joker was the stuff was never on the shelves. If you were out of something and they didn't have it, you had to keep going back until they did have it. Three hours each trip. There were four rows about 20 people deep shopping. But we never complained. We had only to look at the people on the streets to count our blessings.

Lucille managed to find time to join some of the wives in painting classes with a German artist, but materials were hard to find, communication difficult, as the teacher spoke no English, and class attendance dwindled.

Living in Nuremberg was truly a great experience, and though the war had left its indelible scars, there was much that was interesting and humorous at times.

There we learned that cuckoo birds were not all confined to clocks. The first time we heard the familiar coo-coo we looked for the cockoo clock in our house. Finding none, we decided it must be in the house next door. The next morning came the same repetitious coo-coo right outside our window. It was a real bird, and he came to our trees daily to remind us we were in the land that inspired the clock in his honor.

The chimney sweep—kaminkehrer—was an institution. Employed by the state and providing fire protection, he was a person of high standing in his community. As our home had a fireplace as well as a furnace, we were favored with a visit from our chimney sweep once a month. He arrived, covered from head to foot with black soot, carrying his pails, brooms and wire coils. We'd been advised to resign ourselves to the fine soot he inevitably sent down the chimney, but he was so jolly, in spite of doing life's dirtiest job, he made the occasion a gala one.

He told us he inherited his profession; that those born to the trade were considered fortunate in their communities. At 14 he started as an apprentice (lehrling) and received about 12 marks a week for his labor. When trained, he spent the next six years as a gesell with increased pay. He then received a diploma and became a master in the district assigned to him by the state or the burgermeister. He surely earned the food we gave him for his family.

In Dambach, the farming village near our house, we visited with Georg and Gretel. Gretel looked tired, for she worked in the fields beside her husband all day. Like all the farmers, though, they were wealthy and had a new sewing machine, refrigerator and radio. Their dooryard was typical of others we've described with the farm animals, a large turkey gobbler strutting among the chickens and geese, wagons, carts and the ever-present manure pile. The pear trees espaliered along the side of their large house were covered with white blossoms. They told us the sour smell from the lean-to off the kitchen was their barrel of mash. All their potato peelings went into the barrel, and eventually they distilled the mixture for a strong schnapps.

Our maid, Greta, told us her mother worked very hard for food. The father was a cobbler, and her mother sewed, mended, knitted, did anything she could for the farmers. Every three weeks she rode her bicycle some 12 kilometers out to Ansbach, carrying shoes that had been repaired which she exchanged for loaves of farm bread, eggs, potatoes and apples.

Because of the extremely heavy work load, both at home and in court, we didn't have a busy social life, and when the recesses came, we were on the road to see what we could see on the other side of the mountains. We did enjoy our contacts with friends we made among the German people, and occasionally there were dinner parties with the judges and wives. One evening was particularly interesting.

We had been invited to a dinner given by an army colonel and his wife. Their home was one of the finer ones taken over by the American government for families serving in the Army of Occupation. It had a beautiful formal garden surrounded by high walls with locked gates and the usual sign: "Eintritt Verboten." The Bavarian guard who met us at the gate looked more like a guide one might find high in the Alps. He had a fine Alpine hat decorated with a gembspart (a brush made of chamois whiskers) and ornaments carved from antlers, a green Bavarian suit with appliqued woolen designs and fancy buttons. He smoked a long Bavarian pipe and had well-groomed long white whiskers. He'd been photographed many times.

A liveried butler opened the door, and the ladies were escorted to the dressing room by one of the several maids and announced on their return. Our host and hostess had been stationed there for some time, and the colonel's lady, a collector of antiques, had acquired some beautiful pieces. All the wives were collecting something, and since Lucille's hobby was old pewter, she told them about what to look for in the way of guild markings. This proved to be a mistake because in no time pewter practically disappeared from the shops. It was interesting to learn that most of the old pewter seen in the barter marts and antique shops had Hungarian guild marks. Apparently it had been looted in Hungary and was just then finding its way to the markets.

It took the army to get things done. Shortly before we were to go home, the wife of the commanding general called on us, asking to see the house, as they were considering it for their quarters after we left. Apparently she'd seen the pile of cans and trash our American army neighbors left on the public road to Forsthausstrasse and said she would report it. The next day two German civilians were cleaning up the mess as we drove by and Lucille said: "Stop! They should be rewarded." While she was giving them chocolate bars, about 20 little German children appeared from behind trees and bushes beside the road. They weren't begging but it was a pleasure to invite them to wait until we could go home to our supply box and bring them some candy bars too.

We had a similar experience one lovely summer evening when a group of young people in Bavarian dress came to the vacant lot next to us for fun in the moonlight. They danced and sang to the music of accordions for several hours. We enjoyed it so much we made another raid on the supply box and were rewarded by big smiles. Lord Inverchapel was right. Smiles are understood in any language.

Sometime after we moved from the Grand Hotel a homemade bomb exploded on a window ledge outside the hotel dining room during the dinner hour, causing considerable damage but no injuries. The police concluded the blast was the work of a crank. The Army's newspaper stated:

> Recent legal fights in the courthouse, particularly in the case against Alfried Krupp and eleven of his business colleagues, gave rise to an immediate rumor that the bomb might have been aimed at members of that court. However, no members of the Tribunal were within range of the bomb when it went off.

A traumatic time came when the Russians blockaded the corridor leading to the three western sectors of Berlin, and took over Czechoslovakia. The town of Hof on the Czechoslovakian border was, after all, only a two-hour drive from Nuremberg.

At one of our judges' meetings concern was expressed in case the Commies decided to move farther west into Germany. Judge John C. Young from Colorado was sent to see General Clay to ascertain if there were plans to evacuate our families in that event. General Clay reassured him and said to tell the judges to have no worry in that regard. Several judges' dependents did go home, including Mrs. Daly and her daughter, Mary Lou, but Lucille decided to stay with me.

General Clay was a courageous man and proved to be the right man in the right place at the right time. In June, 1948, when the Russians commenced their blockade by land and water, he remained steadfast and immediately alerted General LeMay, the air force commander at Weisbaden, to assign all C-47's available to an air lift into Berlin. These were two engine planes with a 2½-ton capacity. LeMay had 100 of them and made all available for the Berlin run. In the three western sectors of Berlin there were 2,500,000 people to whom all rail and water traffic was cut off. The C-47's brought in a daily airlift of 4,000 tons for the German people and 500 tons for the allied occupation forces. Soon 160 larger C-54's were making the Berlin run, each carrying 10 tons of cargo. In General Clay's own words:

> The air lift was the reply to the challenge of totalitarianism which was willing to destroy through starvation thousands of men, women and children in an effort to control their souls and minds.*

*"Decision in Germany" by General Lucius D. Clay, Doubleday, 1950

In the spring of 1949 the British and Americans achieved a daily average of 8,000 tons, which was as much as had been brought in by rail and water prior to the blockade. This was accomplished by the utilization of 224 C-54's, the C-47's having been withdrawn. This enormous air lift broke the Russian blockade, which was lifted in May, 1949.

On leaving Germany later that year General Clay gave credit to the valor of the people of Berlin and the British and American airmen who gave their lives to the air lift, 28 Americans in all. I pay tribute to the courage of General Clay who stood up to the Russians, and to his firmness in upholding the decision of our tribunal that tried the Krupp Munitions case.

Judges were given the "assimilated" rank of an army major general, assigned olive drab Chevrolet sedans which flew an American flag on the right fender, and provided with chauffeurs. We were lucky in that we also inherited, with our house, a car and driver, Ewald Havist, a displaced person from Estonia who was an excellent mechanic we could thoroughly trust. Everyone in our household became very fond of him.

Twenty-six, strong and sturdy, Ewald had a gentle amiable disposition and a great sense of humor. He was with the Estonian Army when it tried to stop the invading Russian attack on September 22, 1944, was wounded in the chin and neck by shrapnel and put aboard a hospital ship leaving Estonia for Danzig. Although painted white with the large red cross indicating a hospital ship, it was bombed by Russian planes. The ship sank within 15 minutes, and only 750 of the 4,500 on board were saved.

As the stern was sinking, Ewald grabbed a small line hanging over the bow; during his descent another evacuee came down on top of him, and his hands were badly injured on the rope. He couldn't swim but a life preserver enabled him to stay afloat. He and four comrades managed to grab part of a wooden structure from the galley and clung to it in the icy water of the Baltic Sea for five hours until they were rescued and taken to Danzig. In time he landed in the British Zone of Occupation. There the Estonians were formed into a "truck company" and, as expert mechanics, were selected for the motor pool at Nuremberg where they were known as the Nuremberg Military Courthouse Motor Pool. The car provided us had seen better years, but Ewald's skill as a mechanic kept it running like a top.

On learning of the food served at the DP camp, we felt it was inadequate and instructed Lisa and Greta to give Ewald a high protein breakfast on his arrival each morning—ham or bacon and eggs and the jams and fruits available at the commissary. The staff liked our white bread, called it cake, and often exchanged it for their ration of dark whole rye which we considered a treat.

Ewald's skill was tested on a weekend excursion to Fulda, where we were taking a box of food to a relative of a longtime Seattle friend. Heavy rains had caused flooding of streams and rivers, and one detour after another impeded our progress. When we came to the last river to cross before Fulda, it was running high and muddy with water over the bridge and approaches. Since there was a 6-inch separation between the bridge proper and the abutment we wondered if we'd have to turn back. Ewald got out, looked over the situation, came back and said: "We can make it." He revved the engine and away we went, practically flying over the water.

One Sunday morning Ewald failed to appear and everyone was concerned. About 11 Greta came in, eyes wide.

"Aye-valt ist here!" she exclaimed.

When Aye-valt came in, the dark glasses didn't hide his beautiful shiner. We couldn't resist the time-worn question:

"How does the other fellow look?"

"He's in the hospital," he said. "He stole my shoes!"

Realizing serious trouble could result, I suggested he go at once to see his friend, offer apologies and make amends. It was a great relief to learn the friend's injuries were not as serious as they might have been.

So there we were in our second "hitch" in a decade, comfortably settled in a house with two maids, a car and driver at our disposal, and all that scenery. But those were busy days. I worked long hours, both at court and at home, at one of the most exciting, grueling, challenging experiences of my life. Like the good soldier she is, Lucille had the problems of running a house in a war-torn foreign land well in hand. It was, indeed, a time to remember.

Bagpipe Band Serenades Pair

Bagpipe Band Serenades Pair. (Newspaper print)

The "Stafford" skipper presents a painting.

CHAPTER VIII

Nuremberg: The Krupp Trial (1947-1948)

The recent showing of "Holocaust" on national television revived the fading memories of over 35 years ago; of Hitler's Nazi Germany where whole families were ruthlessly murdered because of their racial extraction or political beliefs, where flagrant wrongs were committed.

At the Yalta Conference in November of 1943 discussion took place about setting up procedures for the trial of war criminals and the creation of International Military Tribunals to try them. Toward the close of World War II the London Agreement and Charter were drawn up in August 1945 by the Allies and their associates providing for the creation of such tribunals.

The first trial was held at Nuremberg, the tribunal consisting of British, French, Russian and American judges. Twenty-one Nazis, including Goering, Hess, Ribbentrip, Doenitz, Keitel, Speer and others, were tried before that tribunal. The night before he was to be executed, Goering committed suicide by drinking a small vial of poison which he had hidden in the vast recesses of his bellybutton, eluding the watchful eyes of American guards during the shakedown that evening. This act was considered by his fellow prisoners a great victory for "our Hermann" by thus depriving his prosecutors of the privilege of taking his life.

Gustav Krupp von Bohlen und Halbach was among those indicted and scheduled for that trial, but a question arose as to his mental condition. A committee of doctors was appointed by the tribunal to examine him; they found him senile and unable mentally to participate in his defense. As a result, Gustav was not placed on trial before that tribunal nor before ours, as we received a similar report on both his physical and mental condition. He was permitted to remain in his castle in Austria where he lived with his wife, Bertha, until his death in 1950.

The Big Gustav guns used in the siege of Sevastopol, and the Big Berthas used in World War I were named after Gustav and his wife Bertha. I saw firsthand the terrible damage the Big Berthas did to the beautiful city of Paris in World War I. They could hit a target over 74 miles away.

Thirteen cases were tried at Nuremberg: the IMT trial just mentioned and 12 succeeding ones, tribunals composed solely of American trial and appellate judges, 32 in all. The prevalent feeling was that American judges, farther removed from the devastation of war, would be more impartial. Other war criminals were tried by the British, French and Russians in their respective zones. Some in the American zone were tried by our army courts-martial, among them Ilsa Koch, who was accused of making lampshades from human skin.

One hundred and ninety-nine leading Nazis were tried before these 13 tribunals. Ten others had been indicted but were not tried due to illness or suicide after charges were filed. Of the 199 tried, 38 were acquitted, 36 were sentenced to death but only 18 executed. Twenty-three were sentenced to life imprisonment and 102 were sentenced to terms varying from 1½ to 25 years. All 12 cases tried by American judges were of exceptional interest and made an impact on history and international law. Hess today is the sole remaining prisoner, held in Spandau Prison.

Case number 1 involved the trial of the medical doctors who performed inhuman experiments on inmates of concentration camps. Justice Walter Beals of our state supreme court was a member of that tribunal.

Case number 3 involved the trial of leading judges, public prosecutors of the so-called "People's Courts" and high officials of the Department of Justice. The motion picture, "Judgment at Nuremberg," was based on this case. Spencer Tracy played the part of the American judge, Bert Lancaster that of one of the German judges, and Marlene Dietrich the wife of the Nazi general in prison in whose house the American judge lived. The picture was fairly factual in representing the forces in play at Nuremberg.

While that picture was in production, a letter came from the script writer, Abby Mann, in which he asked if I would be willing to go to Hollywood to meet with Spencer Tracy and help in an advisory capacity or see him if he came to Seattle. I replied that I would be pleased to cooperate, but knowing Mr. Tracy's capabilities, I surmised he needed no advice and would probably do a better job than a real judge, which proved to be true. A special showing of the picture was given for judges and lawyers in Seattle as a courtesy to me.

Later I learned Professor John Fried of New York University, a specialist in international law and a member of the bar of Vienna who served as my chief assistant at Nuremberg, had suggested my name to Mr. Mann. John said the idea of Tracy living in the imprisoned Nazi general's house came from my situation in Nuremberg.

One day during July, 1948, while writing my part of the opinion regarding "plunder of occupied territories," our maid Greta announced the wife of the owner of our house was at the door and wished to see me. Since the army had charge of all housing, I had had no direct dealing with the general's wife. I had no desire to be involved in something over which I had no control and suggested Greta tell the general's wife to see the American army captain in charge. After seeing the picture with glamorous Marlene as the Nazi general's wife, I wondered if I'd made a mistake.

Mr. Justice Brand of the Supreme Court of Oregon, a member of the tribunal which tried case number 3, told an interesting story. As was the custom, the former prosecutors and judges were brought into court 30 days prior to the commencement of the trial for the purpose of having the indictments read to them and a copy served on each.

After the marshal finished reading the indictments and started to escort the defendants back to their cells, the leading former Nazi judge spoke up. "Before you sentence us, could I please say just a word in behalf of myself and associates?" He was amazed to learn the trial was not then being held and, under the rules, they would all have at least 30 days in which to consult with their lawyers and prepare their defense. Obviously there was some difference in the American system and the Nazi concept of justice!

Case number 4 was known as the "SS" (Schultzstaffeln—"Storm Troopers") case. The evidence before that tribunal disclosed that of the 9,600,000 Jews living in Germany and occupied territories more than 6,000,000 perished in the gas chambers or at the hands of the SS. In a letter placed in evidence, Himmler in 1943 boasted:

> Only the SS was equal to the task of exterminating the Jewish people. Others talked about it but had too many reservations. To have completed such a mission is an unwritten page of honor in the history of the SS."

Other trials were known as the Hostage case, the High Command case, the Ministries case, as well as the three Industrial cases: I.G. Farben, Flick Industries, and the Krupp Munitions cases.

An indictment had been filed against Alfried Krupp von Bohlen und Halbach, Gustav's son, and 11 other members of the Vorstand (Board of Directors) of the Krupp firm* on August 16, 1947, alleging that these defendants committed crimes against peace, war crimes and crimes against humanity, and participated in a common plan and conspiracy to commit those crimes. Specifically:

1. Participation in the preparation, initiation and waging of aggressive war.
2. Spoliation and plunder of occupied territories.
3. Unlawful use of and mistreatment of slave labor including prisoners of war.
4. Conspiracy.

On November 17, 1947, within a week after the assignment of the Krupp case to Tribunal III by General Clay, Alfried Krupp von Bohlen und Halbach and his 11 associates were brought before the tribunal for arraignment. All men entered a plea of not guilty to the four counts of the indictment. Earlier we had appointed two German lawyers to represent each defendant. Dr. Otto Kranzbuehler, their chief counsel, was a brilliant lawyer who spoke fluent English as did three other German lawyers, but they always addressed the court in German. They all appeared to have had considerable court experience. Kranzbuehler had served as judge advocate of the German navy during the war and as chief counsel for Admiral Doenitz in the IMT trial. In all, 33 lawyers represented the 12 defendants throughout the trial. An American lawyer, Joseph S. Robinson represented the defendant Von Buelow.

The German lawyers wore long black robes similar to those worn by judges in America. They all carried the title of herr doktor and referred to themselves and addressed each other as such. They were appointed by the court at the specific request of the defendants and were paid 3,500 marks a month by the German government—the equivalent of 350 American dollars. Often the comment was made these lawyers were most interested in the carton of cigarettes issued each week and the one free meal served them each day by the American government.

On December 8, 1947, the Krupp Munitions case came on for trial and was assigned to Room 600, the largest courtroom in the Palace of Justice. This room was used by all the courts on ceremonial occasions such as the opening of an important trial or at sentencing, etc. We

*Ewald Loeser, Eduard Houdremont, Erich Mueller, Frederich Jannsen, Karl Pfirsch, Max Ihn, Karl Eberhardt, Heinrich Korschan, Frederick Von Buelow, Heinrich Lehman and Hans Kupke.

remained in that courtroom for two weeks, and the pictures of the trial were taken there. We were then assigned to Room 196 but returned to Room 600 in the last days of the trial.

The great courtroom was paneled in fine wood, the indentations of each panel finished in a hand-crafted spindled design. The judges sat on a dais, behind them the American flag, in front, a full length polished wood slab with footroom below. On this, before each judge, was an earphone to hear translations from German or other languages into English, a glass of water, a gavel and any notebooks or reference papers needed including copies of exhibits.

A hush came over the courtroom as Judge Anderson, Judge Daly and I took our places on the dais that day. I am sure all three of us felt an emotional impact—the solemnity of the occasion, the gravity of the responsibilities we were assuming. Then the senior marshal, an American army colonel, broke the silence with these words:

"The Honorable, the Judges of Military Tribunal III! Military Tribunal III is now in session. God save the United States of America and this Honorable Tribunal."

At that moment I was keenly aware of the part I was to play in this historic proceeding and its importance in international law. I was grateful to have the opportunity and, mindful of the long way I had traveled to get there, extremely humble. For the country boy from a small hard-rock mining town in northern Michigan the wheels of fortune had turned many a round.

The two accompanying pictures were taken by the United States Army Signal Corps. The first shows the judges of the tribunal, from left to right, Judge Daly, Judge Anderson, Judge Wilkins. Brigadier General Telford Taylor, chief counsel for war crimes, one of the most brilliant lawyers ever to appear before me, who headed up a most capable staff of American lawyers, is seen standing at the podium making the opening statement for the prosecution.*

In front of the tribunal are court reporters, both German and American, who were relieved by their associates every 30 minutes. Meantime the reporters excused from the courtroom wrote up the testimony for the preceding 30 minutes, so, at the end of the day, we had before us copies of all testimony presented that day. At the counsel table to the left are French and British lawyers and other personnel; on the far right are assistant American counsel.

The second picture shows Alfried Krupp, the principal defendant,

*Brigadier General Taylor was assisted by Joseph W. Kaufman, deputy chief counsel, and Russell Thayer, chief of the Krupp trial team; Rawlings Ragland, Cecelia Goetz, Max Mandellaub and Benjamin Ferencz, among others.

seated on the left of the front row in the box in the same seat held by Hermann Goering a few months before. With him are the other defendants named in the indictment. In front of the prisoners are German lawyers in their black robes.

A story was told about an attractive blond German court reporter. During Goering's trial he watched her every movement, his eyes following her from the time she came into the courtroom until she left. The result was, as suggested by his lawyer, to exclude her for the balance of the trial, so Goering could keep his mind on the case. Hermann, it was reported, had a weakness for blondes.

To our right was a glassed-in cage where the translators and interpreters sat, usually in teams of five, two of whom served as monitors. All speaking fluently in six or seven languages, they were picked from Britain, France, the United States, Czechoslovakia and Germany. The trials were conducted simultaneously in German and English with some witnesses testifying in French, Belgian, German, Dutch, Yugoslavian, Czechoslovakian and Russian. The interpreters and translators were so efficient that, at the same time we observed a witness on the stand testifying in his native tongue, the English translation came to us through our earphones. If the witness made a gesture in connection with his testimony we were then able to understand the relationship to that testimony. Many of these competent translators went on to similar work at the United Nations.

Immediately after a witness was sworn he was advised: "Mr. Witness, you will note on the podium in front of you an amber light and a red light. When the amber light flashes, it indicates you are talking too rapidly for the translators and must slow down. When the red light flashes, you must stop." During the trial seldom did either light flash.

Two hundred and fifty-two witnesses were heard during the trial. Exhibits totaling 4,935 were admitted. The transcripts of all the evidence presented used 15,000 typed pages.

An unusual episode occurred during our trial. The German lawyers went on strike! On Friday, January 16, we listened for a long time to arguments from both prosecution and defense lawyers regarding our decision to appoint qualified men as commissioners to take testimony of a purely cumulative nature from witnesses from both sides. We had been advised by the judges of other tribunals, with whom we met at luncheon every day, that defense counsel would utilize dilatory tactics and the appointment of commissioners would be expeditious. Some of the judges were available for this purpose as were other competent American lawyers; the testimony taken by commissioners was written up and immediately available to us.

Following the arguments, we announced our adherence to our

ruling that commissioners would be utilized on occasions when our court was not in session. (As a rule, court was held six days a week.)

About 11:45 a.m. one of the defense counsel took the podium and stated, "Dr. Schilf speaking for the defendant Janssen." Thereupon he began to discuss the same subject matter of the commissioners we had disposed of earlier. Judge Daly, who was presiding that morning, interrupted to tell Dr. Schilf the matter had been thoroughly discussed earlier and we did not propose to change our ruling. Still Dr. Schilf persisted. After the sixth time Judge Daly told him to take his seat or the marshal would remove him from the courtroom. Dr. Schilf's reply was: "I request that you do that." The marshal then escorted him from the room. At the same time all the German lawyers arose and left the room in a body.

We ignored it, adjourned at our usual time of 12:15 and took up again at 1:30 p.m. *No defense counsel were present!* At two o'clock we advised the marshal to find defense counsel and tell them they were needed in court. When he returned, he said all of them were gathered in an upstairs room preparing a statement. They wanted to know if it was an order or a request they return. We instructed the marshal to tell them it was an order, and they finally returned. Their leader took the podium and started to read a paper, but we had decided we must take some action to indicate to them *we* were running our court, not *they.*

We adjudged them guilty of contempt committed in the presence of the court and instructed the marshal to take them to jail and hold them there until Monday morning, on which day all but one apologized, agreeing their actions were contemptuous. The one who refused to apologize, Guenter Geisseler, a former Nazi platoon leader, vitriolic and discourteous, was removed from the case and his courthouse pass taken away.

German counsel were then paid the highest salaries in Germany; consequently they became experts at prolonging trials. Taking Geisseler's pass away prevented him from entering the courthouse; it also deprived him of his one free hot meal each day plus a ration of one carton of cigarettes a week. We had no further trouble with German defense counsel.

Following this incident Judges Anderson and Daly suggested I establish a liaison with the German defense lawyers to try and work out an understanding of their problems. Every Friday afternoon a committee of five of them, together with members of the prosecution staff, came to my chambers where the marshal served coffee, tea and cookies. They told me they enjoyed these visits, and we talked freely of their problems and gripes.

They were honorable men, and we all worked hard to communicate and reach a better understanding of each other's positions. Even in pre-Hitler days, German defense lawyers in the trial of cases never had the freedom that American lawyers enjoy and knew very little of the art of cross-examination. They were required to pass their portfolios containing their questions up to the judge who, in his discretion, put the questions to the witness. During the Hitler period, as is well known, defense counsel were even more restricted.

The tribunal concluded that our liaison efforts established a better rapport all round and really paid off.

The history of the Krupp firm as revealed by the evidence is a fascinating one. The family was established in Essen in the heart of the Ruhr industrial area in 1587. They built their first cast steel plant in 1811; during the 19th century and into the 20th they produced the vast amount of armament for the building of Germany's armed might during the Franco-Prussian and two world wars.

They made the guns mounted on wheels first used to batter the walls around the city of Liege, Belgium, in 1914. The submarine *Deutschland,* built by Krupp, touched in at an American port in 1916 before our entry into World War I. In 1918 the long-range guns built by Krupp, the Big Berthas, shelled Paris in the closing days of the war, killing many civilians.

Defendant No. 4—Erich Mueller—was a designer of cannons and, according to our marshal, was known as "Cannon" Mueller. An American army colonel, an ordnance expert, testified that the Big Gustav gun used by the Nazis in the siege of Sevastopol, was a monstrosity. Immediately Mueller became very agitated, half rose from his seat, shaking his head, and even his associates seemed amused over Mueller's efforts to show his anger. His pride was hurt!

The death of her father in 1906 left Bertha the last of the Krupp line. At 20 she married a German diplomat named Gustav von Bohlen und Halbach. When the kaiser attended the wedding, he gave Gustav the right to use the name of Krupp and pass it along to the eldest son. "The purpose," the kaiser said, "is to preserve the famous name of Krupp." Thereafter Gustav became known as Gustav Krupp von Bohlen und Halbach. Alfried, the eldest son, on trial at Nuremberg, was born August 13, 1907.

Following the signing of the Versailles Treaty in 1919, an Inter-Allied Control Commission composed of three members, French, British and American, had been stationed at Essen since 1920 to enforce the provisions of the treaty. Brigadier General John H. Morgan, one of the original members, testified before us. The commission was withdrawn from Germany in 1926, at which time Germany joined the League of Nations and pledged its desire to live in peace with its neighbors.

In support of the charge of aggressive war, the evidence showed that Gustav, as head of the firm, worked clandestinely with the German navy to establish a secret shipyard in Holland in 1923. There they worked on designs to improve the type of submarines used in World War I. As a result, when Hitler came to power in 1933, the Nazis were able to produce, in short order, a superior fleet of submarines which raised havoc with shipping on the outbreak of World War II. The designs were perfected during the days of the Weimar Republic long before Hitler. Thus Germany was able to outwit the Allied Control Commission.

"Even the Allied Snoop Commissioners," Gustav boasted, "were duped!"

He further wrote:

> Our company decided to preserve the precious experience irreplaceable for the war potential of our people. This we did as the trustee of an historical heritage . . . in order to be ready to execute armament orders when the time came.

In March 1941 Gustav wrote:

> Through years of secret work the scientific and basic groundwork was laid in order to be ready again to work for the German armed forces at the appointed hour without loss of time or experience.

The evidence continued to pile up. In the year 1929 it was shown the Krupp firm, working in conjunction with the German army, supposedly built agricultural tractors according to their books. They took the parts of those so-called agricultural tractors in a sealed train to the distant Ukraine where the Krupp employees, dressed as Soviet Red soldiers, assembled and tried out the "tractors" in the field with the Soviet Red Army. These were the forerunners of the famous "Tiger" tanks used so effectively in the invasion of Poland in September 1939 and later in North Africa.

Further evidence revealed that in 1932 Hitler and Goering addressed a meeting of top industrialists and bankers of the Ruhr area gathered together by Gustav Krupp, the chairman. At this assembly, according to the minutes, Hitler and Goering told of the aims and aspirations of the Nazi party, to which Gustav responded that the views of those present coincided with those expressed by Hitler and Goering. The group of industrialists and businessmen then raised a tremendous sum of money known as the Adolph Hitler Fund, which fund made it possible for the Nazi gangsters to come to power a year later.

At numerous other public meetings and conferences Gustav continued to carry the torch for Hitler and the Nazi party, raising vast sums of money. Admitted in evidence was a document prepared by the Krupp firm in July 1940 which stated, in part:

> Without government orders and merely out of the conviction that *Germany must again fight to rise,* the Krupp firm has, from the years 1918 to 1933 maintained employees and workshops and preserved their experience in the manufacture of war materials at their own cost....The basic plan of a reconversion to war production was retained....But only this procedure made it possible at the beginning of the rearmament period to produce straight away heavy artillery, armor plates, tanks and such like in large quantities....

The chiefs of the German army and navy played exactly the same game. They worked closely with the Krupp firm as disclosed by another exhibit, a letter from Joseph Wirth, who was chancellor of the German Weimar Republic in 1921 and 1922. In 1940 in a letter to Gustav Krupp at the time Hitler's army was at the height of its success he stated:

> I recall with satisfaction the years of 1920 and 1923 when, together with Mr. Director Dr. Weidtfeld (a Krupp director), both of us were able to lay new foundations for the development of the German armament technique through your great and most significant firm.
>
> Mr. Reich-President von Hindenburg, as is well known, had been informed of it. His reaction also was very creditable though nothing of this has as yet been disclosed in public.
>
> I also write down these lines to add them to my files, which already contain the well known letter of Dr. Weidtfeld of 1921, stating that your most respected firm was assured of ten years service for the government on account of my initiative as the Reich chancellor and Reich minister of finance by releasing considerable means of the Reich for the preservation of German armament technique.
>
> I report these matters in a purely personal and confidential way without thinking of making these lines available to the public. The fact being that, approximately two years ago the Reich government made it known through the ambassador in Paris, that any publication about previous preparations for the recovery of national freedom would be discouraged.

These, briefly, were some of the reasons why Gustav Krupp was named as a defendant in the first IMT trial with Goering and the other top Nazis.

In June 1943 Gustav suffered a heart attack while viewing the terrific damage to the Krupp plants by a British air raid the night before. The following November he retired as the head of the firm. Hitler issued a special decree, known as "Lex Krupp," in recognition of Krupp's "incomparable efforts to boost the military potential of Germany" and of Krupp's status as a family enterprise for family ownership with certain tax and other privileges. With express Nazi approval Alfried was permitted to take over the properties signed over to him by his mother, Bertha, who was then the owner, and became chairman of the board.

Considering that Alfried had not taken full charge of the company until June 1943 when Gustav became ill, recognizing that at that time Hitler had already embarked on his aggressive wars, not wishing to visit on Alfried the sins, so to speak, of his father, and giving Alfried and his board of directors the benefit of the doubt, we dismissed the charge of participation in the initiation, preparation and waging of aggressive war, and of conspiracy, (counts 1 and 4) as to all defendants. Had Gustav or the Krupp firm as such been before us, the ruling would have been quite different.

Alfried became a member of the Nazi party in 1938 and received the honorary title of colonel of the Nazi Flying Corps that same year. He became a member of the Krupp board of directors in 1939.

When, on April 5, 1948 we granted the motion to dismiss, I reserved the right to file a special concurring opinion. I quote from it briefly:

> In my opinion the evidence has shown that the basic policy of the Krupp concern which proved to be of such substantial assistance to Hitler's aggressive projects, was established immediately after the first war, that it was carried on during the Weimar Republic, and that it was greatly intensified during those first years of the Hitler regime when none of the present defendants occupied a position of policymaking responsibility in the Krupp combine.... The man who stood at the apex of Krupp's huge industrial combine until June 1943 was Gustav Krupp. At that time all the wars of aggression had started and were well under way.... Giving the defendants the benefit of what may be called a very slight doubt, and although the evidence with respect to some of them was extraordinarily strong, I concurred that, in view of Gustav Krupp's overriding authority in the Krupp enterprises, the extent of the actual influence of the present defendants was not as substantial as to warrant finding them guilty of crimes against peace.... In the light of the available evidence, the conclusion is inescapable that the Krupp firm under the leadership of Gustav Krupp played a vital and very substantial role in preparing Germany for its wars of aggression, as well as in the waging of these wars, and that prior to the attack on Poland in September 1939 the huge armament production of the firm was contemplated to be used for purposes of aggression.

As to the other two charges, namely, plunder of occupied territories and employment of forced slave labor, the evidence which came largely from Krupp's own records and the testimony of several of their employees was overwhelming. In the Krupp case the prosecution labored two years to accumulate the evidence which was presented in an attempt to substantiate the charges set forth in the indictment. Much of the evidence obtained by the prosecution—correspondence, documents and other papers of an incriminating nature—had been secreted in salt mines, mountain hideouts and other inaccessible places. One witness testified that on the day the American troops entered Essen the defendant Von Buelow was seen burning papers in the yard outside the administration building.

Article 45-46 of The Hague Regulations of 1907, to which Germany was signatory, provides that:

> ...private property must be respected and cannot be confiscated .... Pillage is formally forbidden.... An occupying army may make requisition in kind only for the needs of the Army of Occupation and they shall be in proportion to the resources of the country and of such a nature as not to involve the inhabitants in the obligation of taking part in military operations against their own country.

Requisitions could be made for such things as hay for horses, gas for automobiles, billets and food for soldiers.

The judges in the IMT case made this observation:

> The evidence in this case has established that the territories occupied by Germany were exploited for the German war effort in the most ruthless way, without consideration of the local economy and in consequence of a deliberate design and policy. There was, in truth, a systematic plunder of public and private property.

One courageous witness on the charge of plunder and spoliation was Arthur Ruemann, director of the art museum at Munich. He stated that on May 18, 1940 he called on an acquaintance at Dusseldorf who was interested in a certain work of art. While there, his host Mr. Luebs served luncheon to him and two other men. Later they were joined by Alfried Krupp. One of the other two men was the director of Henkel, a well known manufacturer. Ruemann's host and the three other industrialists gathered around a map of Holland while listening to the war news over the radio. With the steady advance of the German army through Holland, they concluded from the news the situation in that country had been so consolidated there was a possibility members of the German economy could go to Holland.

At the conclusion of the broadcast they all began to talk at once, their voices raised, their fingers pointing to certain villages and factories. "This one is yours!" one man stated excitedly. "That one is yours. That one we will have arrested. He has *two* factories." One of the men, identified as Lipps, then telephoned his office to contact the military authority to obtain passports for Holland for two of them the next day.

"They were like vultures," Ruemann said, "about to descend on their prey. Being an artist, I could not countenance such greed. I was amazed with what ruthlessness these people, all of whom were educated people, divided the *people* and *property* of a foreign country. I was so disgusted I put my hand on the shoulder of my host and said, 'Mr. Luebs, may I take my leave? I don't seem to be in the right place here.'" Ruemann definitely identified Alfried Krupp, the defendant in the box as one of the four men he had seen.

Milos Celap testified about his brother-in-law, a Yugoslavian Jew named Robert Rothschild. He refused to sell his plant in occupied France—the Austin Plant in Liancourt—to Krupp and was shipped to Auschwitz in 1944, never to be heard from again.

Voluminous evidence was given of plunder in the occupied territories. We were satisfied that all the pertinent provisions of the Geneva Convention had been violated by the defendants.

Ample evidence justified our finding that it was in this spirit the Krupp firm, working closely with the German army, took over various plants and their contents in Holland, France, Yugoslavia and Russia, the loot consisting of raw materials, tools and machines which were taken back to the Krupp plant at Essen. I wrote that portion of the opinion relating to "plunder of occupied territories and quote in summation one paragraph:

> It is abundantly clear from the credible evidence that those directing the Krupp firm during the war years were motivated by one main desire; that upon the successful termination of the war the Krupp concern would be firmly established with permanent plants in the conquered territories and even beyond the seas. This was more than a dream. It was nearing completion with each successful thrust of the Wehrmacht. That this expansion on the part of the Krupp firm was due in large measure to the favored position it held with Hitler there can be little doubt.

On the charge of slave labor—the Nazis called them free workers—it was established that 100,000 forced foreign workers and 25,000 prisoners of war worked at the Krupp plants. These so-called "free workers" were seized on the streets of occupied countries by the

Krupp people working in conjunction with the German army. The conditions under which the conscripted slave laborers lived and worked, herded together by their guards, the SS using whips freely, were almost unbelievable. Some survivors testified before us.

Father Alphonse Come, then a chaplain in the Belgian army, testified as follows: "On August 15, 1944...at 5:10 a.m. I was just preparing to go to church when a truck arrived with German soldiers and they surrounded the vicarage.... They blocked all the exits.... They rang, I answered.... They entered and said, 'You are a prisoner.' I asked why and the only answer I got was, 'That is an order.' Ten people were taken from our village, among them the mayor, the village clerk, two magistrates. In the neighboring village 10 more were taken.... We were taken to the railroad station at Essen where we formed ranks and the German sergeant in charge laughed as he said, 'Now you are to work at Krupp, and for you that is going to be boom! boom! I mean bombing!' We were marched to the camp of Dechenschule."

On cross-examination he was asked: "Were you yourself a member of the resistance movement?" His reply: "This is the first time a German asked me that question.... Now that you ask it I will answer it. As a Catholic priest it was my duty to oppose the tendency of turning the world into pagans in the haven of the German Army...."

He further stated: "My clothes were taken from me and I got the blue or gray clothes with yellow stripes that is the uniform of a convict.... Another priest...had his priest's habit taken from him at the camp. We were not allowed to conduct religious services.

"We were locked in our camp from 8:30 p.m. to 4:30 a.m.... with lock and chain. At 4 a.m. the guard would shout, 'Get up!' He would come in with a piece of rubber hose which he would use for those who were not quick enough for his taste. We were marched to the factory where work started at 6 a.m. Work stopped between 5:30 and 6 p.m. with short breaks at 9 and 1 when we were marched back to camp in silence. Then the first soup distribution took place, followed by roll call and the second ladle of soup and also of the bread ration which had to last to the next evening."

Another Belgian witness stated that they were so hungry he and an associate caught a mouse and ate it raw.

More evidence disclosed that Krupp personnel had gone to Auschwitz and, in conjunction with the SS, selected 520 Hungarian Jewesses from several thousand women awaiting the gas chambers there and took them to work in the Krupp plant. The women, each individually picked, were young and strong, between 15 and 25 years old. They lived under intolerable conditions, and their working situation at the plant was equally as bad. In both the factory and in the camp these girls were beaten by SS guards who carried heavy-butted leather truncheons resembling what we call a bullwhip, one of which was brought into court as evidence.

As the American army approached Essen, these women were shipped back to Auschwitz for extermination in the gas chambers. Six of them, with the help of friendly Germans, escaped. Two of them—the Roth sisters, now living in America—testified before us regarding their treatment. Their testimony was heartrending. A part of Elizabeth Roth's testimony follows:

"In August, when we arrived at Essen, we lived in wooden barracks. On 23 October there was an air raid; the barracks were burned. Then we were moved into one barrack—all 500 of us—where the kitchen was before. We stayed there until 12 January when there was another air raid. We moved into the cellar...no light, no heat, no baths, nothing at all.... We slept on the floor. We were lucky when we could find a piece of wood, take it down to the cellar and sleep on the wood.... We were 500, but if there were 30 mattresses, it was much.... We had the dispensary where very, very sick people could go with a very high temperature; I could say, half dead. Most of us were frightened to say that we were sick...since we would be taken to the gas chamber.... We were beaten in the factory and beaten in the camp. We were kicked. We were beaten by the SS men; not by the soldiers but by the SS men in the factory.... Every SS man had that (identified the leather whip placed in evidence). I got it once on the face. The camp leader—his only pleasure was to hit anybody in the eyes.... One evening I came home. I was tired, staying in line for my food. I don't know why and how it happened but one of the SS soldiers walked up to me and hit me over my face....

"In the factory they used to kick us with the SS boots.... There was no one in the camp who didn't feel that who doesn't know what it is. I was lucky I got it only once but I have seen people blue and red on the whole body. They couldn't get up and still they kicked them."

Finally she told of her escape from the camp with her sister, two cousins and two friends.

"I heard the American army was approaching Essen, so we knew it is just a question of a few days they will be in Essen. I always wanted to escape but it was very hard. It was just impossible.... I heard they wanted to take us to Buchenwald.... I said to my sister, 'I don't want to go. I can't.... I know that if they take me to Buchenwald I won't live any more.'.... The SS had threatened for the past few months that if the Allied troops entered Essen, the women would be killed within five minutes."

Peter Gutersohn had worked for Krupp since 1912. In an affidavit filed with the court, he stated:

"Following the middle of October, 1944, we also received an allocation of concentration camp women, Hungarian Jewesses. These women were in very run-down condition. They had to load rubbish and cart it away on wheelbarrows and carry iron girders.... They had neither work clothes nor protective gloves for these jobs. Their entire clothing consisted of one ragged dress made of burlap. They wore wooden slippers on their naked feet.... In winter the Jewesses had to come to work in the worst weather dressed in their wet rags with simply their thoroughly soaked blankets on their shoulders."

Later he testified: "After the shift there was an alert. We had to go to the air raid shelters. At that time I saw these women for the first time quite near because I had been sent to our air raid shelter. I was deeply shocked when I saw these women. I must say I was really ashamed to be a German when I saw what had been done to these women."

Gerhardt Marquart, who was employed at the Krupp plant since 1920, succeeded in helping the six women survive during the two weeks before the American army arrived. His testimony follows:

"When the girls were employed in our plant, I often gave them bread and some articles of clothing...whatever I could get because their own clothing was so very inferior.... One of the workers in rolling mill 2 had promised to take them in. He didn't do so in the end because he thought it was too early and he was afraid he would be found out.... The first night I put them in the mortuary in the Jewish cemetery.... Then I put them in another house that had been gutted.... I kept them there about two weeks...I had to be very careful in case they found out because the SS had said, 'If we ever find the man who is giving shelter to the girls we will certainly hang him....' I procured some potatoes which had been kept in the gas broiler in Essen that had been damaged. So I took some potatoes out of it...which I could give them. I gave them some bread and I later slaughtered a sheep some of which I gave the girls....

"They were glad to have left the Auschwitz camp, and they told me that at Auschwitz people had been incinerated, but I didn't want to believe it because I hadn't any previous knowledge about Auschwitz. However, when the girls told me that, I had to believe them. They said that they presumed their parents were all dead...."

In concluding this coverage of the evidence relating to slave labor, mistreatment of foreign workers and prisoners of war, and spoliation of occupied territories, I have but scratched the surface. More material can be found in Volume IX of "The Trials of War Criminals" published by the United States Printing Office in 1950 (1,539 pages).

One of the issues raised in defense of the Krupp firm during the trial was that one of our Allies—Russia—was guilty of the same two charges—plunder of occupied territories and slave labor. Our court excluded such testimony because it was not pertinent to the guilt or innocence of the defendants before us.

The testimony was concluded and final arguments completed June 30, 1948, at which time the case was taken under advisement. None of the defendants took the witness stand; therefore they were not subject to cross-examination.

Judgment was rendered July 31, 1948. All the defendants except Kupke and Lehmann were charged under count 2 with plunder and spoliation. Six of the 10 were found guilty under that count.

All the defendants were charged with war crimes and crimes against humanity in connection with the slave labor program, and all defendants except Pfirsch, who alone was acquitted, were found guilty under that count.

We three judges spent days carefully reviewing the evidence against all defendants and the extent of their personal guilt. We gave much thought to what would be appropriate sentences to impose upon the 11 defendants who were found guilty. Coming from widely separated areas in America (Judge Daly from Connecticut, Judge Anderson from Tennessee and I from Washington State), we sought not only to impose a sentence that would fit the guilt of the individual defendant but also bring about uniformity in the sentences which we judges strive to obtain throughout this country. We concluded that the most culpable defendants were Alfried Krupp, Erich Mueller and Frederick Von Buelow, all three of whom we sentenced to 12 years imprisonment.

In addition, all of the Krupp properties were ordered confiscated on behalf of the Allies. This was authorized under the London Agreement of August 8, 1945, and the Allied Control Council Law No. 10, both of which spelled out our basic authority for the order of confiscation. Judge Anderson dissented.

This order of confiscation was based on Gustav's and Alfried's close alliance with Hitler, an alliance which not only assured his coming to power, but made possible the plundering of the occupied countries by and for the Krupp firm.

As to the other defendants we determined on sentences as follows: Edward Houdremont and Frederick Jannsen—10 years each; Max Ihn and Karl Eberhardt—9 years each; Ewald Loeser—7 years; Heinrich Korschan and Heinrich Lehmann—6 years each; and Hans

Kupke—2 years and 10 months, and who was released the day sentence was imposed.

As to Loeser, although he was the number 2 defendant and an active member of the Vorstand for several years, it was shown that toward the close of the war he was involved in the anti-Hitler plot. As a result, Judge Anderson felt that, despite Loeser's guilt on the two charges of slave labor and plunder of occupied territories, he should be released forthwith, with credit for time served. Judge Daly and I agreed we should consider his anti-Hitler involvement and accordingly concluded that, instead of sentencing him to 12 years as we did in the cases of Krupp, Mueller and Von Buelow, we impose a sentence of seven years. If the members of the prosecution staff had recommended we release Loeser forthwith, I would personally have joined with Judge Anderson in releasing him. However, in our final order on sentencing we stated, for the record, that Loeser had been excused from attendance at court on different occasions because of his health, and we wrote to General Clay calling his attention to Loeser's health problems.

Counsel for the sentenced defendants filed appeals before General Clay, the military governor, petitioning that the sentences and order of confiscation be set aside or modified. General Clay appointed a panel of three able lawyers to review the entire record of trial, which I am advised was done. On February 28, 1949 Joseph W. Kaufman of the prosecution staff filed with the panel an excellent brief on behalf of United States Senator James E. Murray and other United States senators in support of the confiscation order. On the basis of the panel's recommendations, following a thorough review of the entire record of trial, General Clay on April 1, 1949 confirmed the jail sentences imposed on all defendants. He also confirmed the order of confiscation of the Krupp properties with only one slight modification.

At the time General Clay reviewed the sentences and the order of confiscation, the Allied Control Council no longer was functioning, so his confiscation order declared the Krupp properties in each zone subject to forfeiture by the individual commander in each zone.

I wish to make it clear that the defendants in this case were not indicted nor convicted for making guns, submarines, tanks or other munitions of war. Such activities in behalf of one's country in time of war is proper and legitimate and has not been declared to be illegal nor condemned by any of the Nuremberg tribunals.

The 32 American trial and appellate judges who staffed the tribunals at Nuremberg sought to conduct the trials with the same fairness, courtesy and dignity one has the right to expect in our own courts, giving the defendants the following rights:

1. Appointment of counsel of their own choosing
2. Presumption of innocence
3. Guilt must be proven beyond all reasonable doubt
4. Right of defendants to meet their accusers face to face
5. Proof of individual guilt

As an example of extending the right of the defendants to face their accusers, which is inherent in our Constitution, six Polish witnesses whose testimony was important for the prosecution on the question of slave labor were held up by the Russians in East Berlin and were not allowed to come to Nuremberg to testify. The Berlin air lift was then on. The prosecution had affidavits of those six Polish witnesses and offered them in evidence in lieu of their nonappearance. Although these affidavits were admissible under international law, under the rules by which we were operating, we sustained the defense's objections to the admission as we felt to admit them would be contrary to our training and our American system of justice. We never lost sight of the fact that the record on which we judged those defendants would be the record on which history would judge us.

In the words of the late justice of the United States Supreme Court, Mr. Justice Robert Jackson, who was appointed to be the chief prosecutor for the trials, "These trials commend themselves to posterity as fulfilling humanity's aspirations to do justice."

Imagine my surprise one day in February 1951 to read in the newspaper that John J. McCloy, the high commissioner to Germany, had taken an action reducing the sentences of Alfried Krupp and his associates to time served, a reduction of six years for Alfried, and restoring all the Krupp properties that had been ordered confiscated!

This was such a variance from ordinary legal court procedure that I felt impelled to write Mr. McCloy inquiring as to the reasons upon which he based his decisions, to which he replied with a courteous letter setting forth the things that motivated his actions, as well as a copy of the "Landsberg Report" which contained the final decisions of the high commissioner, McCloy, in all the Nuremberg cases.

I believed then and I believe now that *political expediency* dictated his decision. The Russian blockade and Berlin air lift had been on. East Germany was in Communist hands. Czechoslovakia had been overrun. And the wall was being built in Berlin.

Instead of advising Mr. McCloy that I had no criticism of his action, I should have been more forthright and at that time questioned his decisions.

I was then, however, an active member of the trial bench in Seattle and the philosophy of trial judges has always been never to voice criticism of an appellate court for reversing or overturning your decision. Moreover, I assumed Mr. McCloy or the "Judge Peck Panel" which he appointed to advise him had reviewed the entire record of our trial which apparently was not the case. In any event, I am now retired and have no qualms about speaking my mind.

So, in retrospect, I feel obliged to speak up in an endeavor to set the record straight. This must be done on behalf of, in respect for, and in fairness to General Clay, one of the greatest military administrators in our history, and also for my two associates, Judges Anderson and Daly, able, experienced and dedicated jurists. All three above named are now deceased, so I speak up not only for myself, but for them as well.

It is unfortunate that General Clay did not continue as military governor of the American zone of occupation instead of being replaced by John J. McCloy as "High Commissioner for Germany." I am confident the sentences which we three judges carefully considered on each of the ten defendants would not have been reduced, nor would the Krupp properties which we had ordered forfeited have been returned to the main defendant, Alfried Krupp von Bohlen und Halbach.

General Clay had the advantage of having a committee of three lawyers review the complete record of trial including the exhibits which had been admitted. That committee, finding no errors of fact or law in our trial record, recommended to General Clay that he approve the prision sentences imposed and the order of confiscation of the Krupp properties, which he did. Inasmuch as General Clay had made his decision and affirmed our action after a careful study of the evidence, why was it necessary for Mr. McCloy, within a brief period thereafter, to take any action in the Krupp case unless it was a matter of *political expediency?*

One can understand that the high commissioner for Germany might have the authority to consider clemency proceedings for the war criminals so far as prison terms were concerned, but the order returning the property to Alfried Krupp which had been ordered forfeited, in my opinion, does not come within the category of clemency. By his action on the forfeiture of the property, he expressly overturned and reversed the order of our tribunal and the subsequent affirming order of General Clay. So, the question is raised: "Did Mr. McCloy exceed his authority?"

Alfried's claim to the properties was based on "Lex Krupp," a law passed by Hitler which was his way of rewarding Gustav and Alfried "in recognition of Krupp's incomparable efforts to boost the military potential of Germany and of Krupp's status as a family enterprise for 132 years." Thus, by returning the Krupp properties to Alfried, Mr. McCloy recognized Hitler's Lex Krupp decree as valid.

OFFICE OF MILITARY GOVERNMENT FOR GERMANY (U. S.)
Office of the Military Governor
APO 742

Berlin, Germany
9 October 1948

The Honorable William J. Wilkins
Superior Court for the Court of King
Seattle 4, Washington

Dear Judge Wilkins:

I appreciate very much the sentiments expressed in your letter of 17 September. It is very encouraging to know that our policies are meeting with favor.

Let me take this opportunity to express to you my great appreciation for the services that you rendered as Judge of Military Tribunal No. III in the trial of the Krupp case.

As you know, I have always felt it essential that the U.S. Military Tribunals establish a high example in Germany. Without the willingness of men of your high standing to participate in the work this objective would have been impossible. I am grateful to you for your contribution which has lived up in every way to the American tradition for justice.

Sincerely yours,

LUCIUS D. CLAY
General, U.S. Army
Military Governor

In the Landsberg Report he states, "I can find no personal guilt in defendant Krupp, based upon the charges in this case, sufficient to distinguish him above all others sentenced by the Nuremberg courts." Had he permitted members of the prosecution staff to submit briefs and oral arguments, as was done by General Clay and is customarily done in our courts, Alfried's *personal* guilt would have been readily pointed out. In our final decree we said: "In examining the evidence in this case and in reaching our conclusions stated herein, we have done so realizing that there can be no conviction without proof of *personal guilt*."

A careful review of the full record of the trial including the exhibits admitted would serve to spell out for Mr. McCloy the *individual* guilt of Alfried. I can only assume that neither he nor the "Judge Peck Panel" which he appointed to advise him read the complete transcript of the evidence that was before us. It reveals that Alfried Krupp became a member of the Nazi party in 1938 and received the honorary title of colonel in the Nazi Flying Corps. He spent many years as an apprentice of the Krupp firm before becoming a deputy member of the board in 1936 and a full member in 1938. In June 1943, his father Gustav suffered a heart attack, and Alfried then succeeded him as chairman of the board and was in complete charge of the firm from then on. One has only to read the testimony of a few witnesses, namely, the Roth sisters (Hungarian Jewesses) the Belgian priest (Father Come) and other Belgian and Dutch so-called "free workers" to understand why we found Alfried *personally* guilty of the charges of slave labor and plunder of occupied territories.

More than 100,000 foreign workers worked at the Krupp plants including 25,000 prisoners of war and 5,000 concentration camp workers. The treatment they received and the conditions under which they lived and worked were almost unbelievable. In Krupp's principal plant at Essen, consisting of close to 100 factories where Alfried physically presided, there were thousands of these pathetic people to be seen traveling to and from and working in the plants. Longtime German employees of Krupp testified and confirmed those deplorable conditions.

On the charge of spoliation and plunder of occupied territories one should read the testimony of the German witness, Ruemann, curator of the art museum at Munich, to understand that Alfried was *personally* involved in the plunder of Holland and France. One should read of his involvement in taking over the Austin plant at Liancourt, France. When the owner Robert Rothschild, a Jew, did not fully cooperate, he was arrested and sent to Auschwitz, never to return. Alfried *personally* inspected this plant and he *personally* participated in a coordinated scheme to take over various French properties, not for Germany, but for *Krupp private profit*. One should read also of the plunder of the Elmag plant at Mulhouse, France, and of the looting of a shipyard in Holland. The evidence of the wholesale carting away of machinery from France, Holland and Belgium to the Krupp plants was well established.

On the invasion of a country lists were prepared of needed machines and equipment; the Krupp people moved into the territory and obtained selected machines and raw materials, with the aid of the military, and brought them back to the Krupp plants. This was in clear violation of The Hague Regulations and the Geneva Convention, to which Germany was signatory.

One of the main reasons which prompted Judge Daly and me to order the confiscation of the Krupp properties was because much of it was stolen and pillaged from the occupied countries. Control Council Law No. 10 provided, among other things, for: (1) forfeiture of property and (2) restitution of property wrongfully acquired. How much more fair it would have been to sell the confiscated Krupp properties, as we had hoped, to peaceful-minded people, the proceeds to be distributed to the thousands of slave laborers who were forced to work and live under the most detestable conditions and to the owners of the stolen property.

Instead, all the Krupp properties, valued in the hundreds of millions, which we had ordered confiscated, were returned to Alfried Krupp, who at the time of his death in 1968 was reputed to be the richest man in Europe. Certainly that would not have happened had General Clay remained longer in Germany and the Allied Control Council continued to exist and operate. What is your guess? Was the early release of the Krupp defendants and the cancellation of the confiscation order by Mr. McCloy a matter of *political expediency?*

Again in retrospect, I feel obliged to state that if Mr. McCloy objected to our order of confiscation for the *sole reason that no other Nuremberg tribunal issued such an order,* then he missed a golden opportunity when he later commuted the sentences imposed upon Alfried and his co-defendants and overturned our order of confiscation, to attach conditions imposing fines of several million dollars to be paid as restitution and damages to those unfortunate kidnapped slave laborers and the citizens of the occupied countries whose properties were stolen by and on behalf of the Krupp firm. Our order of confiscation was not only justified under all of the evidence but also was legal under International Law which governed our proceedings. Moreover, the order of confiscation had already been approved by General Clay.

It is interesting to note the final decisions in the Landsberg Report mention all Krupp defendants confined at Landsberg prison except Ewald Loeser, the number 2 defendant whom Judge Anderson wanted to release forthwith because of his connection with the anti-Hitler conspiracy. He alone remained after the release of Alfried and his associates. Friction between Alfried Krupp and Loeser during the trial was noted, so I can only assume that the Krupp lawyers purposely did not represent Loeser on the appeal. In view of what happened, I now regret that I did not join Judge Anderson in releasing Loeser at the time of our judgment.

I have since learned that associated with Dr. Kranzbuehler on the appeal before Mr. McCloy was an American lawyer named Earl Carroll. Mr. Carroll attempted to enter the case before us in the early stages of the trial as an associate of Dr. Kranzbuehler. It was then brought to our attention that Mr. Carroll, who had served as a captain in the American army in Germany, was under orders from General Clay, the military governor, to leave the American Zone of Occupation. The reasons stated to us in open court related to his participation in some military courts-martial cases and had nothing to do with the trials at Nuremberg. Our court decided that under the circumstances Mr. Carroll, being illegally in the zone, should not be permitted to join with the 32 lawyers including one American then representing the Krupp defendants.

Professor William Manchester, who did exhaustive research for his superb and interesting book, "The Arms of Krupp" (Little, Brown), on page 679 says:

> In the fall of 1946 he (Carroll) had fled home under the threat of a court-martial. Now he was rich.
>
> The size of his (Carroll's) Krupp commission is a matter of dispute, but it was certainly historic. In 1954 a magazine interviewed him and reported that "The terms of Carroll's employment were simple. He was to get Krupp out of prison and get his property restored. The fee was to be 5 percent of everything he could recover. Carroll got Krupp out and his fortune returned, receiving for his five-year job a fee of, roughly, $25 million..." Three members of the firm's legal staff concede that while the fee was "very high" it wasn't *that* high. They hint at a figure somewhere between two and three million....

My two associates were honorable ethical judges. Judge Anderson was a solid southern conservative who expected the lawyers appearing before him to be ever mindful of the obligations resting upon them as members of an honorable profession. Unethical conduct was not countenanced. We all took offense at Mr. Carrol's attempt to barge into the case, and in our discussions which took place in chambers, I well remember Judge Anderson referring to Carroll as an "ambulance chaser." His contempt for him was demonstrated in open court when he used the team "this alleged attorney." I wonder what Judge Anderson would say if he knew Mr. Carroll received millions to persuade Mr. McCloy to release Alfried Krupp and restore his properties to him. My guess is he would turn over in his grave!

In March 1963 Professor Manchester addressed a letter to me, the sole survivor of the tribunal, stating that he was engaged in a study of the "Krupps of Essen" and would appreciate any material or any thoughts I might have on the Krupp trial. He had been referred to me by General Telford Taylor. I was pleased to send him all pertinent papers then in my possession, and we corresponded off and on through the years. During that interim he wrote the celebrated book, "The Death of a President," which gained him national recognition.

On December 25, 1968 I received a letter from him in which he stated; "As a small token of my appreciation I have just mailed an inscribed copy of the book. . .a rather special copy—the third of 75,000 to come off the press." It was a copy of "The Arms of Krupp," beautifully inscribed in poetic words.

How could I adequately express my appreciation? It is the most treasured book in my library. As I have told him, "The Arms of Krupp" is a masterpiece. The portrayal of the proceedings at Nuremberg is fair and factual, and the book is a valuable review of the Krupp dynasty.

Recently the West German government has voted to remove the statute of limitations on charges of murder filed against Nazi war criminals. Almost 35 years have passed since the close of the war, and it is highly unlikely that any arrests will be made of those who have been in hiding. However, it is good that the restriction has been removed just in case some of those wanted come out from cover. No country should have a statute of limitations for the crime of murder.

The chimney sweep

The walls and gates and towers of Nuremberg. (newspaper)

Seattle Jurist Sitting at Nuernberg Trials. (newspaper)

At the Krupp trial, the five leading defendents are shown at their arraignment.

House at Dambach

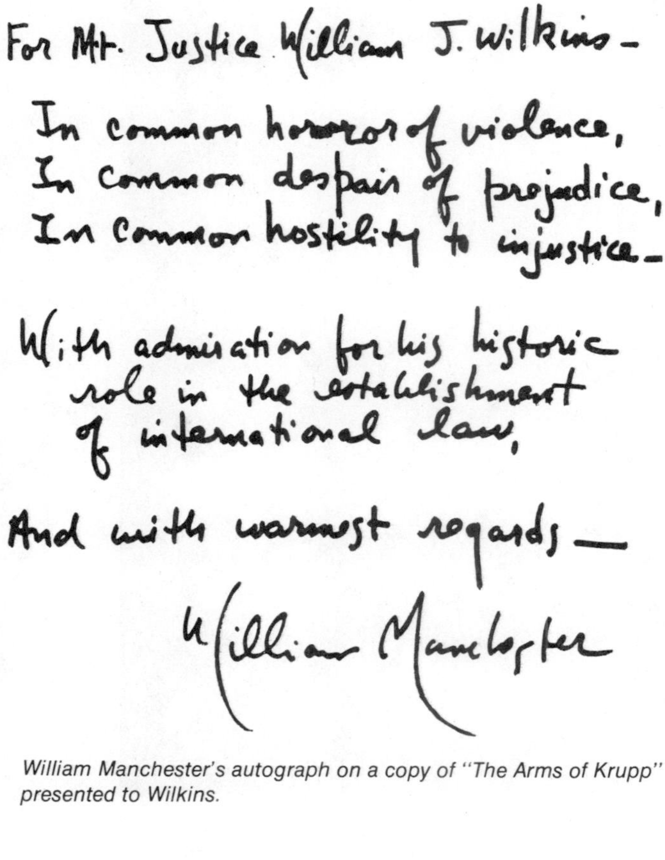

For Mr. Justice William J. Wilkins –

In common horror of violence,
In common despair of prejudice,
In common hostility to injustice –

With admiration for his historic
role in the establishment
of international law,

And with warmest regards —

William Manchester

William Manchester's autograph on a copy of "The Arms of Krupp" presented to Wilkins.

American judges at war crimes trials, Nuremberg, Germany, 1947-1948. Front Row: Judges Carter (Montana); Crawford (Oklahoma); Wyatt (Georgia); Musmanno (Pennsylvania); Anderson (Tennessee); Shake (Indiana); Wennerstrom (Iowa); Christianson (Minnesota); Phillips (North Carolina); Wilkins (Washington); Speight (Alabama); O'Connell (Massachusetts). Back Row: Colonel Ray (Secretary General); McGuire (Oregon); Daly (Connecticut); Hebert (Louisiana); Merrell (Indiana); Dixon (North Carolina); Morris (North Dakota); Burke (Michigan); Hale (Tennessee); Richman (Indiana); Harding (Ohio); and Colonel Metcalf (Marshall).

The courthouse at Nuremberg

Gustav and Alfried Krupp with Hitler

Gustav and Alfried Krupp with Hitler

CHAPTER IX

Nuremberg: Our Goings Out

(1947-1948)

In a long involved trial like the Krupp case, with 33 lawyers for the defense and 16 for the prosecution, delays and recesses were inevitable. And since no man can work steadily, Sundays and all, without some respite, when those recesses came, the bags were packed, and because of the short distances between countries in Europe, we were able to visit several.

The first of the many delays came before the case even got underway. Having been told the Iron Curtain was being drawn tighter, we decided to go to Prague before it might be closed. Although the war in Europe had been over for almost three years, the highways of Czechoslovakia were strewn with evidence of the struggle—burned-out tanks, weapons carriers and guns. At the intersection where one road leads to Karlsbad (called Karlovy-Vary by the Czechs) and one to Pilsen, there is a beautiful memorial shaft erected to the boys of our First Division which marks the farthest eastward advance of the American army. Apparently the Czech people had not forgotten their liberators, for there were fresh flowers at the base.

After the ruined cities of Germany, Karlsbad, a famous resort city, was a delight, and Prague, a city of over a million inhabitants, stood whole, untouched by weapons of war. Historic and of great beauty, it was called "the golden city." In the older section the cobblestoned streets were too narrow for automobiles, and the tall old medieval buildings seemed to lean toward each other, denying any penetration of the sun. The Moldau River, which flows through the city, was crossed by several old ornate stone bridges. After a drive up a very steep hill, we came to the famous square with the cathedral, castle and palace, the older parts of which were built before 1000 A.D. The newer part with President Eduard Benes' palace, looked comparatively modern.

Old castles and cathedrals fascinated us; we never tired of exploring them, and this castle was no disappointment. There was a jousting room where knights of olde held their tournaments, the king's throne room glittering with gold, an ornate chapel, dungeons and torture chambers, and towered battlements. The cathedral was Gothic with fine stained glass windows and a splendor to rival Notre Dame, although the many variations in architecture and additions through the years detracted from its beauty.

When we expressed our gratitude these old buildings had been spared for posterity, our guide took us to a bronze plaque on which were the names of 21 Czech heroes. Knowing the main square had been mined, at the last minute they were able to prevent the retreating Nazis from setting off the charge but lost their lives in the ensuing struggle.

The trip up that steep hill had some scary moments; the trip down was a real hair-raiser! Evidently the brakes had failed, and our driver was depending on the emergency brake. In an effort to save gas, he had been coasting for some time, building up considerable speed. Toward the end when he needed the emergency—and needed it badly—that too was gone. Tires screamed as we careened around curves on two wheels at 60 miles an hour or more, finally ending up in a vacant lot, upright and without a scratch.

From castle and cathedral to the near deserted ghetto in an ancient part of the city was a trip, not only in miles, but years. Through those years 47,000 Jews had come here and made it their home, such as it was. As we stood there our guide told us the entire population—47,000—had been taken away by the Germans and only 6,000 returned; 41,000 had been slaughtered! The ghetto was a bleak and empty place, a sad picture of what had been repeated over and over during the war. The hard reality was born on us then that 6,000,000 people in conquered territories and in Germany had met the same fate.

Ten miles out of the city was the site where the little town of Lidice had been. Before us was an ordinary meadow with a small fence surrounding the common grave of all the citizens of that doomed village.

Photographs of Stalin were widely displayed in Prague. One building was draped with huge red flags over each side of the entrance with enormous pictures of Stalin and Benes. Crowds of young people of about high school age stood in line a block long waiting to enter the hall. For educational purposes, no doubt.

Hotels were overcrowded; we were shunted from our reservation to a second-class hotel with no heat. Our first and only meal there consisted of a thin borscht and five kinds of potatoes, all dark in color—boiled, scalloped, fried, mashed and pickled raw! The next day some good eating places were found where the ingenuity of the restauranteurs conjured up meat and fresh vegetables in that land of scarcity. Coffee was not potable and milk was unheard of.

There were shops but the operative word was *were*. The Americans, with their sought after dollars worth 220 to 250 Czech kronin on the parallel market (black market), had emptied the shops. By then they were mere skeletons, the articles in the window displays all marked "sold." The shelves were bare; in the windows, though, were the things we'd always associated with the craftsmen of Czechoslovakia—fine crystal and glassware, china, costume jewelry, leather goods, linens, evening bags, embroidered peasant blouses, painted woodenware, toys.

The Communist-dominated Czech government had passed border regulations to discourage Army of Occupation weekenders to visit that country. Each visitor was required to purchase $20 worth of kronin before entry and $10 worth each day thereafter. At the legal exchange rate of 50 kronin for $1 and prices pegged at the black market, it was understandable Americans would be reluctant to pay such exorbitant prices.

Although the Czech people were behind the Iron Curtain, they were very friendly. The Russians might dominate, but they remembered it was an American president who helped create their nation after World War I, and years later, the Americans who played a major part in freeing them from the Nazi yoke.

So it was, with grateful hearts for our priceless gift of freedom, mixed with sadness for these people who had had so little security in their history, that we came back to Nuremberg and the job at hand.

During the Thanksgiving recess we drove to Garmisch, south of Nuremberg. Here was true Bavaria—picturesque, with small villages nestled among the high Alpine mountains, and charming old Bavarian houses of gleaming white stucco with great overhanging eaves, heavy ornately carved timbers and balconies on two sides, the shutters carved and painted with gay designs. Red down comforters hung over every balcony, woodpiles were stacked under the eaves, and the inevitable chickens and geese dawdled in every dooryard. Huge pumps were circled by wooden tubs and blue earthernware pitchers and jugs. Often a little shrine with a crucifix under a shelter invited a moment of silence. Cattle and sheep grazed the mountainsides, and farming incomes were supplemented by crafts, especially the exquisite woodcarving for which the country is famous.

A cog railway trip to the Snow House, a resort near the top of the Zugspitz, the highest mountain in Germany, provided a view across the Alp country to Switzerland, Austria and Italy. From there a basket car hanging from a cable took us up to the very top of the mountain. Skiing was excellent, and teams were trying out there for the Olympics.

Later, at the ancient monastery of Ettal, a little old monk who had studied in Ireland and spoke with a real Irish brogue was the guide. In the beautiful rococo church, the skeletons of canonized early Christian martyrs dressed in gorgeous Renaissance clothes—bejewelled satins and brocades—had been placed on fancy couches in glass ornamented cabinets. Many 15th century paintings were on the walls. This was near one of Ludwig II's palaces—Linderhof, a small but complete castle in every respect, a perfect gem.

Ludwig II was a renowned builder of castles, each exquisite in its own particular way; the one called Neuschwanstein was thrilling. A winding tortuous road led up the mountain to where it stands on top of a great granite rock, its white marble towers reaching to the sky, a waterfall in the background; below were two emerald green Alpine lakes and, in the distance, Hohenschwangau Castle and two small villages. Gazing up at it, Lucille said: "Now, if I were the Sleeping Beauty, *that's* the fairytale castle I'd have chosen to wander into." Ludwig built it in the 1870s as an example of the romantic era, the days of the old Germanic legends—Wotan, Brunhild, Siegfried, Lohengrin. Paintings of these legends covered whole walls; the furniture was heavily carved oak.

Though the Passion Play would not be done again until 1950, Oberammergau was worthwhile. The houses, generally Bavarian in style, had been influenced by the Italians; many religious paintings were on the exteriors. Carved balconies and shutters revealed the natives' special woodcarving talent. The people are very devout, chosen for their parts in the Passion Play by reason of their exemplary lives. In a shop Lucille wanted to buy a wooden bowl around the edge of which was carved: "Gieb Uns Heute Unser Taglich Brot" (give us this day our daily bread). When she started to pay with marks, the artist said, "I do not want marks. I would rather have a carton of cigarettes." We had our PX ration books with us, so we went there and returned with our ration, happy to have the bowl and hoping the shopkeeper's black market deal would not exclude him from the next religious play.

Nearby Berchtesgaden was a must—a beautiful summer resort, world famous because it was chosen by Hitler for his summer residence and retreat. At the Berchtesgadenerhof (hotel) Bavarian entertainers, in their native costumes, danced the native dances, and the yodeling excelled any we heard while in Germany or Switzerland. Their native dress is beautiful and everyone dons it on Sundays for church and a promenade.

Hitler's chalet, the Berghof, was a short distance up the mountain road. In April 1945 a bombing raid gutted the house, but it had been so soundly built we could walk through the huge rooms and see the view of the Bavarian mountains through the huge window in the famous conference chamber. The underground passageway that connected the Berghof with the homes of many top Nazis and the great SS barracks was then filled with water. Later, the whole area was completely demolished after anything worth salvaging had been removed.

The return route passed Chiemsee, a large lake where a cruiser took us out to an island where Ludwig II had built his largest castle in 1878. An exact replica of Versailles, it looked as if everything had been put in place that week. An admirer of King Louis XIV of France, King Ludwig emulated the decor of that period, using fleur de lis, portraits of Louis XIV, the Bourbon crest, busts of mistresses of the Bourbon kings, and ornate hand-carved wood covered with gold. The Hall of Mirrors, 36 × 330 × 42 feet high scintillated by day, and one can imagine the sight of the hall and 35 chandeliers all aglow. Some rooms were filled with the finest work of the Meissen craftsmen. Ludwig II, friend and benefactor of Richard Wagner, loved glory and splendor and beauty; on the other hand, he had an almost insane tendency to absolute solitude. These loves were culminated, with all his dreams of power, in the castle on the Herrenchiemsee.

Christmas is probably the most important fete in Germany and is celebrated the entire month of December beginning with the fourth Sunday before Christmas. On the first Sunday the Adventkranz (wreath), made of fragrant evergreens and holding four candles, is hung by four strings over the dining room table. One candle is lighted at dinner the first Sunday, two the next Sunday; by the fourth Sunday all four candles are lighted.

Candles were then hard to come by, so we bought eight—our ration—to have when the electricity failed, a common occurrence, but when our little maid bemoaned the fact they had no candles for Advent, we gave her four. At the watch repair shop the man's wife asked if we could pay with one candle she could melt down to make four small ones, so there went the fifth candle.

Goose is the traditional bird for Christmas. St. Nicholas is like our Santa Claus in every respect except he visits the children on December 6. He wears the same red coat and cap trimmed in white fur, long white whiskers and black boots, visits with the family, asks if the children have been good and makes a list which he delivers to Kris Kindle.

Kris Kindle is the one who really delivers the goods on Christmas Eve. Originally Kris Kindle meant Christ Child; the word Kindle is a kind of pet name like "kid," so it might be said he is "the angel for the kids." He is never seen by anyone; in pictures he is shown wearing a cloak of gold, with golden wings and glowing gold hair. On Christmas Eve he comes quietly and unseen, leaving toys and presents the children ordered from St. Nicholas.

The Americans in Nuremberg went all out to make Christmas a merry one. Among the military tribunals $1,500 was raised to provide food, clothing and presents for orphaned children. American women made up food boxes for their German help and their families.

It was miraculous how, just before Christmas, the windows of the usually barren shops were filled with tinsel and evergreens, sparkling incongruously against the background of bombed-out buildings.

Then, toys had to be made at home or imported. Nonetheless, the old spirit and traditions of the people lived on. The Kris Kindle Market opened as usual. Here all the decorations, toys and trinkets which had been made in the homes were taken to booths and sold to the people who came from near and far to Olde Nuremberg to acquire the trappings for Christmas. It was apparent that, though for the most part life had become a matter of survival, the German people were going to make as much of Christmas as they could.

We left Nuremberg in the throes of Christmas and took the Prague-to-Paris Express, an overnight trip; our compartment surely excelled the one on the Bremerhaven to Frankfurt trip! We'd been prepared to find a not so "Gay Paree," but it was still fun and exciting. No matter how weary and care-worn the French people were after four long years of occupation, they greeted us with warm friendly smiles. The very music of their language gave us a lift, and the famous old landmarks had not changed.

One day while having a glass of wine in a cafe in the Montmartre section, we struck up a conversation with an elderly artist who reminded Lucille of her Grandpère LaBissoniere. He invited us to visit him, and a few days later found us climbing the stairs to his studio in the old section of Montmartre on the top of one of the medieval buildings. The stairs wound round the outside, giving us a fascinating vista of the whole of that part of Paris. His name was André Utter, and in his late years he had married one of Paris's most famous models, an artist in her own right—Suzanne Valadon. Her son by one of her former marriages was Maurice Utrillo. He had lived with the Utters in his last years, and we were shown his room, the bed still as he had slept in it and the few of his paintings Utter still owned.

In April 1948 the prosecution rested in the Krupp case, and the

German counsel were granted a four-week recess to prepare their defense. We took the opportunity to go to Italy, where we visited all the cities and places of interest in the guide books.

We carried a letter of introduction in Italian from one of the court reporters who was of Italian descent and often drove to Italy on weekends. As the American army had left, the Italians were again in charge of customs. When our turn came in Bolzano, I handed over the letter. The result was amazing; in fact, disconcerting.

An Italian sergeant and a squad of soldiers appeared from nowhere and went over every inch of the car. Cushions were removed, sides and doors tapped, every piece of luggage examined. With an American army car flying an American flag on the right fender and a GI driver in *uniform* we thought it strange to be treated like smugglers with a carload of contraband. Finally we were waved on.

Upon return to Nuremberg we heard rumors that our Italian friend had been caught at the border with olive oil, scarce and valuable then, and some choice Italian wines. If true, the letter may have sparked the search. Everywhere we went were the constant reminders of the terrible human cost of two World Wars. Of course, the recent scars were wider and deeper and were going to take time to heal, but it was our fervent prayer that heal they would.

Compared with Germany where so little recovery had been made, Italy seemed rich. Stores bulged with merchandise. Beautiful window displays and shelves piled high with linens, silks, woolens, leather goods, silver objects, laces, glass, every type of craft for which the Italians are famous, not to mention radios, washing machines and every kind of electrical gadget. And nothing was rationed! All the people needed was lire, and inflation was rampant; only the rich could afford to buy. The railroads had been electrified and the new trains were all streamlined. Cities had electric trackless trolleys; all intracity buses were the latest model. On the highways we saw new mammoth trucks and trailers; we took our lives in our hands every time we tried to pass them—the Italians lived up to their reputation as terrible drivers, took the middle of the road and stayed there.

In spite of the few touristy adjustments, memories of the beauty and historic treasures of Italy will long be remembered.

Another excursion took us through Wiesbaden and Essen to Holland, up to Verdun and my old battlefields of World War I. In France, from the high ground overlooking Bruielles-sur-Meuse, we viewed the place where Companies E and G were given the mission to cross the Meuse and the canal beyond and establish a bridgehead on the eastern bank. Then to the town of Velosnes where my men and I completed that mission. We sat at an outdoor table at a cafe close to the bank of the river and studied the route I had pursued all the way back to the bridgehead. I admit, we both shed a few tears.

We drove on to the old gravel pit outside the town of Jametz where my men and I spent the night of November 10, 1918. It was there, in the eerie silence of November 11 following the cease fire, we collected our dead comrades, covered their bodies with olive drab blankets and laid them to rest under a small apple tree. It was now much larger, and nearby, at the corner of the road by the gravel pit, within 100 feet of the fox hole where I lay that night, was a monument—a shaft 15 feet high. On it was engraved the insignia of the "Red Diamond" 5th Division and these words:

> This point marks the outpost line 6th Infantry, Col. H.J. Hunt commanding 10th Brigade, 5th U.S. Division at the time the Armistice was declared 11 hours—November 11, 1918.

As we viewed the large cemeteries at Romagne Sous Montfaucon where lay the fallen heroes of World War I, including several of my buddies, we both expressed the terrible tragedy of lives lost—for what? In less than 25 years we'd had to do it all over again. Would the world ever learn that nobody wins a war?

Farther on were found some of the old trenches where I warmed up for the Meuse-Argonne offensive. At Oberbruck in the Vosges mountains where the Doller River flows through the town, we found the house where I'd been billeted; the same family still lived there. The same small girl of seven had grown into a mature woman who said she remembered well the American soldiers who gave her chocolate. She led us up to the hayloft where I slept in 1918. More nostalgia!

Back in Nuremberg we stayed close to home. The trial was winding down, and since I was to write the decision on plunder and spoliation, time was needed to thoroughly review the testimony. Sawhorses were put up in an upstairs room and long planks laid across them to form several tables. Here were all my notes and papers—everything pertaining to the case including copies of hundreds of pertinent exhibits. Rising at 6 every morning afforded some quiet hours of work and study before going to the Palace of Justice. Social life came to a halt.

In June when the defense requested a two weeks' recess in which to prepare arguments, we took a long anticipated trip to Britain. General LeMay had an army plane going to London via Paris and, hearing we planned a trip to England, was nice enough to invite us to join one of his generals and other military personnel. The Special Services Bureau, which was most accommodating to all the judges, had made reservations for us at The Bailey in London, a charming Victorian hotel where, so we were told, "they had the best supply of food." Even so, we were surprised and touched to have a plate of bacon and eggs, toast with marmalade—items we knew were scarce—on our breakfast tray.

We marveled at the sight of St. Paul's Cathedral standing untouched midst the rubble of flattened buildings. To this day it remains a miracle and a mystery, as other revered edifices had not been so lucky. There was the usual sightseeing, but the thing that impressed us most was the stoicism of the British people. It was hard to realize how close they were to being invaded and sad to think they might have become mere slaves to the Nazi regime. However, one Britisher told us, "Of course, we British would never have given up the fight. Did you know plans had been made to move to Canada and continue the war from there?" Remembering Dunkirk, we could believe it.

In Devon a minister friend of my Uncle Will had made reservations at the Northcliff Hotel in Lynton, a resort spot on the Bristol Sea, snuggled close to the water amid wild rocky ravines and tumbling streams with a view across the sea to Cardiff in Wales. That was the place we wished we could stay the whole two weeks, get into some old clothes and hike and fish; time there, however, was to mean far more.

Setting out to find the minister friend and inquire how to get in touch with Uncle Will, a man stopped us and asked, "You wouldn't be the Wilkins, would you?" *He* was the minister. Later, over tea in the manse, Pastor Belcher told us he'd spotted us by the "new look" and my snap brim American hat. After tea he drove us out to see Aunt Agnes and Uncle Will. As a parting gift the pastor gave me a picture of Christ in a neat leather frame which I packed carefully in my bag.

As Aunt Agnes was infirm, the next morning we returned to their home early enough to help with the washing. Lucille took over the washboard, and I turned the old-fashioned hand wringer. The next day she wielded the "sad" irons, the kind you heat on the wood-burning stove. Uncle Will, my mother's youngest brother, told about their family history. He remembered the trip he and his father made to Liverpool to say goodbye to his sister Selina Ann when she left with her two small children, George, Jr. and Ada, to join her husband in America. The last night we gave a dinner party for all the relatives and friends we visited there, all dear people with a wonderful sense of humor—a soul-satisfying experience.

Then on to see "kissin' cousins" Susie and Jim Rodda in Cornwall. (Susie's sister, Lillian, was married to my brother Howard.) They'd lived in Cornwall 30 years, and Susie was hungry for news from America. Jim was a farmer and cattleman, the best business in England, had a new car and plenty of petrol. They drove us all over that lovely country, the background of many novels and legends, traversing the length of the majestic coast of Cornwall to Land's End and picnicking on Cornish pasties and strawberries with Devonshire cream. In Penzance of pirate fame our hotel room overlooked St. Michael's Mount off the English Channel—a great spot for pirates.

Susie and Jim left us at Aunt Lydia's, father's sister, who lived in a charming antique stone house at Cambrose near Camborne Hill. Many's the time I'd heard the Cousin Jacks in Michigan sing that old Cornish song:

> Going up Camborne 'ill, coming down,
> Going up Camborne 'ill, coming down,
> The 'orse stopped still and the wheels went 'round,
> Going up Camborne 'ill, coming down.

In Scotland we visited Nané Brennen's mother, Mrs. Middleton Borland, at her home, Kincardine Castle, at Auchterarder in Perthshire, for a long memorable weekend. The castle was built in the 18th century on the site of the ruins of a historic castle, that of the Duke of Montrose, stones from which were used to build the church at Auchterarder. An old yew tree still stands from which, it is reputed, 11 men were hanged in 1690 while the battle between the Church of Scotland and the Church of England raged during Charles II's reign.

In Nané's father's time several thousand acres of land were operated as an arable farm with prize sheep and Aberdeen-Angus cattle. Now thousands of game birds were raised each year and turned loose for the shooting season. One section was still kept for the grazing and breeding of a prize herd of Aberdeen-Angus.

Near the castle a stream of crystal clear water tumbled through a glen straddled with tall trees. The rhododendrons and azaleas were in bloom, and the fields, rolling away from the castle as far as we could see, were a soft misty green.

The butler had unpacked the bags and placed the picture of Christ on the night stand. On retiring, Lucille looked at it and said with a twinkle in her eye, "Ah! Thom must have sensed the Methodist background in you."

The return trip was on a C-47 picked up through the embassy in London. After crossing the channel, within sight of Belgium, we ran into thunderheads, and the plane was struck by a lightning bolt with a resounding crash as if we'd hit the tops of a stand of trees. Evidently it did no damage except to put the radio out of commission, but we were pretty nervous.

On removing the picture of Christ from my bag I said, "From now on I'll carry that picture in my bag when we're traveling." The thought then came that the next trip would take us home.

And so I settled down for the final act in the drama of the Krupp Munitions case which came to a close on July 31, 1948.

Then, at last, came the final "going out." Many dear friends had been made during that year in Nuremberg—British, French, American and German. It had been a year of discovery, of learning new values and relearning some old ones. It had been a time of joy and a kind of bittersweet sorrow at the things we had seen. It had taught us lessons we would never forget, and we hoped in some measure that in our coming in we had been able to help, and that on our going out, we would be missed. Anxious as we were to return to the farm and friends—I to my place on the bench and Lucille to our own home—it was hard to say, "Auf Wiedersehen."

Greta and Elizabeth cried, but no doubt our gift of surplus food, gadgets and paraphernalia of living accumulated over the months helped assuage their grief.

Parting with Ewald was hard, but happiness came in the knowledge he would be coming to America. Since Russia had swallowed up the little country of Estonia, Ewald and his fellow compatriots did not dare return, as they would be considered "capitalists." They were all looking for a chance to go to Canada, Australia or the United States; since the latter's immigration laws were the more stringent, most of them went to Canada or Australia, but Ewald held out for his chance to go to America. Before leaving, we drove to Munich to see the American consul-general where Ewald filed his application to immigrate to America and I signed as his sponsor. In August 1948 he drove us to Bremerhaven and our parting words were: "Till we meet again."

That dream came true within a year when he arrived at the Union Station in Seattle, where I met him and took him home to live with us at PunkinBill Farm for several months. He studied English which he'd started to learn from our *Life* magazines with pictures in Nuremberg. The farm jeep was his transportation. He got a job operating a blueberry farm and continued his studies; today he is chief engineer for Van de Kamp's Bakery. Since 1969 he has been a volunteer member of the Rescue Ski Patrol. He and his wife, Marge, have two children in college; he certainly justified our faith in him, and we take great pride in what he has accomplished.

The voyage home was quite different than the one in October 1947. The *General Patrick* was a troop carrier during the war, but we were told $6,000,000 had been spent to reconvert her to a luxury liner, and that she was. Judge Anderson and his wife and Judge Daly were with us, and we spent many hours reminiscing about life in Germany.

Before we sailed, we were called to the purser's office where all army script was changed into real cash—American money! It was good to see those familiar greenbacks again—they seemed worth more.

Then came the last day when we stood on deck and saw America's Great Lady holding up her lamp to light our way home! I wondered if any American, having that same experience, doesn't say a quiet prayer of thanks for the privilege of being one. I thought of the millions to whom America has given sanctuary—the tired, the poor, the homeless and tempest-tossed.

After a visit with Zorka and Don Oenslager in New York, we went on to Michigan to visit with all the family; also Dean Bates at Ann Arbor, who said, "Aren't you glad you decided to be a lawyer instead of a cheerleader?" What a memory!

Then west, stopping in Yakima for a reunion with Lucille's family, and finally home to PunkinBill Farm.

Yes, the land kept!

5th Division Monument

Revisit (1948) to the billet at Oberbruck in 1918.

The gravel pit in 1948.

Susie serving Cornish pasties.

Aunt Agnes and Uncle Will

First and Last House in England

Uncle Will and John

CHAPTER X

And Then There Were Seven

(1952)

Late in the fall of 1951, while I was sitting as judge on the probate calendar, an old friend came to me asking for help. He had been appointed the guardian of a family of five children whose mother and father died while we were in Nuremberg.

"Bill," he said, "this is a tragic situation. There's an elderly housekeeper who hires a flock of help in that big old house of theirs, but nothing is done for the children's happiness. My wife and I go there to collect the monthly bills and check on the household management; she cries when we leave and is depressed for days. Frankly, so am I. Something *has* to be done."

Lucille and I spent hours discussing the situation, our hearts filled with concern. Perhaps our solicitude was greater because we'd known the children's parents in a lawyer-client relationship and of their deaths within three months of each other. Friends who might be interested were called. Couples who might be willing to take on the job as foster parents were interviewed with no success. One day, as we sat talking about the possible fate of those children, Lucille sat bolt upright and said: "Why don't *we* adopt them?"

To say the least, the idea was a startling one. I was 55; Lucille was 46. Married for 24 years, we had developed a completeness between ourselves. A solo duet, so to speak. This would be a whole new chorus to learn and direct. To this point we'd been free agents to pick up and go where we pleased, or stay home by the fire and do nothing. Content and secure with our lot in life, did we want to change it? The more we talked, though, the more it seemed a part of our destiny. That it was *meant*. We didn't think of it as a job that had to be done; rather, an opportunity to extend and share the happiness with which we had been so richly blessed.

From then on it became "The Great Adventure." We believed we could be objective enough to make important decisions in the lives of these youngsters. . .*but*. . .we would *not* act impulsively. So we set up a plan.

First, we visited the children to get acquainted. On several occasions we collected them and brought them out to the farm for picnics as well as Thanksgiving dinner. Christmas day we went to their house about 6:30 expecting to find a group of happy children around a Christmas tree. Instead, we found the housekeeper in the dining room with her own relatives, the maid clearing the table for them. We wished them a Merry Christmas, then asked, "Where are the children?"

"Oh," the housekeeper said, "they're upstairs." We found each child in his or her own room, moping and forlorn. Some were reading; some experimented with a new toy. When we left them, our hearts ached. As we reached the car, Lucille was crying.

"*Next* Christmas," she said, with feeling, "things at our house will be *very different!*"

So, the decision was made. Never a thought for the psychological impact, the change in lifestyle, the extra hours of devotion to young lives and the attendant responsibilities and important daily decisions. Some of our friends said we were crazy; others, noble. It was neither. Actually, looking back, we know it was selfish. We wouldn't be young parents. We had, perhaps, more wisdom, but certainly neither the endurance nor the viewpoint of younger parents from which to base those decisions. We just *wanted* to be of help.

On their next visit to the farm we all sat around a bonfire and roasted weinies. Dennis was 15; Jay 13; Jensen 11; Jeannie 8 and Virginia (Ginger) 5. When we asked them if they would like to be adopted by us, take our name and come to live with us, the chorus was "Yes!" Loud and unanimous. They even solemnly promised they would not be house wreckers!

Fortunately, the children's father had left a trust fund which provided for their education, summer camps and other activities under the supervision of the trustee.

Then came another remodeling job, and a mortgage on the "free and clear" PunkinBill Farm. The little house was to become a big house. An architect drew plans for additions—three bedrooms for the boys on the first level, dormers upstairs to create a bedroom and playroom for the girls, more bathrooms, a large extension to the old living room with view windows and a fireplace wall, a recreation room and workshop under the new living room and bedroom wing. The old living room became the dining room, the large kitchen stayed the same, the laundry was moved downstairs, and the room and bath off the kitchen became quarters for the help. One of our first decisions had been that there had to be a live-in babysitter.

Later a large studio room with a Pullman kitchen at one end was added to the guesthouse which had been built a few years earlier. From a church he'd recently completed, our builder procured some beautiful large surplus beams with which to erect the high cathedral ceiling. A free-standing circulating fireplace was decorative as well as utilitarian. Here was Lucille's studio and a quiet retreat for us when the kids had the TV or radio blasting.

During the remodeling Lucille and I moved in with the children in their house in town. They had had so many changes in authority we knew they were more apprehensive about us than we were about them, so we tried to be permissive—with discretion. The banister in the front hall was a prime example. It was a long run with several graceful curves—a temptation to any child—but we suspected hitherto it had been forbidden territory. Seeing the gleam in Jeannie's eyes one day, we said, "Go ahead, try it." We were *in* like Flynn. Until the day we moved back to the farm, they never walked down the stairs. Just to hear their shouts of laughter as they rode down gave us as much pleasure as it did them.

Religion was an important concern. The court's guardian had had all the children baptized at St. Mark's Episcopal Cathedral. Why not us too? The catechism was studied, and we were baptized by Bishop Stephen Bayne. Our regular church near PunkinBill Farm was to be St. Thomas.

The parishoners—many of them our neighbors—must have had mixed thoughts when they saw us march in with five children! Father Arthur A. Vall Spinosa, our neighbor of many years, kissed Lucille. A member of the congregation who had seven children told us tears came to his eyes when he saw us. Later he told us, "I said to myself then—they don't know what they're getting into!"

Until they felt secure enough to call us Mom and Dad, the children settled for Bill and Punkie. Several times they teased me by addressing me as "Wootsie" after they heard Lucille use it. They were fascinated with her vivacious, enthusiastic, sometimes volatile personality. Lucille Ball was then in her heyday, and they watched the "I Love Lucy" show every night. Often we'd hear them laugh and yell: "Just like Punkie! Just like Punkie!"

Weather permitting, I'd drive to the farm after court, build a fire and do some clean-up work. When school was out, Lucille filled a portable oven with hot food, piled the kids in the car, and they joined me for a work session and a picnic dinner. To them, the city house had been a prison; the farm was a fun place with pets which they'd never had and real country outdoors living filled with constant activity.

During the years they'd lived without parents, the natural instinct was to look after each other. Dennis was the father figure; little Jeannie mothered the brood. She still does. Through the years the togetherness we developed as a family has grown stronger. Hardly a day passes the children are not in communication with each other either by phone or a visit. The grapevine brings us the news of all happenings. If it's bad news, they have worked the problem out together, and it sounds fair to good by the time it gets to us.

We vowed we'd be objective, but we couldn't help getting emotionally involved. Those moppets wormed their way into our hearts, and we came to love them as dearly as we would our own. The only regret was there were never enough hours in the day, nor enough strength, to do as much as we would have liked for them. How many parents can find the time to sit down and listen to all the problems, big or little, that crop up daily? We coped with them each day as best we could, and as the children came to trust us, they knew they could come to us at any time, if they needed help.

We soon learned, as in every family, the real brunt of child rearing is the mother's. Fathers, at best, are the backup part of the team, but a team it must be and one that pulls together. Lucille studied child psychology and took instruction at the "Y" in Brownie and Girl Scout leadership. These groups met in our rec room where art classes were also held.

The boys were boarding students at Lakeside School, coming home for occasional weekends and holidays. Lucien Perrot, a bachelor friend, "uncle" by adoption, who taught French at Cornish School, and Lucille's sister, Aunt Sally, loved our boys and devoted many hours to them.

I don't pretend it was an *easy* process. We had troubles; we encountered the usual bouts of hostility. We had our escape hatches where we went to catch our breath and recharge our batteries. We had all the ups and downs of the average family except we all tried harder because of the circumstances of our coming together. In memory, the things Lucille and I cherish are the happy faces of our kids, their good health and vitality and appreciation of happiness, their good minds and their achievements. This is the real reward.

There was Ginger who used to go into a tantrum when Lucille combed her tangled hair. On such occasions, applying her child psychology, Lucille took Ginger, arms and legs flailing, in her arms and hugged her tight until the outburst subsided. And it worked!

There was the morning our first week back at the farm, as we were sitting down to breakfast, when someone said: "I smell smoke!" We all rushed upstairs to find flames in Jeannie and Ginger's playroom. They'd taken a chenille bedspread from the storage closet to make the roof of their "tent" and draped it over a lighted floor lamp. It had smoldered for some time and only then burst into flames, scorching a door. A handy fire extinguisher saved the day. And one more lesson was learned.

In the San Juan Islands, Four Winds, a camp for girls on Orcas where a fabulous inspiring leader, Ruth Brown, was the owner and director, and Hendersons' Camp for boys on Lopez, where Lucille and Frank Henderson (affectionately called by the kids "Rabbit and Tyee") gave their all in unexcelled leadership, were wonderful childhood adventures. That first summer, while we were still bogged down in the remodeling job, Jeannie and Ginger left for camp, pale and wan, timid about a new experience. Three weeks later when we visited Four Winds we found them tanned and rosy-cheeked. As we drove to the island inn where we all spent the weekend, they laughed and sang the camp songs they'd learned. It was their first camping experience and a great success.

The same was true of Dennis, Jay and Jensen at Hendersons' where they were kept active from morning till night. There they learned to participate in sports—riding, sailing, canoeing, swimming, hiking, baseball—and crafts. Our kids have never forgotten camp life.

Dennis became a counselor during his last year. A few years later Ginger was invited to be a counselor at Four Winds with complete charge of the string of horses. She took her own horse along, went up two weeks early and repaired all the harness and gear. She even trained her horse to pull the gig Ruth Brown had brought from Ireland and drove it, piled with kids, to get the mail each day. Once, when "Christmas" was declared because of rain, Ginger arrived with a load of kids as Santa Claus bounded out of the bushes. Frightened by the sudden movement, the horse bolted and ran. The gig tipped over, spilling kids in all directions, but no one was hurt.

By the end of the first camp season the house at PunkinBill Farm was finished. Lucille and I had moved the children's bedroom furniture, all their toys and "sacred paraphernalia"—books, bric-a-brac, "junque," you name it—as well as what furniture could be used in the house, especially those pieces of sentimental value to them. When the kids came home from camp, everything was in place, and we settled down to life on the farm.

We soon learned that Dennis, along with being big BIG brother, was an avid reader and enthusiastic woodworker. Every spare moment found him deep in a book—science fiction especially—or in the workshop creating *something*. He became adept with all kinds of sophisticated tools, and this love of craftsmanship developed from a hobby to the building of fine homes. His good reading habits doubtless helped put his name on the honor roll.

Jay was the mechanic. He spent hours taking things apart, sometimes to our consternation, but always got them back together and running smoothly even though a few loose screws and bolts were lying about when he finished. He loved gadgets, and now that he can afford to indulge his hobby, his minifarm and home are equipped with every mechanical device for convenience, all kept in tiptop condition.

He was often referred to by his teachers at Lakeside as "the Plugger." He always made the grade albeit he had to struggle at times. A good football player, he received his varsity letter the year of his graduation.

Dexter Strong, headmaster of Lakeside, told us a good story about Jay. On filling out an inquiry given to seniors as to a choice of college, Jay wrote: "I have already been *excepted* by Menlo."

Jensen was the nature lover. This became evident while he was at Hendersons' Camp on Lopez Island, where he found some interesting fossils and artifacts while spending hours exploring the woods and streams. His greatest love was fishing. He could sit patiently hour after hour dangling his baited hook. It seemed to make little difference to him whether he hooked a small bullhead or a big salmon just so long as he could play the fish on his line. Once, while trolling with small herring on our lines, a seagull swooped down and grabbed Jensen's bait. Jensen had himself a seagull and was filled with joy, but I had to cut his line to free the gull.

He was also a tease and thoroughly enjoyed badgering his two little sisters. When a couple of mattresses were delivered, he suggested the big cardboard boxes they came in would make fine boats for the small pond. Looking out the window, we spied the girls in the middle of the pond, shouting to Jensen as the water seeped in and ran over the edges. Within moments they went down with their ship. Since the water wasn't deep and the weather was warm, there wasn't any real danger. I have to confess we laughted almost as hard as Jensen while he danced around, pointing at the girls who wallowed out, dripping mud.

At eight Jeannie was an active child and born athlete. Give her water to swim in, a mountain to ski down, a tennis court to play on, a horse to ride—she could do it! There at PunkinBill Farm she had plenty of room to release all that activity. She and Ginger, who was five when they came to us, turned to horses and in time became skilled equestriennes. Jeannie's abilities in other sports, however, opened up new fields for her to conquer. She went in for competitive swimming and was recognized early by her ski instructors as Olympic Games material, but gave it up to become a wife and mother.

As a young child, Ginger was first an artist. Recognizing her love for painting, we provided plenty of art supplies for her busy little hands. She also loved animals, and they her, so it was natural she would go for the horses at Four Winds—a hobby she rode for years. Later, she went back to her art studies and became a talented painter.

That first Christmas was certainly different. Preparations began months ahead. The workshop door was locked and declared "out of bounds." Here the presents and wrappings piled up until Mr. and Mrs. Claus had time to wrap them. The biggest tree possible was found for the living room, one for the rec room, and a tree of branches was made on the dining room wall to hang the Christmas cards on with bright red ribbons. The kids spent hours stringing popcorn and cranberries, and the whole house was redolent with the endless Christmas baking.

When The Day came, our youngest was almost hysterical with excitement, but by the time the bird, plump and golden brown, came from the oven, she'd calmed down. It was truly a wonderful day for all of us!

As parents we learned to give and take too. One summer we collected Ginger in the cruiser we'd bought, which also occasionally served as an escape hatch. After visiting the boys at Hendersons' Camp, we anchored the first night at Mud Bay off Lopez Island. At daybreak we woke to find the boat listing to starboard, high and dry. The tide was unusually low, and clams were squirting all over the beach. Ginger, who was very fond of steamed clams, looked longingly at all that largesse. She knew, however, that I loved those extra hours of sleep on holidays. Peering through the porthole, she couldn't restrain herself longer.

"Please," she said in a small plaintive voice no father could refuse, "couldn't we take naps this afternoon and go clamming *now?*" So out came the shovels and we bagged a big sackful. There were some anxious moments waiting for our boat to right itself. Ginger had taken the small dingy to row along the shore line, when an oar lock broke off, and she was at the mercy of the current which was gradually taking her out to wide water. What a relief when the tide rose high enough for us to start the motor and cruise out to collect that kid and start for home!

In sharing memories of our childhood, I had told Lucille of my glee on those rare occasions when I came home from school to find a jar of jam and a fresh loaf of bread on the kitchen table for us to eat, of the times I'd sneak into the pantry and filch a handful of raisins from the baking supplies. She said their table was always loaded with goodies for the hungry home-from-school gang. So another decision was to give our kids carte blanche to the storeroom with its shelves filled with canned fruit and jams and jellies—the bounty of our labors. No greater appreciation could be shown than the rapid disappearance of the hoard.

Part of the children's experience in the new house was learning about the antiques and collectables we had gathered during our 24 years together.

Lucille told them about the pioneer background of the old bedroom set. She also explained about the fruitwood "rope" bed, circa 1780, with pineapple posters and the wooden knobs still on the hand-turned rails which were originally used to string rope to support a straw mattress. No box springs in those days. After that the kids used to tease: "Punkie sleeps on old antiques!"

White Cloud and Ranger were the first horses to inhabit the barn, an old converted chicken house. The girls brought them home to board for the winter when they returned from Four Winds; we called them the hay-balers. Everybody rode, the only mishap when Ranger ran with Ginger on his back under an apple tree and she got a bad bump on her head.

The next year we found a beautiful palomino mare named Venus for Jeannie and a Welsh pony for Ginger which she named Buster. He was a character. In his stubborn way he loved children; he never bit or kicked and allowed kids to pile on his back to play "cops and robbers" or "Indians," but he sure knew how to indicate when he'd had enough of games. He seldom bucked but had a trick of making a sudden turn and unseating everyone but Ginger. In spite of his mischievousness everyone adored him. He was swift and strong and had no problem keeping up with the neighborhood children's horses. When he got too obstreperous because he'd not been ridden for a while, he was tied by his halter to the back of the jeep and given a fast run.

Wheels spelled happiness for the kids. The jeep provided the most fun and hours of entertainment for them all. Each one in turn learned to drive. Dennis was the first, under the mandate it was not to be driven outside the fenced-in farm. A secondhand gang mower we bought from a golf course cut the grass, the jeep pulling it all over the upper six acres. It took expert handling to sashay around the trees in the orchard, but Dennis was a natural. All the kids piled in for the ride with the admonition: "Keep your *fannies* on the *seats!*"

There were two mishaps. The first, the day Mary Ashley ran over a peach tree. However, it straightened up and produced a bountiful crop! The other happened during the boys' picnic for their Lakeside friends when Timmy Leffler fell out of the overcrowded jeep and the rear wheels ran over his legs. He came limping in to the house and rested a while, but there were no signs of serious injury and soon he rejoined the gang. With some embarrassment I called his father to report the incident. The next day he called back to say Timmy was fine!

During the winter the jeep, with its four-wheel drive, was a blessing. When it snowed, the hillside street was roped off against traffic and the kids had great sledding. The jeep would be waiting at the bottom of the hill to drag a flock of sleds back up for the next run. At Christmas time it took us caroling to all the neighbors' homes.

A huge old maple on the "lower five" was an ideal setting for a tree house. The kids spent one whole summer building it, and their efforts provided many hours of fun. Jeannie was the only one to fall out of it, with resultant bruises, of course. The day they painted the house they insisted on sleeping in it that night. The next morning their sleeping bags looked as if they'd been used for camouflage.

A sandy patch at the top of the farm made an attractive play area. One day the kids invited us to come see the sandcastle they'd built. As we came nearer for a close inspection, down we toppled! They'd made a tiger trap, a dugout 2 × 4 feet and about 2 feet deep filled with crumpled newspaper and covered with a sheet of brown wrapping paper camouflaged with a thin layer of sand. A whole day's entertainment—at our expense! We were learning that parents as well as children had to be tough to survive.

The boys were constantly playing jokes on me. Restaurant dinners were a great treat. As I was paying the check one night at a well known restaurant where we often had dinner, the cashier gave me a strange, very cool stare. When I discovered several pieces of silverware protruding from the lapel pocket of my jacket, all three boys roared with laughter. Fortunately, the cashier had a sense of humor.

On opening a drawer to get out my pajamas one evening, I saw two garden snakes slither over the clean clothes. The instigator of such tricks could never be detected; they all remained close-mouthed. No tattletales in our family. One for all and all for one was their motto.

Skiing was a must activity—the greatest. The Hendersons operated a ski camp at Snoqualmie where all five kids learned to ski. It was a thrill for us to visit there on a Sunday and observe the happy rosy faces in that winter wonderland. As they grew older, they joined various skiing groups that took them to the high slopes in buses.

During those active years of parenthood, as well as court work, the pressure of activities in the Shrine where I then had the position of High Priest and Prophet were increasing. Having joined the Masonic Lodge in Michigan in 1919 and affiliated with La Fayette Lodge in Seattle soon after my arrival, I eventually joined the Shrine. Nile Temple was made up of a splendid group of public spirited men, and the meetings and social activities were enjoyable. In 1951 I had been elected Oriental Guide, the position on the bottom of the ladder of the elective Divan leading to the office of Potentate in four years.

Without question, one of the most thrilling events of my life occurred when I was asked by our Potentate, Ray Eckman, to respond to an address by General Douglas MacArthur, who had been initiated into Nile Temple while our Potentate and his Divan were in the Philippines on an official visit.

Since World War I when General MacArthur commanded a Brigade of the famous 42nd (Rainbow) Division, I'd been an ardent admirer of his. With great humility I accepted Ray Eckman's request. On November 14, 1951, MacArthur made his first visit to his home Temple where thousands of members of Nile extended him an outstanding ovation. His address at that time was most inspiring.

As I stood at the podium to give my response to General Mac Arthur, I looked out over our Shrine auditorium, and it seemed as if Nobles in their red fezzes were, literally, hanging from the rafters. Some 5,000 yelling enthusiastic Shriners were whooping it up as only they can. Yet my heart pounded so hard in my ears it all but drowned the screams of the crowd. The accompanying letter from General MacArthur is one of my prized possessions.

However, though the functions of the Divan were inspiring and socially great fun, Lucille and I found we were attending cocktail parties, Shrine club meetings, official visits with dinners and dancing afterward, as she put it: "eight nights a week." Sometimes we had to ferry across Puget Sound late at night from some function only to have to get up early the next morning to face our new responsibilities along with the old ones. Finally, with deep regret, I decided to resign from the Divan and submitted my resignation.

Years passed before Lucille finally found time to paint. But when the Frye Art Museum presented scholarship classes under the direction of Gerald Grace, an inspiring teacher, she was invited to join and attended weekly sessions. She learned many new techniques and skills and has many times expressed her gratitude to the museum for the privilege of studying with Gerald Grace.

By the late 1950s our young horsewomen had graduated to riding in Bridle Trails State Park where there were 52 miles of trails. Involving increased traffic and the crossing of a narrow railroad overpass, the route to the park had become hazardous for riders. Often on the way we'd noticed a place called Tripple Creek Ranch—a paraphrase on Cripple Creek in Colorado. Ten and a half acres had been developed especially for horse lovers with pastures, meadows, three streams and a training ring, all nestled against a background of old cedar and maple trees laced with delicate vine maples that sent their flame through the woods in autumn. The rambling ranch house had a large all-purpose room with kitchen and fireplace. This was separated from the large box stalls for the horses by hay storage and tack rooms.

Acting on impulse at Christmas 1958, we wrote a note on our card to Ross Sweet, owner of the place and former neighbor in Broadmoor. "If you ever want to sell Tripple Creek Ranch, will you let us know?" He shot back a reply. "I do, and you can have first crack at it." Several months before, Dick Montgomery, a neighbor with seven young sons, had asked if we wanted to sell PunkinBill Farm. We did a three-way switch in record time. Ross got the money, we got Tripple Creek Ranch and Dick got the house and an acre of PunkinBill Farm.

It all happened so fast we'd had no time to seriously consider the ramifications—another remodeling job—though we were, by then, real veterans at restoration. What better hobby? Dennis and Jay were married and Jensen about to be, so we didn't require as large a house. At least, on looking at a picture of that house and seeing the expanse of roof, I can say we didn't require as many *rooms*.

Lucille had already spotted another log house across the road from Tripple Creek Ranch. Built by an early pioneer, it had long since been abandoned but those boys built well.

"Can't you imagine," Lucille said the day she took me to see it, "how *charming* that would look in this new setting?"

I laughed. "I can imagine the *charm,* darling," I said, "but it'll be a devil of a job moving the thing. But you go ahead and see what you can do."

That was all she needed. With her, to think is to act; all obstacles seem to fall away before her determination and enthusiasm. She located the owner of the log house who was glad to sell it for, as he put it, "one year's rental."

If that old log house could talk, it would tell of the Alvin Goff family who crossed the plains in a covered wagon and eventually took a homestead of 120 acres at that location in 1884. Always, with pioneers, the first thought is a permanent shelter. Using the oxen team that brought their wagon west, the Goffs built a skid road, cut the large old cedar trees on the place, then hand-adzed the logs down to a standard thickness of 8 inches so the walls would be straight-sided and level. Helped by pulleys and hoists, the oxen pulled the heavy timbers into place. Uncle Dan, a millwright who made the trek west with the Goffs, did the skillful adzing and mortising of the corners into a tight rainproof job.

The house would tell too of the housewarming, the births, the deaths, the weddings, Thanksgivings and Christmases and Easters, the children and grandchildren—all the sad and glad events that make up life.

We hired a man who'd had considerable experience in moving houses when the Seattle freeway was built to move the house across the road and set it on a concrete foundation. Later, another job entailed moving the studio-guest house from Clyde Hill, annexing it to the log house and converting it to a library, dining room and kitchen.

With the assistance of John Rushmore & Associates, architects, the group of assorted structures was brought together harmoniously into a rambling ranch house with covered decks, carport, porches, and a hand-split shake roof covering all. I have always thought the architects first looked at our plans, then at us as if we were freaks. In an age when most people tore down the old and started all over again, here were people who had moved two buildings—one a log house almost 100 years old—from two different spots and wanted to incorporate them with a third. But, as the job progressed, I'm sure they not only looked on it as a challenge but actually enjoyed it as much as we did.

It was then up to us to adapt the old log house to life in the 1960s. Partitions were ripped out, making the four rooms on the first floor into a living room over 20 × 30 feet; the same for one large upstairs bedroom and sitting room. Logs between windows were removed to open up a vista of the stream, meadows and woods. Our main carpenter, Bill Bailey, had constructed log houses of hardwood in Oklahoma, and he worked on ours as a labor of love. We teased him about the old song: "Bill Bailey, Won't You Please Come Home?" He stayed until the job was completed, then he did go home.

Then began the same process of bringing the old logs to life. Layers of wallpaper, newspaper, building paper and burlap were ripped off. Endless numbers of tacks were dug out. The cedar logs then got the Fels Naphtha and brush routine until they were a soft light brown. The hand-adzed ceiling beams had been varnished and blackened, and it was necessary to use varnish remover to clean them. That was a job! The moss chinking was ripper out and replaced with a layer of fine cement, then plastered. Lucille glazed it with a mixture to match the color of the logs.

The log house and Clyde Hill structure were placed beside the stream with a carport connecting them to the remodeled existing ranch house now called the teenagers' wing where Jeannie and Ginger would be and the family room left about the same. That wing was made into cedar-paneled bedrooms, baths and laundry.

The trick gate copied from "Duel in the Sun" was moved next as well as the weathervane—the "gockel," or rooster—a handcrafted copy of the one on the oldest church in Nuremberg, the steeple of which had fallen topside up during a bombing raid where it was standing in 1947.

One day the man who'd moved the houses called and said: "You've got to come out to Georgetown now. We're taking something out of a Thriftway Frontier Village building you must have." What we found was an architect's dream—an old Western "false front," complete with real antique signs: "General Store" and "Rooms." We moved it along with a collection of old wagon wheels, a hitching post and early "junque." When we heard the barracks buildings on an old Nike site were for sale, we bought one, moved it across a second stream in a clearing in the woods and placed it behind the false front.

The interior walls were covered with burlap, a hugh pot-bellied stove provided heat and there was Lucille's new studio, 25 × 50, where she "painted up a storm!" Painting friends came for classes and as a group gave some benefit art shows. Lucille had painted oils, caseins, acrylics and collages throughout the years; now she learned a new technique when she was introduced to May Lee Mok, an artist from China, the wife of the Chinese ambassador to the Philippines who lost his life the fateful day in 1941 that the Japanese landed there. Befriended by her neighbor in Manila, General Douglas MacArthur, May Lee Mok eventually got to America and taught classes in Chinese calligraphy and ink brush painting. She once said to me, "Loo-see-oo has a Chinese way with the brush!" I agreed, and am proud of some of the beautiful paintings she has achieved with her simple ink-stone, ink-stick and brushes which are a length of bamboo into which are fixed the hairs of various animals.

That studio was put to many uses. Jensen set up his potter's wheel and kiln in one corner. There were teenagers' parties, charity parties, Christmas parties, judges' parties, and a Bonanza party to raise money for Overlake Memorial Hospital.

Lucille could hardly wait to get to the job of decorating the house—the frosting on the cake. And that was some cake! Our collection of Early Americana and furniture fit in so well it was a moot question whether they'd been designed for the house or the house for them. There was a special window with glass shelves in the entry to hold the colored hobnail glass, also built-in shelves in the living room for the pewter collection. There was a spot for a new Hammond organ and the spinet, which Lucille painted for PunkinBill Farm, to provide music and song.

A summer of beachcombing provided materials for the mural Lucille made from small pieces of driftwood—36 inches high and 96 inches wide—to face the cupboard that divided the dining room and kitchen area. With pictures from *Gourmet* Magazine she made a collage to cover the sliding doors on the kitchen side. Burlap was used for curtains and to cover some rough wood areas, pleated and tacked into place.

Throughout the house were Lucille's paintings, old Bavarian cookie molds, jugs, bottles, weeds, vegetables and fruits, the latter changing with the seasons.

Since horses were the reason for all this activity, they naturally played a big part in life at Tripple Creek Ranch. Neighbors came visiting on their mounts. Jeannie and Ginger rode to Jimmy Rainwater's riding academy for classes and all through Bridle Trails State Park. They were also involved in training their horses and competing in gymkhanas and shows. In time they found a pair of beautiful matched blacks they named Nanki Poo and Yum Yum.

The setting itself was so picturesque little landscaping was called for. A memorable trip to eastern Washington was made with the jeep and trailer to collect giant sagebrush. Long poles were taken along to poke around the bushes in case a rattlesnake rested there. On our first poke we flushed a big bull snake! Harmless, but a good alert. More snakes were encountered but none with rattles.

When the trailer was piled high and wide with the pungent lacy fronds, we tied them down and headed for home. As we drove merrily along, satisfied with our day's labor, a state patrol officer arrested us for carrying *too wide* a load and gave me a ticket. What price sagebrush? When it was arranged in large barrels along the covered porch, though, the smoky gray against the dark burnt-shingle brown of the board-and-batten construction was most effective. Crushed rock was laid in the entry court to cut back on maintenance and that was our landscaping job!

The waving grasses themselves were a part of the landscaping. In spring and summer the meadow was a continuous ripple of color as the grass heads turned mauve and yellow and brown; buttercups, dandelions, lady-slippers, gentian, clover, vetch and other wildflowers all sought their place in the sun. In autumn when the leaves in the wood turned, we had the lovely yellows and golds and oranges, russet, scarlet and red mixed with all shades of green.

After several months of house-moving, putting the parts together in a whole, remodeling and decorating, we finally moved in. As we sat in the new old living room of our old new log house, we all agreed it was the most delightful, funfull house we'd ever had.

The last touch was to come when we passed a lumber yard and spied a truckload of hand-split cedar rails salvaged from an old farm on Orcas Island. We bought the lot and built the fence that was a perfect frame for the new-old-antique-moved-remodeled "homestead" ranch house.

In 1962 the opportunity came to visit Spain, a country we passed up while in Nuremberg because of unsettled conditions. Dennis, Jay and Jensen had married, one after the other, according to their ages. Jeannie was in college which would have left Ginger home alone for the time we would be gone. With her enthusiastic cooperation Ginger was enrolled in school in Montreux, Switzerland. Lucille went over with her, then studied for two months with Ramon Nadal, a well-known artist in Palma, Majorca, where I joined her, along with Ginger and two school friends, at Thanksgiving.

The girls had a great time exploring the city and the beaches. When we chided them for their greediness at table, we got the reply, "Well, at our school, if you don't grab, you don't get!" They had said their holiday was two weeks, which seemed a bit long for Thanksgiving with the Christmas holiday coming up soon, and when mail from home eventually caught up with us, there was a frantic letter from the headmistress inquiring *where* the girls were as they'd been given only a four-day holiday. Those scamps had gone AWOL!

After they returned to school, Lucille and I explored the island of Majorca and the Iberian Peninsula, then settled down for the rest of our time in Torremolinos on the Costa del Sol. The Pez Espada was then the finest hotel there, but we saw the beginning of the great hotel-building era. With amazement we watched an endless string of donkeys carrying great leather bags filled with sand which workmen had scooped from the beach, shells and all. It was hard to believe this was the sand which made the cement which built all those modern high-rise hotels.

Ginger came for Christmas, this time for a legitimate two weeks, and we had a lovely fun time in sunny Spain worshipping sun and sea.

Great adventures in friendship came to us at Torremolinos. One day, while collecting shells on the beach, we met four handsome young men on holiday from the University of Madrid and invited them for luncheon to meet Ginger and her English school friend from London. In turn, Carlos Espejo, who soon gained the inside track with Ginger, introduced us to his family.

They were charming people. Colonel Espejo, quartermaster general of the Spanish army, had trained with the American army in West Virginia. He was proud of his American training and fond of Americans. The Espejos had a winter home, La Paloma, at Torremolinos and an apartment in Madrid where he was stationed. His wife and daughter joined us along with the "four musketeers," one of whom was Pedro Garcia-Pelayo, and British friends of ours for the gala Christmas party given by our hotel, also a week later for the New Year's Eve celebration. That was some celebration. So much confetti was thrown it came to our knees!

We had wonderful times with these new friends. When we arrived at the airport in Madrid, they were all there to meet us, invited us to their home and shared our sightseeing adventures. On our departure at the end of the holiday Colonel Espejo, resplendent in full Spanish army uniform, came with the boys to say goodbye. He had heard the Mitch Miller songs while in West Virginia, and on our return we sent him all the Mitch Miller records, which he loved.

The most rewarding part of our trip, however, was making the acquaintance of Pedro Garcia-Pelayo, who was graduating from the university in hotel management. His parents died early in his youth, and his brothers had helped him while in college, but after that he would be on his own. Learning of his desire to go to America, one shared by most young men there, we sponsored him to come to the United States. Through the help of Lynn Himmelman of Western Hotels, Pedro was assured a job in Seattle. Within a year he arrived with his lovely bride Wanda. As the last of our kids were off to college or married, he and Wanda moved into the teenagers' wing for several months.

Pedro is another success story. Long hours of study, hard work and enterprise proved that America is still "the land of opportunity." He now owns and operates with Wanda's help three successful antique shops. Wanda, an artist who met Pedro in Madrid while on an art scholarship from Buenos Aires, and Lucille share art as their common hobby, painted together, and were invited to give a two-person show at the Cellar Art Gallery in Kirkland. Pedro was also to play an important role in a real crisis in our lives.

From my own experience I knew the importance of a good education, but not until I was a parent, keenly aware of our children's progress from day to day, did I realize what a large role schools play in molding the minds and character of students. Adequate praise cannot be given to those men and women who dedicate their lives to teaching, and we can never fully express our gratitude for the help good schools gave our kids. All of them went on to college.

After receiving his BA and law degrees at the University of Washington, Dennis went into the army through ROTC and had courses at the Infantry, Intelligence and German Language schools. Being fluent in German, he was assigned to Germany where he served as a captain in counter-intelligence. His wife Kathy and young son Bob were in Germany with him. With less than a year to serve, he was suddenly transferred to Viet Nam where he spoke neither French or Vietnamese. He served a year and was decorated by the then Vietnamese government. He was a good soldier, quite a contrast to the protestors, especially those who went to Canada to avoid serving their country! He is now with Williams Instrumentation Consultants.

Jay's warm and friendly personality grew stronger through the years and, no doubt, helped him become a successful businessman. He is adored by his three children and his many nieces and nephews. On weekends his recreation vehicle is piled with kids going camping, canoeing down the Yakima River, water-skiing, snow skiing and many other sport activities. Eating is always a great part of every occasion with Uncle Jay stopping at drive-ins for hamburgers, French fries, ice cream, popcorn and candy! He and Marianne recently bought a house with considerable acreage near Issaquah. They have a large vegetable garden and are enjoying their hobby.

Jensen's creative talent, which won him art awards in high school, was expressed at the potter's wheel. Those years of potting culminated in the building of a large studio on his home acreage at Woodinville. There he has several large kilns and creates beautiful designs and glazes. The quality of his work is indicated by the reputation he has in the Pacific Northwest with more invitations to exhibit than he is able to accept. His wife Karen spends long hours in the studio creating designs and as general handylady. With four kids to support they have to keep the potter's wheel turning.

Jeannie continues to mother the whole family along with her three kids. Like Dennis, she is a prolific reader and our mentor as to the worth of bestsellers. She and her husband Don have a large home on acreage at Woodinville with a swimming pool, horses and dogs, and love country life. Jeannie has also been successful in investing and developing real estate.

Today Ginger has some outstanding paintings to her credit, has won many awards, is a successful commercial artist and holds art classes for children on Saturdays. Her daughter, whom we call Cinnamon, already shows signs of having inherited her mother's talent. On four acres at Olivenhain in San Diego County Ginger and Colby have a home which they designed and built with their own hands, the first room finished being the "Studio." There is, of course, a corral and ring for horses, and rail fences. As part of the landscaping they created a small lake with a stone house in the middle—safe from coyotes—for their tame ducks.

Out of five weddings we had the fun of planning and producing—and I use that word advisedly—two weddings. Jeannie wanted to be married at Tripple Creek Ranch with just family and a few intimate friends. It was a small wedding but *not* a quiet one. The family had grown, and all those dear young people filled the house with laughter.

Ginger was married by Father Vall Spinosa in St. Thomas Episcopal Church with a reception at home. Once again the house was filled with family and good friends. There was never any concern about guests enjoying themselves. That old house was an "ice-breaker" and conversation piece. It didn't need embellishment, but the flowers and candlelight and wine added a sparkle to those special occasions.

We are proud of our children and their wives and husbands. We are proud of their accomplishments and the fact they are all living up to their potential. They have done it on their own; all we did was give them love and encouragement and understanding. They are happy kids doing what they like to do. Perhaps the greatest testimonial to the love and energy we put into raising them is the fact they all have chosen country homes with enough land to have pets and the active life they had when they came to PunkinBill Farm.

Now there are 25 of us, adding daughters- and sons-in-law and 13 grandchildren! And speaking of grandchildren, this book would not be complete without one grandchild story.

Recently, while visiting on the phone with one of my granddaughters, I told her we were getting ready to go to the Opera House to hear Pavarotti sing in recital.

"He's the greatest tenor since Caruso," I said. "Do you know who Caruso was?"

There was a pause, then she asked, "Was it Robinson Caruso?"

Family gatherings are frequent happy occasions and communications filled with interesting news. Looking back over 50 happy years together, Lucille and I agree the greatest joy has come to us through *our five kids.*

November, 1952

The gate at PunkinBill Farm.

Dennis

Jay

Jay: charging tackle. (Back, third left)

Jeannie

Jensen in art class.

Children's pet (Virginia)

Jeannie and Ginger on Nanky Poo and Yum Yum.

A few of the grandchildren.

1954

1980

Tripple Creek Ranch–it took a lot of imagination!

The "spread," Tripple Creek Ranch.

A covered deck crosses the stream.

One end of the living room.

Living room.

Original stairway opened to living room.

The guest bedroom moved from PunkinBill Farm becomes a library-music room.

The inherited bedroom set.

The studio becomes a dining room.

Hosts at the "Bonanza" party.

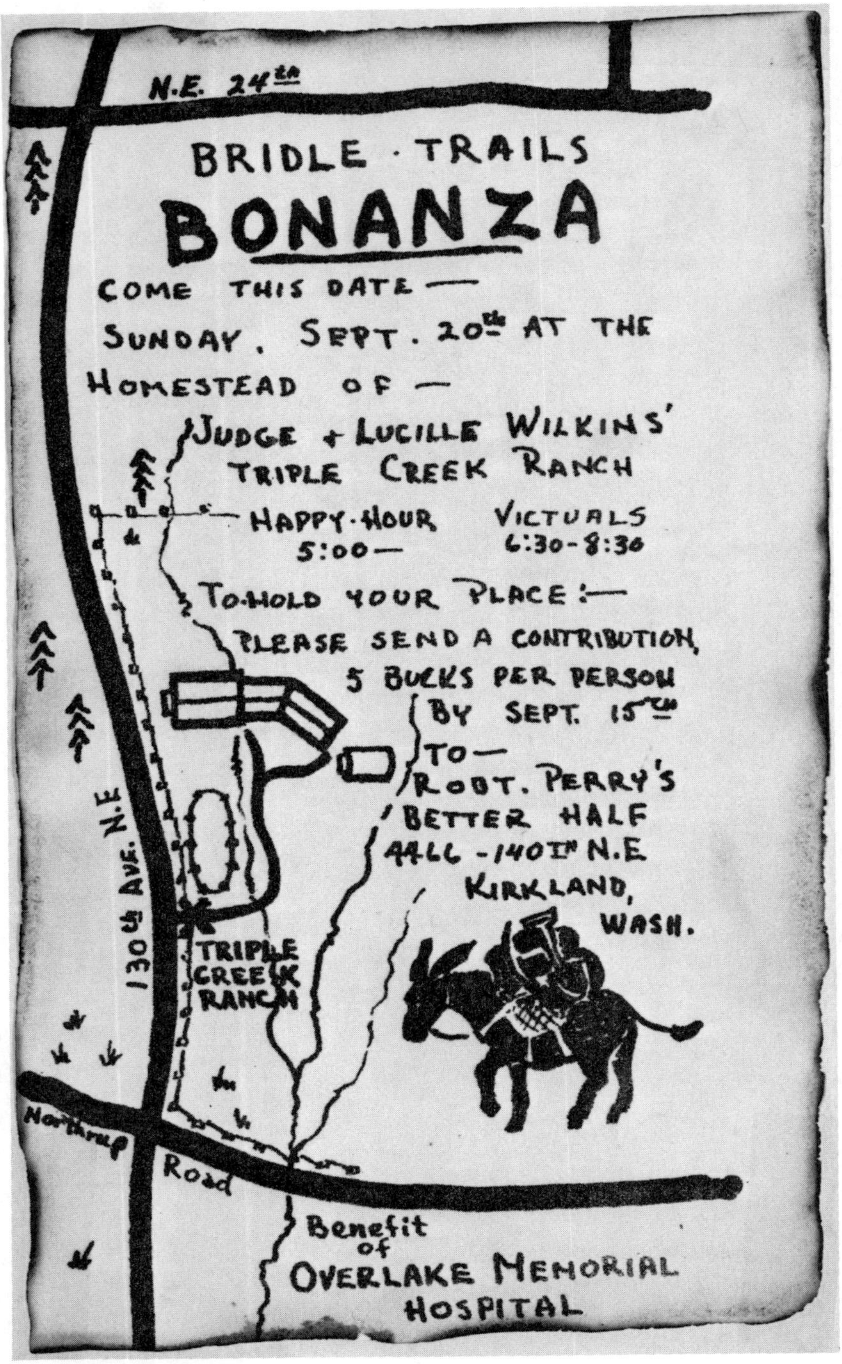

Bridle Trails Bonanza.

The studio.

Twentieth Anniversary of Gen. MacArthur's Visit Here

At this Armistice Day Season we, of Nile Temple, think back to 20 years this November 14, to the visit here of General Douglas MacArthur, one of Nile Temple's all-time most distinguished members.

Judge (Noble) William J. Wilkins gave the address of welcome and said, in part:

"In the years—in the centuries ahead—so long as this Republic of ours continues to exist—and long after the names of those now at the helm of our government have been forgotten—your name, the name of General Douglas MacArthur, will be known to every American school child. The military strategy employed by you in your long, hard victorious trek all the way back from Australia to the Philippines—and on to Japan—in Korea—at Inchon, will be studied, discussed and put into practice by students of Military Science and Tactics throughout the world.

"These American school children will also know that your administration of the civil affairs of Japan following the close of the war in the Pacific was the first successful administration of a conquered country by an occupying army.

"Moreover, history will record that you demonstrated your true greatness as an American when, upon your return to these shores—unselfishly and without rancor—you gave freely of your time, as you did last night, in bringing forcibly to the American people the true conditions, both at home and abroad, as they confront us today—and you have revived our spirits and our will to fight.

"But General MacArthur, we are proud of you because you typify and represent, better than anyone else, the high ideals of Masonry and Shrinedom—you possess to a high degree great moral courage—sterling honesty—a sincere belief in fair play and in your follow man—and, in the words of our Shrine Ritual, you have give us 'an example of a clean, honorable, wholesome and manly life'."

Twentieth anniversary of Gen. MacArthur's visit here.

Douglas MacArthur letter

90 Church Street
New York 7, N.Y.

28 November 1951

Dear Judge Wilkins:

Thank you so much for your note of November 16th and the copy of your remarks at Nile Temple on the 14th. It was a great satisfaction to be able to visit Nile at long last and to be given such a wonderful welcome by my brother Nobles. Please give them all my most cordial good wishes.

With renewed thanks and fraternal greetings,

Yours sincerely,

DOUGLAS MacARTHUR.

CHAPTER XI

The Bench

(1945-1972)

From 1945 through 1972 my return to the bench was interrupted twice—the War Crimes Trial in Nuremberg (1947-1948) and a brief recall to active duty during the Korean conflict in 1950.

Since release from active service in September 1945, I had remained in the Judge Advocate Reserve section of the air force, in charge of the squadron comprising the air judge advocate members in the Seattle area. During that time we were ordered to McChord Field at Tacoma for brief periods of active duty. In 1950 after another military leave was granted, I reported to the commanding general of the Fourth Air Force at Hamilton Field, California, and was assigned by Major General Alvan C. Kincaid to be the deferment officer.

Air reservists were being called up on short notice, a hardship for many. Those needing additional time to put their businesses and homes in order reported to me. Most requests for deferment were for short periods—a matter of days—the average request being for a week or 10 days. No permanent deferments were requested. The morale of those air reservists was high, and their enthusiasm and spirit were commendable.

Lucille decided to stay in Bellevue, so I was assigned to bachelor officers quarters where I met Colonel James L. Tarr, then adjutant general of the Fourth Air Force. After three months the recall of air reservists slowed down, and I was released from active duty to return to the bench. Lucille drove down to collect me, accompanied by her sister Cathy from Yakima, a widow for some years. Jim Tarr and I had become good friends, and before we left, he invited us on a fishing trip in

San Francisco Bay. The weather was good, the company congenial and the fish were biting, all of which combined to make a most enjoyable trip. It was then the mutual attraction between Cathy and Jim began, one that eventually blossomed into romance and marriage. They were married in October 1951 in our home in Bellevue.

Jim, at one time a star end on the football team at the University of Missouri, had a distinguished military career in World War II, in the army and the air force to which he subsequently transferred. After their marriage he and Cathy were stationed in Tokyo where Jim was adjutant general of the Fifth Air Force, then in Washington, DC where he was the air adjutant general. Among the many medals he received were the Legion of Merit with four oak leaf clusters and the French Legion of Honor and croix de guerre. They have since retired and live in Vista, California.

A highlight of my first year back in harness was the privilege of acting as one of the hosts to Admiral Halsey in 1946 when he was the honor guest of the Fourth of July celebration sponsored by the American Legion, Seattle Post No. 1. Elliott Burdett, our Legion commander and I, as general chairman, had the honor of riding in Admiral Halsey's car in the parade. We thoroughly enjoyed our visit with him, and that ride through the streets of cheering citizens was a real thrill.

Perched above and behind us on the back of the rear seat, Admiral Halsey, too, obviously enjoyed the tremendous welcome given him all along the parade route. He laughed heartily as he waved an acknowledgment of the warm greeting of the crowds. He was truly a great hero.

After the parade Emil Sick and his wife gave a cocktail party and supper for the admiral. It was a gala affair, and Lucille bought a new "costume" for the occasion—a dusty pink dress with black embroidery and a pink *hat* with a large black bow across the back. Hats were very "in" then, she tells me. Toward the end of the evening and time for us to leave, I looked around for her and eventually found her, sitting on a sofa beside the admiral, listening to his amusing stories of navy life.

The Seattle earthquake of 1940 was strong enough to sway the antique hanging lamp in our bedroom, the glass prisms jangling in a curiously discordant tune, but there was no structural damage. The one in 1950, however, registered over 7.0 on the Richter scale, and considerable damage was reported all over the area—cracks in walls, toppled chimneys, falling bricks and stone from buildings.

I remember it well. The time was 5 minutes before 12 noon. I was on the bench in my seventh floor courtroom with a jury case in progress when suddenly a violent temblor shook the whole courthouse. This continued, accompanied by loud cracking noises. Without due process I arose and said "Let's get out of here in a hurry. Go quickly down the back stairway to the south courthouse lawn." Discarding my robe, I dashed after them. On my descent Judge Lloyd Shorett, 6′ 4″, bounded past me, his long black robe flying behind him like Superman's toga. When we again assembled at 1:30, we found two long cracks in the wall behind my bench.

In 1952 the Superior Court Judges Association of the State of Washington elected me president. In a letter to the 63 members I stated, in part:

> The president-judge is authorized under the statute to assign judges of the Superior Court to other counties where calendars are congested...I ask you to so arrange your calendars far enough in advance to permit you to assist judges in other counties...OUR OBJECTIVE SHOULD BE TO REDUCE TO THE LOWEST PRACTICABLE MINIMUM THE TIME INTERVAL BETWEEN THE DATE OF OCCURRENCE OUT OF WHICH THE LITIGATION ARISES AND THE DATE OF TRIAL AND DECISION IN THE SUPERIOR COURT. The accomplishment of such objective makes for the best public relations for both the Bench and Bar...We must constantly be on the alert for new ways to oil the wheels of justice. The serious task for all of us—judges, lawyers and lay people alike—who love justice is to make it more speedily available to more people and with greater efficiency and less expense.
>
> A truly successful court system must command the respect and have the confidence of the people it serves...We must see to it that justice in our courts is a search for truth and not just a mere battle of wits...Let us all constantly strive for the improvement of the administration of justice in our state.

The cooperation of the judges in Washington State resulted in a material reduction of our backlog. In time the judiciary was enlarged to take care of increased filings. Younger men were appointed or elected, and through the years many fine judges joined us.

If anyone doubts humor in judges, let me give you a few examples that prove otherwise.

Judge Jim Hodson, a good judge endowed with a sense of humor, was a master in equitation and often presided as ringmaster at gymkhanas and horse shows. In his well-tailored riding clothes, he cut quite a figure on his thoroughbred, Pentago. When Jim and I were on the judges' budget committee, an architect was telling of the plans for the renovation of some of our older courtrooms. He stated that with the installation of air-conditioning the windows of the courtrooms would be blocked out. Jim asked, "You mean to say we would have no *windows?*" The architect said, "Yes." Turning to me in mock-consternation Jim said,

"With no windows, *where* am I going to look when I know a witness is lying like hell?"

With the other judges of the court, Jim and I served as honorary pallbearers at the funeral services for Judge James T. Lawler who was also called Jim and like him (Hodson), a member of the Roman Catholic church. In the course of the service the young Irish priest mentioned that Jim Lawler had lived an exemplary life *but* doubtless he had committed *some* sins which would necessitate his resting in purgatory for a while before the pearly gates opened for him. When we got outside, Jim Hodson said, "Now, boys, old Jim is on the two-yard line. Let's get behind him and push and pray like hell and put him over."

One prank almost backfired on us. Judge Lloyd Shorett was an ardent duck hunter and each fall furnished the ducks for an annual stag duck dinner. That particular year the dinner party was held at the Meydenbauer Bay Yacht Club, where Judge Story Birdseye was a past commodore. Judge Malcolm Douglas, who prided himself on his culinary prowess, left the courthouse shortly after noon on these occasions to prepare the feast along with his friend, Lucien Perrot, who was born and reared in Paris and known as a great gourmet cook. This annual event was great fun—a time for jokes and laughter, for ribbing each other and generally letting down our hair. The real jokesters in the group were Lloyd Shorett and Frank James.

That night Lloyd and Frank had cooked up a joke on Malcolm. They arranged for a deputy sheriff to arrive at a designated time to inquire if any of the judges had been involved in an accident on the way to Bellevue that afternoon. Meanwhile Lloyd and Frank had sprinkled catsup over the right fender of Malcolm's car and given the deputy sheriff the following questions to put to him.

"Are you Judge Malcolm Douglas? Are you the owner of such and such a car? Did you cross the bridge this afternoon? Did you have an accident while on the bridge and severely injure a pedestrian, thereafter driving away from the scene? Is your car license number AAA-100? Then the punch line: "Well, how do you account for the blood on the fender of your car?"

By this time the usually placid Malcolm was quite upset, vigorously denying any part in an accident especially when he observed our thespian officer fingering his handcuffs. According to the script, at this point I was supposed to come to Malcolm's defense, but I was in another part of the club at the time.

Highly excited, Malcolm got very red, and the two jokesters were afraid he might have a stroke. Finally, they all went out to look at the car. Lloyd ran his finger along the fender, put it to his mouth and said: "Catsup, officer. Nothing but catsup."

Colorful Ward Roney, whose hobby was the operation of a successful dairy ranch in the beautiful Redmond valley, was sometimes called our cowboy judge. Dressed in classic western he often gave us a lively number on his harmonica.

We called genial Jim Mifflin our no-nonsense judge. Assigned on occasions to our settlement calendar he was most successful in getting the parties together and reducing our trial calendar backlog.

Because of their expertise Judges Walter McGovern, the late Morrell Sharp and Eugene Wright received promotions to the federal bench, and Judge Robert Utter to the state supreme court.

Early in the practice of law I came to respect judges who were alert, able to keep abreast of the trial and "shoot from the hip," especially those prepared to rule at the conclusion of the evidence rather than take a case under advisement, a custom of some causing delay. Emulating those judges whose procedure I approved, I seldom took a case under advisement even though it meant carrying home a full briefcase at night and burning the midnight oil.

In 1969 I was elected president of the National Conference of Metropolitan Courts, a group composed of presiding judges of the top trial courts in our largest cities. That year the conference met in Seattle with some 75 member judges in attendance. Among the judges' greatest concerns were: (1) backlog of cases, both civil and criminal; (2) lack of uniformity in sentencing; and (3) the steady increase in crime.

Federal District Judge George Boldt was our guest speaker. George had served with the Office of Strategic Services during World War II and was appointed to the federal bench by President Eisenhower. He made a masterful presentation of the problems then confronting trial judges.

Here something should be said about the grand jury. Our grand jury custom goes back about 800 years to the early English common law when people wanted to protect themselves from the king. They came together in assemblies and called themselves grand juries. These grand juries stood as a buffer between the crown and the citizens to prevent unjust prosecution by the crown. The king had to obtain an indictment from the grand jury. A grand jury should not be confused with the regular courtroom "petty" juries which hear cases and bring in verdicts in open court in both civil and criminal cases. The job of a grand jury is to decide *if someone should stand trial—not to determine the person's guilt or innocence.*

In February 1966 while serving as the presiding judge, it became my duty to call a grand jury, summoned at the request of the prosecuting attorney, to examine the high cost of remodeling the county courthouse and the operations of the county assessor's office, Judges Lloyd Shorett and Story Birdseye assisting. I was charged with the duty to see we had an unprejudiced, impartial grand jury. After the 17 members were selected they were required to take an oath to keep their deliberations secret and to avoid "envy, hatred, malice, fear, favor, affection or reward in their studies." After charging the grand jury and appointing a foreman, my duties were completed except for being available to answer legal questions.

On March 4, 1966 an editorial in *The Seattle Times* stated:

> Judge Wilkins advised the jurors that, while they have powers to examine all public records, a generalized, roving examination of all records in the county would probably be wasted; while cautioning the jurors to rely on the advice of the special prosecutors in investigating matters other than those pertaining to the assessor's office and the courthouse remodeling project, he reminded them of their right to look into any area in which they have good reason to suspect wrongdoing.
>
> There were two other points made in the judge's charge worth noting in reference to the courthouse remodeling project. He told the jurors, "I caution you, however, that you must not consider lack of good business judgment to be criminal activity. You should distinguish between the two. Nor should you permit any partisan politics, as such, to have any place in your deliberations." The grand jurors, it seems to us, received some good advice.

After the charge the prosecution presented evidence, interrogated witnesses and provided advice as requested. The secrecy of what goes on inside the jury room is so tight that the law states a grand juror cannot testify in court about what happened behind the closed door during deliberations. If the grand jury does return an indictment, as it did in this case, a warrant is issued by the court for the person's arrest and served by the sheriff. Until the arrest is completed, the indictment remains secret. All grand juries follow the archaic tradition of inspecting the county jail—a good custom.

The experience with that grand jury convinced me that calling one occasionally has a wholesome effect on the community.

Now, something about a few of the cases out of thousands that came before me.

Perhaps one of the most famous cases I presided over was:

The Egg and I Case

In February 1951 a civil jury case came on for trial in which 10 persons, claiming they'd been identified as the real-life counterparts of characters drawn in Betty MacDonald's best-selling book, "The Egg and I," filed libel actions for $975,000 against Betty, her publisher, the Lippincott Company, and the Bon Marche, the local distributor of the book. Plaintiffs were Albert Bishop, his six sons and two daughters, contending they had been identified as the "Kettle" family, and Raymond H. Johnson, said to have been depicted in the book as "Crow-Bar." The plaintiffs maintained they had been subjected to shame and humiliation when their acquaintances identified them with the characters in the book.

Their counsel told the jury that all of them were hard-working, respected members of their communities and were not at all like the Kettle family portrayed by Betty. With the exception of Albert Bishop, who was 87 and in ill health, all the Bishop family were present in court and testified on their behalf. It was claimed the father was depicted as "Paw Kettle," a lazy shiftless individual. The mother, Mrs. Albert Bishop who, they claimed, was identified as "Maw Kettle," had died. Members of the Bishop family testified that, in their opinion, "Maw and Paw Kettle" were inspired by Albert Bishop and his wife. Mrs. Bishop's sister testified that "Paw Kettle" is described as having a lisp and a "thick thatch of stiff gray hair, quite obviously cut at home with a bowl, perched on top of which he wore a black derby hat." She stated further that Albert Bishop did have a lisp and he did wear a derby hat they "always called a dicer."

A brother of the late Mrs. Bishop testified that his sister didn't have time to be "primping herself up" but that she was generally neat in appearance, whereas "Maw Kettle" is described as having "her whole front dirty and spotted." He stated that "Paw Kettle" had, according to the book, "a neckline featuring several layers of dirty underwear and sweaters" but that, in his opinion, Mr. Bishop was "clean in every way I know of."

Under questioning as to whom she believed the Kettles to be in real life, a daughter of the Bishop's said: "The Albert Bishop family—my folks." She also stated that friends and acquaintances associated her with the book and that "we are ashamed to go out—we were hurt very much." Others of the family and friends gave similar testimony.

In her defense Betty MacDonald stated it was some 20 years after she was a neighbor of the Albert Bishop family on the Olympic Peninsula when she wrote the book and she didn't have the "faintest recollection" of what Albert Bishop looked like when she knew him. She also stated she kept no diary, no records and letters associated with her residence there from 1927 to 1931; that she left the farm and her former husband in 1931; that if her description in the book of "Paw Kettle" and the Kettle farm resembled Albert Bishop and his farm, it was a coincidence.

Betty said a book publisher who was a friend of her sister's asked if she knew any authors writing books about the Pacific Northwest, and her sister, Mary Bard Jensen, author of "The Doctor Has Three Faces," arranged the appointment with Lippincott who published the book. Testifying in her own behalf, Betty stated: "I had become very irritated by women who wrote books about living in the country without electric lights and running water and said they just loved it. I thought I would write the other side. My idea in writing the book was to make fun of my incompetence as a farm wife....All those women who loved living in the country without conveniences were very efficient. I was most inefficient. I meant to make fun of myself. I was writing about an imaginary place in an imaginary country." She was emphatic in her denial that she described the Bishop family as the Kettles, and to her knowledge, she had never met Raymond Johnson who claimed he was portrayed as "Crow-Bar" in the book.

Betty, an attractive auburn-haired woman, was a very convincing witness. Throughout the two-weeks' trial the courtroom was crowded with people who were reading the book, following the exploits of the Kettles, and seeking Betty's autograph. It was really quite an ordeal for her. At one time, under cross-examination, she suddenly burst into tears and left the courtroom. The next day, however, she had regained her composure.

The case went to the jury of nine men and three women at 4 p.m. Within 24 hours they returned a unanimous verdict for Betty and her publisher. DeWitt Williams presented and argued a motion to dismiss his client, the Bon Marche, on established law, and I granted the motion prior to submitting the case to the jury. The foreman of the jury explained that the decision of the jury was unanimous on the first ballot but they took time to read the entire book in accordance with my instructions. Betty, of course, was elated over the verdict.

The Wheat-Aiken Murder Case

In October 1965 the first degree murder case of State vs. Wheat and Aiken, involving the killing of three service station attendants within a period of less than a month, came on for trial. A criminal charge had been filed accusing these two defendants jointly with three counts of murder in the first degree. A précis of the evidence follows.

On the evening of March 25, 1965, Owen Fair, 52, was the attendant at a Time Oil service station on Empire Way South in Seattle. His body, riddled with five bullet wounds, was found by the owner of the station at 10 a.m. the following morning in the storeroom beside a blood-smeared white regrigerator.

According to the autopsy surgeon, Mr. Fair had been shot first in the chest. Four other bullets had entered his body, the last between his eyes, the gun held approximately one-half inch above his face. Five spent revolver .22 caliber casings were found near the body. It was apparent a robbery had taken place prior to the killing. Except for a few pennies the cash box was empty. No currency was found in the victim's shirt pocket where he usually kept his paper money. His black wallet, found by the coroner in his hip pocket, was empty. The accounts for the day's receipts had been compiled and laid on the counter, indicating the attendant was getting ready to close the station when murdered.

The Seattle police were called and began their investigation at once but found no clues to the killers. Other than the money, the only thing stolen was a new Exide automobile battery.

On April 12, 1965, 18 days later, Daniel Wolf, 19, a daytime college student, was the night attendant at a courtesy Enco station, also on Empire Way. One of the station's regular customers, a nurse, drove in to the station about one o'clock that morning. Seeing no one around, she went to the office, heard someone moan and found Wolf on the floor bleeding from a head wound. He struggled to get up but without success. She put her arm under his head and was trying to give first aid when she saw the bullet wounds and called the police. Dan was taken by ambulance to King County Hospital where he died on the operating table about 2 a.m. He had sustained two gunshot wounds in the head. The casings of two .22 caliber bullets were found near the place where the nurse found the victim.

The police investigated the case, but other than a stomped-out Pall Mall cigarette stub, no other clues were found. Again it was apparent the killing had occurred during a robbery.

Meanwhile the public became alarmed over these two brutal murders. Fathers whose sons worked nights at gas stations sat in cars close by armed with shotguns. In certain service stations Seattle detectives were secreted behind doors with peep-holes to observe customers as they drove in.

Twelve days later, early on the morning of April 24, Jim Harp was the lone attendant at a service station in the north end of Seattle, just beyond the city limits. He had served in the navy and been discharged six months previously. His brother, Bill Harp, came by about 4 a.m. to fix a spare tire. While he was there, two black airmen drove in. One remained in the car; the other walked past Bill's car and went in the station, asking for the lavatory key which Jim gave him. While he was in the lavatory, Bill closed the trunk of his car and drove away. As the airman returned and put the key on the counter, two young friends of Jim's drove in and walked into the station. The airman pulled out a pack of Pall Malls, leaned against the counter and began to smoke. The three men conversed for a while, then shook hands and Jim's friends left. He went with them to the corner of the building to say goodbye. It was then 4:15 a.m. by the clock on the station window.

Shortly after 5 a.m. Jim's two friends returned, parked their car and went into the station. When they couldn't find Jim, they shouted his name but got no answer. Seeing a spare lavatory key in the desk drawer, they opened the door and found the lifeless body of Jim Harp on the toilet seat, bent over so his head and arms lay in a pool of blood on the floor. There were three gunshot wounds in his head. They ran across the street to summon the owner of the station; soon after, units of the King County sheriff's office and the Seattle police department arrived.

Now they had several clues to the killers. Pall Mall cigarette stubs were found on the pavement close to where the airmen's car had been parked. Bill Harp and the two friends were able to describe the 1954 Ford in which they were riding and the airman with whom they'd visited. The car had a dark brown top, black hood, light brown bottom. A chrome strip was missing from the right front fender in which there were several dents. An "All Points Bulletin" was issued containing this information.

Alert Washington State Trooper Harlan Ritter was one of the lawmen advised of the bulletin. As he was patroling a road on the north side of Paine Field—north of Seattle near Everett— he spotted the 1954 Ford described in the bulletin and the license number. At once, he contacted his radio operator to obtain the name and residence of the owner of the vehicle and found it to be one Antonio Nathaniel Wheat, an airman serving as a cook at the air force base at Paine Field. Having confirmed his findings with the provost marshal's office at the field, Trooper Ritter proceeded to the base with members of the King County Sheriff's Department and Seattle police. About 3 p.m. April 24 Wheat was taken into custody.

As the result of a statement made by Wheat, an "All Points Bulletin" was issued late that evening for the arrest of a man fitting the description of another airman, Arthur Nathaniel Aiken. The following day an immigration official at Blaine on the Canadian border recognized Aiken from the description given. He was sitting in the rear seat of a car returning from Canada. The Border Patrol and the Washington State Patrol were alerted. Together they stopped the car, ordered Aiken out and found a cocked .25 caliber automatic with live bullets in the chamber on his hip. Aiken was transported to the King County jail where Wheat's first statement was read to him. He called for a confrontation with Wheat.

Following his arrest, Wheat made five written statements, one regarding the Owen Fair killing, one about the Daniel Wolf killing, and three covering the Jim Harp killing. Aiken made three statements, one regarding each killing. Both defendants had been warned of their rights before the statements were made.

Both men were charged with three counts of murder in the first degree, and the case came before me for trial. A jury of 12 men and women plus one alternate juror was chosen. Two able and experienced lawyers were appointed for each defendant. The three prosecuting attorneys were likewise extremely capable.

An FBI man came from Washington, DC, to testify the bullets found in the bodies of all three murdered station attendants had been fired from the .22 caliber gun of Italian make which was owned by defendant Aiken and found hidden in defendant Wheat's duffle bag at the base following his arrest. Also found in Wheat's jacket were Jim Harp's wrist watch which was identified by his mother, and an identification card with Wheat's picture thereon with the name of Gary A. White. The evidence showed Wheat had used this identification card at the Seattle Sporting Goods store on Wednesday, April 21 when purchasing a .25 caliber Colt automatic. Further evidence disclosed the Exide battery taken from Owen Fair's station was found in Wheat's car.

It was also shown that earlier, on the evening of Jim Harp's murder, Wheat and Aiken had parked their car at another gas station operated by Maynard Anderson where Seattle detective Kurtilla, on the alert for robbers, was watching through a peep-hole. He observed a man he later identified as Wheat enter the station, stand around a while, place coins in a cigarette machine and obtain a package of Pall Mall cigarettes. He smoked one which he later stomped out before leaving. It was then midnight, and there were several customers in the station. However, after Officer Kurtilla left, Wheat and Aiken returned around 4 a.m. when Anderson had already closed and locked the station. Seeing the two men drive up, he wisely placed the lavatory key outside and relocked the station. By so doing he doubtless saved his life.

The case went to the jury on October 13, 1965 after extensive arguments by all six lawyers. Neither of the defendants took the witness stand. The prosecution requested the jury impose the death penalty, while the four defense lawyers pleaded that the death penalty not be inflicted. Then Wheat requested he also be permitted to argue his case to the jury in his own behalf. I acquiesced, and Wheat was permitted to read a plea which was a request for the jury to vote "No" on the death sentence and permit him to live and prove that he could "use my life in a meaningful and useful manner..."

All the voluntary statements which set forth the defendants' respective versions of these three callous killings were admitted in evidence and were before the jury for their consideration. I quote two statements in part to show how deliberate, brutal and ruthless were these three crimes.

From Aiken's statement of the Daniel Wolf killing:

> We had discussed robbing a gas station, and as we drove by an Enco station Wheat said that looks like a good one, there is only one man there.... I was carrying a .22 cal automatic.... The attendant asked if this was a hold-up when he saw the gun...said he didn't want any trouble and would give us the money.... I picked it up and put in in my pocket.... The attendant said he had more money in the safe...showed Wheat the key.... Wheat reached into the safe, pulling out the money...said 'let's go' and pushed the attendant and we all went back to the lube room.... The attendant said the money was insured, he was very religious and didn't want to die. Wheat pulled out a small switch blade knife and forced him into the small room...said to me, 'do you want to do it or should I?' I said I wouldn't do it. Wheat handed me his knife and I gave him the gun. Wheat pointed the gun at the attendant, the attendant said he wanted to pray...got down on his knees and covered his face with his hands.... I walked toward the front...heard one shot...another shot.... We walked to the car and drove off. He (Wheat) counted the money...around $200...I think I got $94.
>
> From Wheat's third statement of the Harp killing: I talked to the attendant until his two friends drove up and left...asked for change for a $20 bill...pulled the .22 automatic...told him to give me all the money...took the currency...told him to walk in the rest room.... I followed.... He sat on the toilet seat, said, 'Don't kill me'.... I released the safety on the gun...the first shot went off accidentally...He slumped over and I fired two more shots after I aimed at his head...ran to the car.... Aiken was asleep...drove back to the base.... On the way I counted the money...which amounted to $120.

The jury returned to the courtroom at 10:12 the following morning with a unanimous verdict finding both defendants guilty of murder in the first degree on all three counts. In answer to the interrogatory, "Shall the death penalty be inflicted?" the answer was "Yes" on all three counts, which counts and interrogatories were signed by the foreman.

In view of the evidence presented about these three killings, and having in mind the manner in which they were perpetrated, I agreed with the verdict and death sentences and told the jury so. In due course I sentenced both defendants to the penitentiary at Walla Walla "there to be hanged by the neck until dead" and set the date of execution which was deferred pending appeal to our supreme court where the convictions and sentences were affirmed.

An appeal was taken by the defendants to the Supreme Court of the United States. That court, by order of June 17, 1968, vacated the judgments of our courts and remanded the case for further consideration in line with their opinion that our statute regarding the death penalty, vesting wide descretion in the jury, was unconstitutional.

After reviewing the opinion, our supreme court again affirmed the jury verdict as to both defendants. In the end, however, I was required to resentence them to life imprisonment, which I did on each of the three counts of murder, the sentences to be served *consecutively*. It was my feeling that neither Wheat nor Aiken should ever be released.

Both defendants were transported back from Walla Walla to the King County jail for resentencing. Afterwards, while the deputy sheriffs were taking the defendants to the institution at Shelton, Aiken attempted to escape. He is strong, an expert in judo in which he held a "brown belt" and had worked out regularly in the gymnasium at Paine Field. His escape attempt did not succeed, as the courageous deputies were able to overcome him.

The policy in the State of Washington is such that life imprisonment does not mean that per se, and our citizens should be made aware of this. The State Board of Prison Terms and Paroles releases a life prisoner after serving 13⅔ years depending on good conduct and recommendation by the warden. So, by setting sentences consecutively, the judge makes sure the inmate does not start serving on the second sentence until he has served 13⅔ years, likewise with the third sentence. Thus Wheat and Aiken would be required to serve approximately 40 years before being eligible for parole.

During my years on the bench it fell my duty to sentence four men to death by hanging—the three previously mentioned and John D. Canady. As in the case of Wheat and Aiken, his death sentence was ultimately vacated by order of the Supreme Court of the United States.

The Canady Case

An amended information was filed on May 1, 1969 charging Canady in six counts: alleging in count 1, attempted rape on January 4, 1969 of Mary Annabelle Bjornson; count 2, murder in the first degree on the same date, of Mary Annabelle Bjornson by choking and strangling; count 3, rape on January 23, 1969 of Barbara Beresford; and count 4, of assault in the second degree of Barbara with a knife; count 5, with the rape of Lynne Carol Tuski on January 25, 1969; and count 6, with her murder by choking and strangling.

A plea of not guilty by reason of insanity was filed, and three psychiatrists were appointed to examine Canady. All three reported on April 15 that defendant was sane at trial and was at the time the offenses were committed, that he knew the difference between right and wrong, which is the test under our statute, that he was able to appreciate his peril and assist in his defense.

Canady pleaded guilty before me to counts 3 and 4 which related to rape and assault of Barbara Beresford. I sentenced him to life imprisonment and declared him to be a "sexual psychopath" under our statutes. The jury found him guilty on counts 1, 2, 5, and 6 and answered the interrogatory, "Shall the death penalty be inflicted?" with "Yes." I denied the motion for a new trial September 25, 1969. An indigent appeal (defendant being impoverished, destitute, counsel is appointed at state expense) was granted on October 8, 1969.

Final orders from which the appeal was taken sentenced Canady to death on counts 2 and 6 which charged him with the deaths of the two girls, all sentences to be consecutive. Our supreme court affirmed the case except only so far as the death sentence which the court vacated. A final order was signed by my successor, Judge Peter Steere, on September 7, 1972, sentencing Canady to 20 years on count 1, life on count 2, life on count 3, 20 years on count 4, life on count 5, and life on count 6, all sentences to be served *consecutively*.

So Canady is now serving time at Walla Walla for the killing of these two unfortunate women, and Wheat and Aiken presumably are there too for the killing of three innocent men.

The Eighth Amendment to the Constitution of the United States provides: "Excessive bail shall not be required, nor excessive fines imposed, nor cruel and unusual punishment inflicted."

After reading about these cases, ask yourself whether any punishment could be more "cruel and unusual" than that inflicted on those innocent and law-abiding victims.

The Busing Case

On December 9, 1970 a group of Seattle citizens known as "Citizens Against Mandatory Busing" (CAMB) filed an action in superior court seeking injunctive relief from a decision made by the Seattle School Board, entered November 11, 1970, which was a plan to integrate the Seattle schools with the implementation of what was known as the 4-4-4 plan with the commencement of the fall term of 1971. Included in this plan was a requirement of mandatory cross-busing of certain children to achieve the object of the plan.

All the plaintiffs in the case were taxpayers and parents of children living in the Seattle school district.

Shortly after this action was filed, the defendant Seattle School Board successfully filed a motion of removal to the United States District Court for the Western District of Washington. Following a hearing, the federal district court held the case in abeyance awaiting certain decisions of the United States Supreme Court and finally entered an order June 22, 1971 remanding the case to the superior court, holding there was no federal question involved. On July 1, 1971, the case was pre-assigned to me for trial, and having in mind the statute requiring me to hear such an appeal *de novo,* from the beginning, and expeditiously, I immediately set the case for trial July 26, 1971. This recitation of time sequence will explain the delay in the trial of the case filed the previous December seeking to enjoin the implementation of the plan scheduled to take effect within a month of my hearing date.

There were two full weeks of testimony. Many witnesses were called on both sides, and 132 exhibits admitted in evidence. The testimony was completed on Friday, August 6. The lawyers completed their arguments on Monday, August 9, and I rendered my decision by way of a written memorandum of 17 pages the following day.

It would serve no useful purpose to quote the entire decision (copy of which is available under Cause No. 731666 at the King County courthouse). My order *enjoined* the Seattle School Board from carrying out its Phase I plan for a year until further study was made as to the effects of the plan, and the citizens made fully aware of them. I stated that the board's action in moving so hastily without allowing sufficient time for input on the part of the citizens was arbitrary and capricious; that the citizens *had the right to know* all details about costs, facilities and program changes, *so as to be in a position to initiate a referendum or initiative* if they felt aggrieved with the proposed implementation of the plan. I also enjoined the board from busing involuntarily any child to a school other than his neighborhood school, or the school he had been attending during the past school year without the consent of parents or guardians. I quote two paragraphs from my written opinion:

> With the substantial cross-busing planned, many parents with children now attending their neighborhood schools will lose the right to have their children attend those schools. This restriction will affect all children from kindergarten through the 12th grade. In order to reduce existing racial imbalance in Seattle schools, which is its primary object stated by the Seattle School Board, cross-busing will be used extensively. In the first year of the plan, 842 students are to be cross-bused. Costs for the cross-busing will be furnished by the federal government or by the state on the theory that the plan is for desegregation. The second and third phases will be put into effect at a later time which will mean that little children attending kindergarten for the first time cannot be certain

> that they will be in a classroom with their neighborhood playmates whom they have known and associated with during their pre-school years. All parents understand that the first year a child goes to school can be a traumatic experience. That is the time that close liaison is necessary between the teacher and the mother of a small child. Removing a child from the security of his home and neighborhood surroundings during these formative years could have a deleterious effect on his welfare and happiness with obvious slackening of the level of his school performance. Parents have the natural right and responsibility to educate their children, and while they surrender their children to the schools for a few hours each day, this does not deprive them of their rights and duties of parenthood nor does it give the school any of those rights belonging to parents....
>
> What we have here in Seattle is racial imbalance and not *de jure* segregation.... *De jure* segregation comes about because of the willful act of a state or other governmental agency. Its purpose, as it was in the South, was to deliberately segregate the races. The cases decided by the Supreme Court of the United States from *Brown* to the present related only to *de jure* segregation and not to *de facto* segregation.... *De facto* segregation or, as it may more properly be referred to as racial imbalance, as it exists here in Seattle, comes about not because of action by the state, county or city, but purely because of housing patterns....

The citizen response to my opinion was terrific. Within the next few days I received close to 300 personal letters, largely from parents and educators, approving my decision. They all were commendatory and expressed gratitude. Never in my long career as a judge have I received such an enthusiastic expression of approval on a decision rendered by me. I still have those letters and am most grateful for the confidence of my fellow citizens.

There were some, of course, who did not approve. In fact, that was the only time in all my years on the bench I was threatened, and then only by hearsay. Following the rendition of my opinion and during the time counsel were arguing motions for a new trial and certification of the facts preliminary to an appeal, a deputy sheriff called to see me in chambers. He told me the FBI had reported to the sheriff that one of their undercover men heard a rather unsavory looking student at the university say: "Judge Wilkins is going to be massacred." The sheriff wanted to know what I would like in the way of protection. My instructions to him were: "Have a couple of detectives in plain clothes in the courtroom each day the case is being heard; if someone answering that description enters, have one of the detectives sit next to him and keep an eye on him. Call my friend, the chief of police of Redmond and ask him to have his men keep a close lookout day and night while on car patrol passing my home." However, nothing came of the alleged threat.

While at Ferris State College I heard Senator Ferris say: "Never let the federal government get its foot in the door of education." Observe what is taking place: schools of all states must now take dictation from the federal government—the Department of Health, Education and Welfare (HEW)—as to their plans and methods, otherwise the federal bureaucracy cuts off its funds. These are the funds of the taxpayers of all the states. Senator Ferris knew what he was talking about. Now the federal government has a separate Department of Education.

As to busing: How much time on the bus is wasted for children? How much money is spent on buses and their maintenance? How much precious gasoline could be saved if forced busing were outlawed? Perhaps forced busing will stop only when gasoline runs out. Will it be too late?

In the fall of 1978 the Seattle School Board planned to cross-bus close to 12,000 students and an increasing number in 1979. As a result, a group known as the Citizens For Voluntary Integration (CIVIC) filed Initiative No. 350, which provided for the right of parents in the State of Washington to send their children to the nearest neighborhood school.

In the spring election of 1979 the initiative carried by an overwhelming majority of better than two to one. This is the American way of letting the citizens of our state speak.

Despite the expressed wishes of our people, the Seattle School Board brought action in federal court to have the initiative declared unconstitutional. A federal judge agreed and so declared; his decision was subsequently approved by the Ninth Circuit Court of Appeals. In the end it may be necessary for Congress to amend the statutes to recognize the rights of parents to send their children to their own neighborhood schools. Would it not be better to use the money now spent on busing for quality education for all schools, no matter where situated?

A few months before my retirement the judges were guests of the 101 Club at the Washington Athletic Club. One of the "gags in good humor" was the presentation to me of a plaque on which was mounted a toy replica of a yellow school bus below which was a gold plate inscribed thus:

Honorable William J. Wilkins
101 Club—Judges' Night
February 24, 1972

If you travel by bus
Leave the driving to us.
CAMB

I have been asked many times about my judicial philosophy. I suppose you could call me a hardliner. Any man coming before me who has committed a crime while carrying a firearm would not get probation. A firm believer in capital punishment, I think it should be handled in such a way that it is a *deterrent*. Certainly no sentence is going to be a deterrent if it is not imposed until almost a generation after the crime has been committed.

One never knows what penologists will do or recommend; time passes rapidly and memories fade. The innocent victims are forgotten except by their loved ones. Inmates of many penal institutions are now called "residents." Telephone calls are allowed. Some mail is uncensored. Committees of so-called residents have an advisory hand in running the institutions. Some are permitted to attend colleges. A few years ago at Walla Walla the idea was promulgated—"take a 'lifer' to dinner." How many under this program were hosted at dinners outside the walls has not been disclosed, but it is true that on two occasions the "lifers" escaped and thereafter each committed a murder, leaving two more widows in this state, one of a state highway patrolman. Nothing more has been heard of the project. Apparently the sponsors seek anonymity.

Federal judges are now running the public schools and recently are taking over the operation and supervision of state penal institutions. Other federal agencies are directing our lives in almost every endeavor. If this trend continues, what is going to happen to the cherished states' rights of the "free and independent states," the preservation of which brought us together? Isn't it about time to get this creeping expanding federal bureaucracy off our backs and bring about the restoration of *states' rights?*

Thirty-two and a half years is a long time to serve on the trial bench. Through those years I participated in decisions which affected many people—a great responsibility. The job of a trial judge in my opinion is one that cannot be equaled. One is so close to people's problems it is imperative to be forthright and understanding, impartial and honest.

The judiciary is, perhaps, the most important branch of the government. Its primary duty is to *interpret* and *apply* impartially the laws of the land. As long as this is kept in mind and no attempt made to legislate as do some courts, especially the United States Supreme Court, we, the members of the judiciary, will be on safe ground and our unique system of checks and balances will be maintained.

Ten Not Libeled

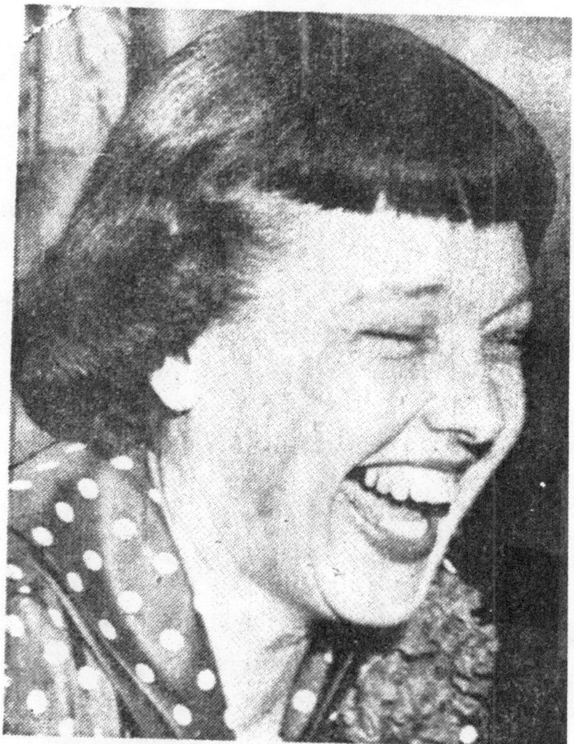

HAPPY—Betty MacDonald, author of "The Egg and I" beams her pleasure at unanimous decision in her favor returned by a jury in the half million dollar libel suit filed by 10 persons who contended she portrayed them in her best-seller.

—(Post-Intelligencer Photo.)

Ten not libeled (Betty MacDonald, newspaper)

Legal Arguments Begin in 'The Egg and I' Trial. (newspaper)

Admiral Halsey, Wilkins, Elliott Burdett

Colonel and Mrs. James L. Tarr

With Colonel Maxey, 4th Air Force, Korean conflict, 1950.

Lucille's paintings of Rothenberg and Nuremberg

Judges, 1970. Back row, L to R: Holman, Smith, Callow, Chan, Elston, Soderland, Thompson, Smith, Dore, Soukup, Howard, Roberts, Noe. Front row, L to R: Ringold, Henry, Walterschirchen, Revelle, Turner, Shorett, Wilkins, Roney, Agnew, Birdseye, Gaines, Mifflin, Stuntz.

CHAPTER XII

Green Pastures

In 1966 we were informed the proposed freeway to Redmond would go right through the house at Tripple Creek! All that planning and preparation, all that work and sweat was going to be just swept away? After the initial shock, though, we paused to ponder. We'd had eight wonderful happy busy years there, but the children were all married with homes of their own so we were back to two. In 1972 I would be retired. Perhaps this was the time to stop, look, and consider if we were ready to give up country living.

We looked at several condominiums in the city, for if we were going to make a change in our lifestyle, the purpose would be to keep commuting and work at a minimum. A high-rise condominium on the city side of Lake Washington was then on the drawing board and after a lot of thought a deposit was made to hold a unit. Days and weeks went by; the condominium project was delayed for various reasons. Meanwhile the freeway wolf was fast approaching.

Every time we talked of it, the idea of a bulldozer gobbling up the historic log house, of giving up the peace and quiet of country living, of not having a bit of land to work or just to feel in our hands was devastating. We discussed the pros and cons, the feasibility of another house-moving job *and* the hazards, of the hard work involved in another remodeling, and never came to a conclusion.

One day we sat on the porch after one of those discussions. Neither spoke. We'd come to the same impasse. I glanced at Lucille and saw her usually bright vivacious face in repose. Her eyes followed the ripples of the grasses on the meadow, up to the treetops to the sky above. The rhythmic hum of insects filled the air. Occasionally the song of a bird came to us. Over all there was that quiet, the sense of being apart from the rest of the world we'd come to cherish.

I inhaled deeply, exhaled, and said: "Let's move it."

Lucille's face was ecstatic. She threw her arms around me and said: "Of course! It's the *only* way to go!" So there we were with a log house and as much or as little of the rest of the house as we chose to get *off* the 10½ acres and *onto* "somewhere." That was the next question. Where to put it? After scouring the countryside we found a beautiful two-acre lot with big cedar trees four miles farther east overlooking Lake Sammamish. There was a clear route for the moving job albeit up and down some rather steep grades. The mover didn't see any problems, though, so again, for us the wheels were going round.

The decision was made to move only the log house and the wing that included the entry, dining room and kitchen, so we could live in the teenagers' wing during the moving job. All the furniture except our bare necessities was put in storage. The hardest part was getting the log structure on the flatbed which would take it to its new location. Finally the great day (in July, 1967) arrived and we watched the parade get under way.

The lead car was one from the highway patrol, its revolving blue lights flashing. Behind that came two utility trucks, men standing in buckets suspended at the top of high jointed arms to raise low wires or cut tree limbs which might impede the progress of our "Mighty Mo." Then came the big old truck that had carted so many homes out of the freeway's clutches, pulling the flatbed with the log house, all bedecked with red flags. Workmen walked along either side. "Like pallbearers," I thought. A back-up truck to serve as a brake to hold the house as it progressed down the hills followed the flatbed. Bringing up the rear was another highway patrol car followed by a flock of dogs and kids on bicycles.

Though the mover had reassured me about the hills, I was still apprehensive about the steep grade on that last long run down Northeast 24th Street to Lake Sammamish Boulevard. With visions of the log house tugging loose and barreling down the hill to end in a pile of hand-adzed, hand-laid, hand-cleaned, hand-polished logs—probably the most expensive bonfire in history—I muttered: "There goes the funeral procession for the old log house." However, all went well, which goes to show it doesn't pay to worry. The next day the procession formed all over again while the other wing was moved and placed on the new lot according to the architect's drawings. The remainder—the teenagers' wing—was left to satiate the appetite of progress. It was a long time before we could go past that area and not be hit by nostalgia.

The excitement of the new project kept us so busy, though, we had no time to brood—just think onward!

With furnishings in place the house would look practically the same as the one at Tripple Creek. The remodeling was almost all new construction involving a large entrance gallery, a breakfast room to the south, a workshop-studio and carport. Large decks and wide sloping terraces, for the most part covered with plastic and beauty bark to reduce gardening to a minimum, gave us ample room to stretch out or entertain large groups when we wished. Thanks to Lucille's creative drive we had another beautiful home, and the log house had been preserved for posterity.

Finally, when the jobs of settling and landscaping were under control, Lucille set up her easel in the big workshop-studio, invited painting pals to join her, and indulged in her hobby, which she claims to be the best one of them all. I agree and am proud of her talent and accomplishments.

We had some memorable times in that house. At some time or other all the judges on the King County bench and their wives were our guests. The year I was president of the National Conference of Metropolitan Courts Lucille entertained all of the judges' wives in our home. Being members of the English-Speaking Union, of which I was a past president, we honored the new British consuls general and their wives and hosted more than one cocktail party for the union. There were the usual art groups, parties for charity, old and new friends and family gatherings throughout the years.

Under the laws of the State of Washington judges are required to retire at the end of the year in which they reach the age of 75. Let us hope such a law will be passed to apply to all judges throughout the country including members of the United States Supreme Court and the members of Congress. My retirement year was 1972.

That year the Seattle *Argus* paper did an article on "Judging the Judges." It stated that only trial lawyers and police keep a sharp eye on judges, hence the public had little information on which to base their votes. The *Argus* asked experienced trial lawyers for their opinion about the judges and compiled a short résumé on each judge of the current panel. Not filing for reelection, I was surprised to see my name included in the survey but pleased to note the following evaluation:

> William J. Wilkins, (retiring) epitomizes the establishment, tends to be rough on defendants. Very able and leader of the old guard faction.

In Washington State retired judges may be called back to sit for short periods of time to help with the trial calendar. This I did for five years but finally gave up the practice with the appointment of six new judges, making a total of 39 superior court judges in King County whereas there were only 15 when I was appointed in 1940.

Thus, in 1975, though retired, I was still having to commute while doing occasional duty on the bench.

Then the time came to take stock. At age 78 and retired, wasn't this the time to enjoy the Golden Years together with less work and responsibility?

Though we'd planned so we could spend minimum time in house and garden work, those most persistent of all growing plants—weeds—had a nasty habit of poking their way up out of the beauty bark, *everywhere!* The stain on the house *had* to be renewed. Plants *had* to be fed and watered, as did our guests. The gravel in the courtyard and parking area *had* to be raked; so did the leaves—a constant demanding hobby. Those were happy times, busy times, ones we would always remember with joy but now could leave with no regrets.

With Seattle undergoing severe growing pains, more and more people were living on the eastside and commuting to the city; increased traffic on the two floating bridges, frequent tie-ups and delays made the drive something to be endured.

With no children at home we had more time to indulge in the cultural advantages offered in the city—the symphony, the opera, the Repertory Theater, the museums. Many of our friends now lived in the city. Commuting was the real obstacle.

In August, 1974 we heard of a new condominium, Fairway Estates, being built on a high hill above Lake Washington with a view of the snow-capped Cascade mountains, shining like a crown of jewels, landscaping which we could enjoy but not labor to maintain, a large swimming pool, exercise rooms, saunas, tennis courts and a sky bridge to the Sand Point Golf and Country Club. It also provided maximum security with only one door to lock when we wanted to take a trip and a gas fireplace with only a button to push to have a bright blaze on our hearth. We looked it over and decided it was for us. What we did not know then was that here we would be surrounded with as kind and charming and stimulating a group of friends and neighbors as we could hope for, which makes for many congenial occasions close to home.

The Day We Moved

Moving day was March 20, 1975. This time we didn't have to move the *house,* but because of this, we had to move our worldly goods *out* of it and *into* the condominium. Though we'd spent weeks going over "things" collected in 47 years of marriage and the raising of five kids—sorting, discarding, what to take, what to give away, what was junk and what was "junque"—it still took the men a full day to load their largest van. We were to meet them at Fairway Estates at 9 the following morning. Meanwhile Pedro (Garcia-Pelayo), who worked at his own antique business during the day but was an auditor and night manager of the Sixth Avenue Motor Hotel, had solved the problem of overnight bed and board by wangling a suite for us on the top floor of the University Towers Hotel.

After a brief rest we showered and dressed and went downstairs to a leisurely cocktail hour and dinner, then early to bed. A few minutes before midnight I woke to the loud clanging of a bell. By the strong smell of smoke I knew it was a firebell. And not a drill; the real thing! Jumping our of bed, I ran to the open window and saw firemen on the street below running to connect hoses. Sirens proclaimed more engines were on the way. Lucille ran to get her robe in the bathroom but found the knob—the whole door, in fact—too hot to touch. She turned and staggered through the pall of smoke that already hung over our room to join me by the window. By that time both of us were coughing and our eyes were filled with tears from the smoke.

Great clouds of it belched from the floor below. Hanging out the window as far as we dared to breathe fresh air, we saw other heads popping out of windows. One of the firemen, using a bull horn, yelled:

"Keep your heads out the window! Don't go *near* your doors *or* the stairway!"

I don't know how long we remained there on our knees, arms around each other while the smoke and heat built up behind us and trapped us there on the 15th floor. Occassionally we saw a long tongue of flame lick a windowsill or climb a wall, but the watchful eyes of those magnificent firemen always spotted it and wiped it out with their powerful hoses.

"I wonder if they'll spread their nets," Lucille said, trying to see the activity below through her tears.

Looking down those 15 floors, I answered: "At our ages, even if we landed in them, we'd probably end up a couple of jellyfish."

It seemed an eternity we knelt there before we heard someone pound on our door. An authoritative voice shouted:

"Seattle Fire Department! Come out!"

I can tell you we didn't lose any time obeying that command. A Seattle police officer and two stalwart young firemen grabbed us and led us to the back stairway. Barefoot and clad only in our nightclothes, we scrambled down 15 flights, through smoke and water, past burned debris and clutter, always supported by those heroic firemen. During the descent the man leading Lucille pressed an oxygen mask to her face.

At the second floor we began to breathe cool clear air again. Lucille was taken to one of the cars where the women were given blankets and treated for smoke inhalation. Some were taken to the hospital for observation. Knowing Lucille was in good hands, I chose to remain on the second floor where I could breathe fresh air from an open door. Dressed as I was—or wasn't—that was plenty cool for me.

As I stood there, retired Battalion Chief Lee of the Fire Department recognized me. "Hello, Judge," he said matter-of-factly. "Wouldn't you like a blanket?" I nodded. In minutes he was back with one and it was most welcome. Shortly after, he returned to say: "I think I can get you back to your room now if you'd like to get dressed. Your wife is well taken care of. I'll take you to her when we come back."

On the 15th floor the air was still heavy with smoke, but the fires had been completely extinguished on the second and 14th floors where an arsonist had gathered flammable materials and set them afire. When I saw the extent of those fires, I knew we were lucky to be alive.

I hurried into my clothes, gathered Lucille's and followed Chief Lee downstairs to one of the large dining rooms where I found her with other hotel guests sipping coffee and receiving "aid and comfort" from the wonderful people in the fire department's Red Cross unit.

Where did we spend the rest of the night? As I passed the desk, a clerk hailed me to say I was wanted on the phone. It was our dear friend Pedro. He'd been listening to the radio and heard about the fire.

"Come down to our hotel, Judge," he said. "We've got a room for you."

At 2:30 a.m. we arrived at the Sixth Avenue Motor Hotel and were welcomed by Pedro with open arms and a stack of towels. We were a sight to behold. Our clothes were smudged with soot and smoke; our legs and feet were as black as India ink, and we were still coughing up a heavy black phlegm from the smoke.

"Only two things we would like, Pedro," I said. "A hot shower, and a good stiff drink to settle our nerves and put us to sleep."

Hot water never felt so good! Try as we did, though, and scrub as hard as we did, we couldn't get all the oily black soot from our pedal extremities. Pedro, however, did manage to find about a quarter of u bottle of Canadian Club to warm our insides. We finally went to bed and slept like kittens.

So, by the grace of God and those dedicated and courageous firemen, we were alive and on hand the next morning to meet our movers at our new home. Had the firemen not been so quick in getting those fires out, we'd have been dead either from flames or smoke inhalation. It was a traumatic adventure; it was also a time, above all else, to count our blessings.

Now entertaining is more relaxed and a real pleasure. Here there is no frantic last-minute drive to pull the weeds, sweep the driveway, pick up the clutter and haul in firewood. Guests come for cocktails, then, after a short walk over the sky bridge, we have a gourmet meal spread before us at the club. After that we return for a songfest with Lucille at the organ and some lively conversation.

In her indomitable way Lucille met the challenge of decorating a modern apartment with Early American antiques. Burlap covers the walls in the hall as a backdrop for a retrospective show of Lucille's paintings. Quiet earth tones prevail. A homespun feeling was achieved by having our son, Dennis, a master craftsman, panel the fireplace end of the living room with old weathered silver barn boards and install a long mantel to display the pewter collection. The organ stands in a niche to one side of the fireplace.

The huge old oak roll-top desk inherited from one of the last of the Spanish-American War veterans, with its many piegonholes and drawers of all sizes, provides a complete functional office in my study. One wall is filled with books. On top of the desk are the 15 volumes published by the Department of the Army containing the important portions of the records of the 12 cases tried at Nuremberg. On the wall above are the framed awards given me through the years. A small glass-covered box on a bookshelf contains miniatures of medals awarded while in military service.

Another room is a compact studio for Lucille. Now, what does she do with her paintings? Sure, she sells some, and feels very smug to know that someone likes her creative efforts well enough to buy them. Does she profit greatly? Well, not if she kept account of the outlay for framing, materials and incidentals, but my guess is she comes out about even and has all that fun! She has given away dozens of paintings, and our kids' and other relatives' houses display many which she calls "on loan." Visitors refer to our entry and hall as an art gallery, and there are paintings in every room, as she says "It's cheaper than wallpaper."

She is a member of the Quad "A" Art Association, attends meetings, and participates in its semi-annual art shows. Painting only when leisure permits, she insists she is still "just a little old hobby painter in tennis shoes!"

One wall of her studio has art books and another a floor-to-ceiling montage depicting our kids in stages of activity from childhood to maturity.

In the bedroom the old Victorian set "still proudly hails," enhanced by a garden of Victorian floral paintings and the early colored hobnail glass.

This move was the right thing at the right time, and we thoroughly enjoy the relaxation from responsibilities and time to visit with friends close by. Brian McKay, an airline captain, and his artist wife, who paints old houses under the name of Gwen Beckman, told us that in the old log house they had found everything they'd ever dreamed of. They bought it, and we know the house is in good hands.

In June, 1975 at Vancouver, BC, following an address on the Nuremberg trials to the alumni association of Alaska and Idaho, I was presented a Distinguished Alumnus Award from George Washington University, for which I am most grateful.

In May 1976 we attended the 50th reunion of my law class at the University of Michigan. Thirty-seven classmates attended, and down the halls echoed the old refrain, "You haven't changed a bit!"

After visiting with members of my family, we went on to Montreal, Trois Rivières and Quebec City. Trois Rivières was our Mecca. For a long time Lucille had wanted to check her mother's genealogy written many years before by a Jesuit priest. The guidebook stated, "The seminary there has the oldest historical records in America." The Abbot Monseigneur Hermann LaPlante, took us behind locked doors and brought out copies of all the old records dating back to Cartier in 1534.

He then invited us to walk with him to the great Gothic cathedral where he opened the vault which contains the *original* books of records, all written in longhand by the early priests. There he took down and placed in Lucille's hands the volume in which was written the record that her ancestor Jules Trotier, in 1630, had come to Trois Rivières from France with a land grant from King Louis XIII.

We spent several days exploring Quebec City and felt nostalgia for Paris.

On January 19, 1979 we would celebrate our 50th wedding anniversary, and we had to make a decision. Would we stay home and let our kids give the "Big Party" they were talking about? Would we forego our usual three months in Hawaii where we enjoy the color and warmth of the Islands? Did we *want* that kind of celebration?

Our 49th had been so smashing we didn't think anything could top it. Seattle and Maui friends came for cocktails on the roof garden of our condominium. There was a big Hawaiian moon, and the sky was filled with stars. There was a Hawaiian guitarist whose wife sang those beautiful Hawaiian songs including the "Hawaiian Wedding Song." There was excitement when a pod of whales came to mate in the protected bay right below us. There was the navy that opened up with a practice bombardment of the tiny island of Kahoolawe across our bay, dropping flares that lighted up the whole island. It was like the Fourth of July!

We compromised. It had been some time since we'd had a good visit with Ginger and her family and Cathy and Jim Tarr, so we opted to rent a condominium at Solana Beach near San Diego for the winter. Our deck extended out over the Pacific; from there we could watch the surfers, whales, porpoises and dolphins—and the spectacular sunsets. Lucille took along her typewriter and we spent many hours working on this book you are now reading.

January 19 found us surrounded by our San Diego families, visiting relatives and a few intimate friends. Ten Downing Street, a restaurant a block away, served a delicious gourmet dinner. There were flowers. There was a beautiful cake sent by all our kids. There was champagne. A simple but soul-satisfying celebration long to be remembered. And all the work and planning had been spared, to say nothing of the bills!

Now our family has grown and there are 13 grandchildren. For the first time we are free to do what we want, not what we must. There is time for reading, for golf, for friends and music and song. Among fondest memories are the great times we have had with our good friends Hazel and Loren Baldwin. Generous Loren, the "Big Fisherman," charters a boat and takes his friends fishing at the mouth of the Columbia at Ilwaco or at Westport, where we always catch salmon, either silvers or kings, sometimes whoppers, as in the accompanying picture.

Blessed with good health, literally able to "eat our cake and have it, too," more happiness would be euphoria.

Moved again, 1968

Final resting place of the log house, overlooking Lake Sammamish

End of living room

View from the condominium

The study

Lucille's painting

Lucille's paintings

Lucille's paintings

Lucille's paintings

Lucille's paintings

Lucille's paintings

Lucille's paintings

Lucille's paintings

Lucille's Chinese ink brush paintings

Lucille's Chinese ink brush paintings

Grandchildren

50th reunion, 1926 law class, Ann Arbor - 1976.

One that didn't get away.

INDEX